The Naga Queen

The Naga Queen

Ursula Graham Bower and her Jungle Warriors, 1939–45

VICKY THOMAS

The History Press

To Peter, who would have been so proud

First published 2012

The History Press
The Mill, Brimscombe Port
Stroud, Gloucestershire, GL5 2QG
www.thehistorypress.co.uk

British Library Cataloguing in Publication Data.
A catalogue record for this book is available from the British Library.

ISBN 978 0 7524 6401 5

Typesetting and origination by The History Press
Printed in Great Britain
Manufacturing managed by Jellyfish Print Solutions Ltd

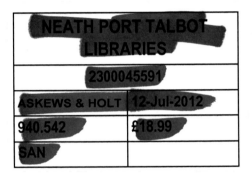

Contents

Acknowledgements

So many people have helped to bring the story of Ursula Graham Bower to light that it's hard to know where to start, but I will begin with Max Arthur, for whom I was carrying out research at the Imperial War Museum when I stumbled on a transcript of an interview with an extraordinary Englishwoman, living alone among tribesmen in the hills of Nagaland. I would probably never have embarked on my own research had it not been for Max's encouragement and enthusiasm for my own project.

After Googling 'Naga Queen' I found a page on the Burma Star website which featured a short synopsis of an as-yet-unwritten biography by Catriona Child (now Kakroo) – Ursula's daughter. To my relief this book had not been started, but after meeting with Catriona we agreed that I should write Ursula's story and she gave me three heavy crates of family documents – letters, diaries and photos. Without the insight and detail from this family archive, *The Naga Queen* would never have been possible – and I thank Catriona for trusting me with such valuable family artefacts and for giving me so much personal information and a string of connections to relatives and friends who added a different perspective to my picture of Ursula.

Among these people who so kindly welcomed me to their homes and regaled me with memories and anecdotes were Ebenezer and Isabel Butler. Despite having recently been flooded out of their Carlisle home, they entertained me royally and shared stories of Eb's time at Ursula's jungle school – she made an impact on him undiminished by the years. Geraldine Hobson was just a child when her father Philip Mills was Governor's Secretary and Director of Ethnography in Assam during Ursula's first visit to Nagaland, having formerly been Subdivisional Officer. He not only encouraged Ursula in her anthropological research but he and his wife became firm family friends – my thanks to Geraldine for an enlightening day sharing her memories and her father's 'Pangsha Letters'.

Then Catriona put me in touch with Ursula's cousin Joan Shenton, who recalled childhood anecdotes and shared family photos. I was privileged to meet Yongkong, then resident in London, who had been part of the Naga delegation to the UK in 1962, and who stayed with Ursula and Tim at their farm on Mull. A very elderly gentleman, sadly now passed away, he embodied the Naga people's deep and long-lasting gratitude and affection for Ursula – another valuable insight into Ursula's relationship with her Naga family.

My thanks go too to Professor Alan Macfarlane, now Emeritus Professor of Anthropological Science and Life Fellow of King's College Cambridge, who generously gave me carte blanche to use material from his 1985 video interview with

Ursula – since it was never possible to meet Ursula in person it was wonderful to hear her recollections in her own voice.

Finally, I want to thank Ryan Gearing of Tommies Guides Military Booksellers and publishers, who brought *Naga Queen* to the notice of Jo de Vries at The History Press, who recognised a remarkable story when she saw one!

To all these people, my profound thanks – it wouldn't have been possible without such generous support and help.

Foreword

Vicky Thomas often shared details of her latest research with me, but in 2003 one story really captivated her, that of Ursula Betts, a lone Englishwoman, living among Naga tribesmen in the remote jungle-covered hills north of Assam on the North-East India-Burma borders during World War II. She eventually tracked down Ursula's daughter and with her co-operation, the help of other friends and family, and with Ursula's dairies and additional research she has now written *The Naga Queen*. Her outstanding research shines from the pages, giving a special insight into the personality and influences that drove Ursula's courageous and pioneering spirit.

It would have been exceptional enough for an Englishman – an outsider – to gain the confidence of the naturally cautious former head-hunters in Nagaland, but for a woman to be so accepted was even more extraordinary. The redoubtable Ursula was not only accepted, but became the leader of these tribesmen in their actions as guerrilla scouts when the advancing Japanese threatened their homeland. The story of Ursula's life among the Nagas unfolds with humour and pathos for hers was a highly unusual relationship with the tribesmen – a blend of employer, mother and friend. But after the Japanese threat was neutralised, Ursula's story becomes an even more romantic one. Still hungry for adventure, Ursula and her husband Tim move into the wild and remote Subansiri territory towards the Himalayas for him to administer as a Political Officer. The area had only recently been charted in 1945 and was home to a number of turbulent warring tribes, which tested the diplomatic and tactical skills of Ursula and Tim to their limits. A new episode opens – again full of personal insight and first-hand detail – a ground-breaking and pioneering tale which not only follows Ursula's life but portrays the historical situation in pre-independence India.

Ursula Betts overcame many obstacles and setbacks to pursue her dream of adventure. I am so glad that Vicky Thomas's excellent new biography has vividly captured Ursula's eventful and pioneering life.

Max Arthur
London, November 2011

Introduction

In the humid October heat of Assam, in the hill town of Dimapur, a Scottish girl in her mid-twenties stood by her car, fanning herself and swatting away the flies. She was waiting for the only train of the day to arrive at the small railhead on the Nagaland border. At last a growing rumble and flurry of local activity heralded the arrival of the train from Bundu, on the Assam plain below. Alexa Macdonald hurried across to where a motley assortment of local Indian traders and British ex-pats were unloading and boarding. As the melee cleared, Alexa picked out a tall girl, standing alone surrounded by smart British luggage, and ran across the dusty track which served as a platform to greet her friend, Ursula Graham Bower.

Travelling alone from London by sea, Ursula's journey had been a long and daunting one since setting out on 25 September 1937. After a long sea crossing, she finally arrived in India at the end of October, and then negotiated her way from Calcutta by train, then steamer into Assam. After crossing the Brahmaputra at Bundu and boarding a final train, Ursula had weathered the last bone-shakingly uncomfortable leg of her journey, cheered by the prospect of joining Alexa and finally being able to relax in familiar company. Alexa's brother, Ranald, was working in the British administration of the Indian Civil Service in Imphal, and when he had asked Alexa to come out and housekeep for him during the winter, her thoughts had turned immediately to her friend Ursula. A trip to India would be just the sort of adventure she would love, and Alexa wrote to Ursula at once, inviting her to come out and keep her company for a few months.

The girls loaded the luggage into the car, Ursula climbed gratefully into the passenger seat and Alexa drove off into the thick surrounding jungle towards Imphal. The scenery and vegetation were like nothing Ursula had ever seen before. Dense forest, draped with tangled creepers blocked the light above the rough road, then, as the route began to climb, they came to more open territory. Cliffs and streams turned eventually to low-ground forest then a wide mountain landscape. The car bumped and bounced over the uneven zigzag road and progress was slow. They had covered some forty tortuous miles when they rounded a bend and there, walking towards them, were four men.

To Ursula's surprise, these were not the slender Assamese of the low country – there was a more Filipino or Indonesian look to them – but on consideration, their closest resemblance was to Mongolians. They were stocky, with the muscles of their copper-coloured shoulders and torsos sharply defined above their native kilts. They stepped aside to let the car pass and Ursula sat back in her seat, stunned.

'Lexie, for goodness sake – who are they?' Alexa looked surprised and said simply, 'Nagas'. Ursula recalled that moment for the rest of her life. Of course… they were Nagas. 'I could not think at the time what I knew about Nagas, or where I had seen Nagas – I didn't know what it was, but it was real déjà vu – which disappeared as soon as it had hit me', she later recalled.

Imprinted on Ursula's mind was the splash of colour of their woven cloths, their shining muscles – it was a flash of something timeless and intriguing. 'Just one look and they were gone, and I was left with my head fairly going round, wondering what on earth had happened to me. I knew Nagas – I was certain I knew Nagas. I just didn't know where I was.'

In that moment Ursula's life was changed forever – things would never be the same again.

1

The Early Years

The year was 1910, and in Portsmouth the Fleet was in as the nation enjoyed a period of peace at the end of the Edwardian age. A large number of naval officers were on shore leave, among them the dashing Commander John Bower of submarine C34, who with his best friend, Noel Laurence, arrived at a party in Fareham. It was an elegant affair, gentlemen in evening dress or dress uniform and young ladies in ball gowns – the latter chaperoned by their mothers or married older sisters as late-Edwardian society demanded.

Casting his eye around the assembled company, John Bower's gaze fell on a girl of extraordinary beauty. He quickly contrived to make her acquaintance, and he and Noel were introduced to Miss Doris and Miss Esme Coghlan White. It was Doris, the younger of the two, who had caught his eye and he spent the rest of the evening with her, under the watchful gaze of the girls' mother. By the time carriages came at the end of the party, John was utterly smitten, and he made sure of Doris's address so as to be able to call on her. His plan was to get to know her better and, after a respectable interval, ask her to marry him.

John Bower was the youngest son of the Bowers of Kincaldrum, a long-established Scottish family whose ancestry could be traced back directly to Henry I of England and, according to family records, as far back as Cerdic who lived 495 to 534. The name 'Bower' stemmed from a knight who distinguished himself in the Third Crusade by repelling a sortie of Saracens, and from who were descended the families of the Archers and the Bowers. The coat of arms of the Bowers features two bows and three quivers of arrows, with the motto, 'Ad Metam' – 'To the mark'.

It was during the nineteenth century that the Bower estates were lost through the defalcations of the family lawyer, and they had to leave the ancestral home. From this time on, the Bower men had to get jobs, so they mainly joined the Navy and some the Indian Army and the family remained associated with those services thereafter. All carved out distinguished careers – at the age of fifteen, Graham John Bower joined the Navy, where he prospered and was awarded a knighthood for his services to the crown. Sir Graham married the Australian beauty, Maude Laidley Mitchell. Although, according to one of the Scottish Bowers, 'Maude was a very stupid woman', she captivated Graham with her stunning good looks. With her cascade of pre-Raphaelite auburn hair, she was the belle of Sydney, and 'stupid' or not, they were soon married. Maude may have been the princess of Sydney society, but she had a strongly religious streak and was apt to throw fits of the vapours at the slightest provocation.

The redoubtable empire-builder and his straight-laced antipodean wife had three children, James, John and Maud, and returned to England, settling at Droxford in Hampshire. John joined the Royal Navy as a midshipman, taking part in the Somaliland Expedition of 1902–04, and then, as the Navy expanded its submarine operations, he joined the new service. Not satisfied with the risks involved in early submarines, he also learned to fly in 1908, taking to the sky at a hair-raising sixty miles an hour in a flimsy aircraft which more resembled a box-kite with a motor bicycle engine on the front than anything dignified by the term 'aeroplane' today. The pioneering Bower alpha males led their family packs and the ladies 'merely followed the drum'.

Doris's family were no less colourful. Before her marriage to Francis Coghlan White, Doris's mother Violet was a Du Croz – a flamboyant family of travellers, adventurers and entrepreneurs. They had made their fortune in Australia, Violet's father Frederick and his brother having set up a very lucrative merchant's business in partnership with the famous Dalgety. The Du Crozes became so successful that they owned considerable areas of Melbourne and were prominent figures in the growing city's best social circles.

Frederick du Croz returned with his wife Margaret to England, to Sussex, where he bought a fine house, Courtlands, at West Hoathly. Margaret was a charming woman, at home in elegant society and happy to throw her money into philanthropic projects, but she had a bullish and obstinate side too. As Joan Shenton, one of Violet's grandchildren, recalled, 'she quarrelled madly with the local vicar, so she built a church of her own – that was the sort of person she was'. Their daughter Violet was born and brought up in Sussex and, while visiting an aunt in the Brighton area, met the Coghlan Whites. Pillars of local society, the Coghlan Whites were an equally eminent family, and it was a matter of great satisfaction to both sides when Violet married Francis, affectionately known as Cog. He took a post as District Officer in the Far East, so committing them to live abroad for some time. Cog cut a dashing figure with his dark hair and trim moustache – and with his tremendous personal charm, he was always surrounded by admiring women – however, in Violet's eyes he could do no wrong, and his flirtations were of no consequence.

While in India, Cog contracted sprue, a tropical disease affecting the mouth, throat and digestion, which could not be cured – but could be improved by removal from the tropical climate. Violet and Cog came back and took up residence with her parents at Courtlands, where Cog, although an invalid, ran the family estate. All the same, he was frequently absent as his sister Frances accompanied him on long cruises for the sake of his health. When Margaret died, the Coghlan Whites moved to Hambledon in Hampshire, not far from Droxford.

In the early 1900s, the daughters of upper-class families were not expected to 'come out' into society until they were eighteen, at which time they would emerge, butterfly-like, from their cocoons. Because of Cog's illness and frequent absences, Violet was almost solely responsible for bringing up their two daughters, Esme and Doris. Once Esme turned eighteen, Violet allowed her to put her hair up and go to balls and parties, and being unusually liberal and modern in her attitudes, she felt it unfair that sixteen-year-old Doris should be denied the same entertainment. So it was that, although technically still in the schoolroom, Doris was allowed out into society – and fate brought her together with Commander John Bower.

Bower was so smitten by the sixteen-year-old siren that he proposed almost immediately. Doris, although taken aback by the suddenness of this development, was bowled over by all the ardour and passion, and threw herself enthusiastically into the whirlwind romance. At this stage, Violet, despite her liberal, modern thinking, put her foot down. She was adamant that Doris was much too young to get engaged at sixteen, so Bower, impulsive and besotted, threatened to shoot himself. It was only with great effort that Noel Laurence dissuaded him.

Violet insisted that they have a very long engagement and not marry until Doris came of age, so eventually Doris and John were married in December 1912 – very shortly after the death of Cog. Young, glamorous, dashing, and very much in love, they lived at the centre of navy social life and Doris eagerly embraced the role of service wife, travelling everywhere with her husband. The world was their oyster.

In November of 1913 Doris Bower discovered she was pregnant – and greeted the news with less than unbounded joy. A baby would cramp her style, just when she and John were having such a wonderful time. Being pregnant would spoil her figure, and what was more, it wouldn't be long before she would have to forego the high life and stay at home, nursing her bump.

Ursula Violet Graham Bower was born on 15 May 1914, and Doris was impatient to return to the social life she'd enjoyed before. Still only twenty-one, Doris had no intention of staying at home with the infant Ursula while John travelled and partied, but fortunately, Violet was happy to look after her grand-daughter. She joined them as live-in nursemaid in the Bower home in the Dovercourt suburb of Harwich where John was based, and Granny Violet – affectionately known by all, for whatever reason, as Humpus – took care of Ursula's upbringing.

Ursula was three months old when the First World War broke out and Harwich, as a major submarine base, became the centre for North Sea E-boat patrols. At the age of two, Ursula's first memory was of looking down from a first-floor window on to a bomb-crater in the seafront road in Dovercourt. Just a few doors away from the Bower home, barriers had been rigged up around it and a solitary policeman stood guard. German Zeppelin airships had legitimately targeted the naval base, but had missed, hitting instead the residential suburb where many naval families lived.

Her second enduring memory was of going to see the wreckage of a Zeppelin which had been shot down. She recalled,

> It must have been the 'Cuffley Zepp', whose destruction was a landmark in World War I. It had been raining, and the grass was wet and brilliantly green. The wreckage lay in a field with many other visitors seeking access to it; the way in lay through a single gate. I remember my father picking me up and carrying me over the muddy and trampled entry. I remember, again vividly, blackened openwork girders towering high up above my head against a showery sky. The Zeppelin had come down in flames and I was told later that a number of the luckless crew had jumped to escape the flames. The ground was presumably soft after rain, and it was noted how extremely deep was the impression made by the Captain's falling body.

It was at Harwich that the Bowers met Rudyard Kipling. At the time, John's forays into writing had remained unpublished, but Kipling encouraged him and nurtured his talent. This was the start of a writing career which was to last for many years, as John wrote under the name 'Klaxon'. Ursula would be the first to admit that much of his verse was clearly derived from Kipling's, but his prose had a much more individual character. Whatever his style, this second career brought new influences to bear, and may have been what inspired Ursula to write in later life.

With Humpus looking after Ursula, Doris was free to enjoy the life of a navy wife – and it occurred to her that two children would be no more incommoding than one. When Ursula was two, Graham was born, and Doris looked after him a great deal of the time, while Ursula stayed mainly with Humpus. She was undoubtedly happy with her – but as she grew older she couldn't avoid feeling that her mother had rejected her, and this conviction coloured much of the rest of Ursula's life. Ursula's own daughter Catriona, almost eighty years later, was brutally honest:

> Mummy, from an early age was quite a plump baby and grew into a tubby toddler... she was indulged by her grandmother, and one of her cousins had an enduring memory of my mother being a plump little girl sitting on a sofa eating a box of violet creams.

Sadly, Ursula didn't match up to Doris's image of the ideal daughter – a petite and elfin moppet she was not.

The life of a navy family was a nomadic one, especially during the war, and in 1917 the Bowers moved to Inverkeithing in Scotland, where John served in the ill-fated K-boat submarines based at Rosyth until the end of the war in 1918. For once, Ursula was left with Doris, as Humpus returned to Hampshire. With submarine warfare still in its infancy, the K-boats were appallingly hazardous, but Bower quickly got to grips with his command of K12, and did well in what was a particularly accident-prone class.

Crews would be on exercises for unspecified periods and, required to observe radio silence, had no means of contacting their families to say when they would be home. John was away for long spells – but Doris would always be at the dockyard when he got back. Their romance had always been a very passionate one, and one might attribute Doris's certainty as to when he would be returning to a mental resonance between them, but a strong psychic ability – a sixth sense – ran in Doris's family. With a sudden intuition, Doris would take the rickety train from Inverkeithing to the dockyard, where the men grew accustomed to seeing the elegant figure of Commander Bower's wife arriving at the submarine base and would comment, 'Ah, K12 is coming home today'. And K12 would turn up, and with her John Bower – but as the war progressed, he was increasingly exhausted and stressed. Just as it was not recognised in the trenches of the Western Front, shell-shock was not acknowledged as the result of weeks cooped up underwater in a vessel of dubious reliability and under sustained exposure to enemy attack – but by the end of the war that was what John Bower was experiencing.

After a short posting in Chatham, K12 was sent to Portsmouth. In one of the most stable periods of Ursula's early childhood, the family settled in Droxford, near John's parents. Humpus also lived in the area, having found a beautiful Queen Anne house just across the road from Sir Graham and Lady Maude. Her home became a family hub as Doris's sister Esme brought her children to live with her while her husband was travelling with the Navy (she was now married to John's best friend, Noel Laurence).

With the Bower family around her, Ursula began to discover first-hand the family's tradition for adventure. Her daughter Catriona summed up the influence that the Bower family had on Ursula's childhood:

> The Bowers were a series of alpha males – accustomed to command and quite tough cookies – good organisers and good servicemen, with a strong adventurous streak. There was all this travel, and the navy – and her great uncle [Sir Graham's brother Hamilton] was an explorer and did some of the early surveys in Tibet. She had all those influences and lots of stories of derring-do and adventure – she was reared on Kipling and Buchan. She breathed all that in – it all passed into her system.

In Droxford Ursula came under two contrasting influences. One was Humpus, who meant well, but by overindulging Ursula's penchant for expensive chocolates, helped to turn an already big-boned child into a large and plump one. Doris, always elegant and immaculately dressed, felt little in common with the daughter who so little resembled her. Equally certainly, Doris was unaware of the lasting sense of rejection Ursula felt.

The other influence was Sir Graham, who would take her for long walks on the Hampshire Downs. These forays awakened her interest in the ancient world and even as a little girl of six or seven she was fascinated by archaeology as a window into the past. In Sir Graham's house the talk was always of travel and adventure. She recalled years later,

> All the time there was coming and going in the house and talk of these service adventures and anecdotes of my grandfather and great uncle. One heard this sort of thing all the time, and it really was most exciting. I was bitterly resentful that I was not a boy. I can remember bursting into floods of tears at the age of three, being quite inconsolable on discovering that I couldn't follow my father into the Navy.

Ursula and Graham grew up with cousins, Joan and Keith, and Ursula became particularly close to the latter, who was about her age. The big nuclear family was completed with plenty of dogs and at least one pony, which the children learned to ride. In addition, her father, with whom she always got on very well, enjoyed taking her out shooting and fishing. She never felt rejected by John as she did by Doris, and she loved the unashamedly boyish activities that they shared. These were tremendously formative years for Ursula, and by the time the family moved on again when she was eight, Ursula was a dyed-in-the-wool Bower. She had become a tomboy, and she was beginning to feel prevented by convention from enjoying the hereditary spirit of adventure which promised to inspire the lives of her brother and cousin.

The next move for the Bowers was to Weymouth where she first went to school – the four cousins in Droxford had previously been taught at home. From here Ursula evinced a desire to go to boarding school, most particularly Roedean, and at last some of her aspirations looked within reach. It was arranged that she would study at Roedean, then go to university – Oxford for choice – and read archaeology.

2

Roedean

Ursula loved Roedean and thrived there. Girls came to board from all over the world and she felt at home among the daughters of travellers, diplomats and aristocrats – one didn't get to go to Roedean without having the financial wherewithal. Perched on the cliffs overlooking the sea to the east of Brighton, and backing on to the South Downs, the situation offered plenty of opportunity to enjoy the countryside – and Ursula was in her element. Here, too, Ursula was removed from the upheavals of naval family life – and from the feeling that she was second best to her brother in her mother's eyes.

Graham too went to boarding school – which suited all concerned – and when John was posted to China, Doris went with him. Recognising the stress that sustained submarine operations inflicted, the admiralty transferred John to surface ships, but he missed the camaraderie. Captaining his new ship, he increasingly found himself alone on the bridge so, far from feeling like part of a team, he became isolated and demoralised. Former athlete, boxing champion and non-drinker, he took to the bottle. This began to affect his behaviour, and he was, as his grand-daughter would later put it, 'messing about with other women and being impossible at dinner parties'. Before long, the unshakeable marriage was on the rocks.

John's drinking and marital problems never stopped him from staying in touch with Ursula, and he wrote to her from all around the world from HMS *Crocus*. In 1927, sweltering in tropical heat, Bower wrote to the thirteen-year-old Ursula with some sound advice:

> I enclose a cheque for £1. I have made it out to our DVB [Doris, currently at home], as I don't know if you have a chequebook yet. She will cash it. Do not put it in the Savings Bank but blue it. These things are meant to be wasted on nonsense when unexpected.
>
> Now, my dear child. I want to impress on you that you must be very good, always obedient to your good, kind mistresses at school. Always remember that your father was very, very good at school, and that your mother (if she had been to school) would have been equally good. You must always – oh, cut it out! I can't keep it up. I'll try something more modern. Keep your hands down and shoulders back, and don't muck the horse's mouth about. Keep your stockings up and always wear them a size too big because then they don't wear out so quickly.

Once the Bowers – their marriage in tatters – returned from China, Ursula saw her mother during her holidays, when she stayed with her or Humpus, who had moved to London. There are photos in the family album of holidays in Cornwall – playing on the beach and picnicking – but Ursula still felt herself under the shadow of being second favourite child.

Ursula prospered at Roedean, where Humpus paid her fees. It was a school with a very strong academic track-record – no mere training ground for marriageable daughters of the well-to-do. As she later remembered,

> You had to work. Standards were extraordinarily high. In my day it was quite difficult to get in. And moving between form and form, you were allowed one slip-up in your promotion. If you failed to get promotion in your exams at the end of the summer term for the second time, you were out. It didn't matter if you were the head girl's younger sister. You were out, to make room for a scholarship girl who was better than you were. There was no nonsense about it. I think it was extremely good for me too.

This was borne out by her report of September 1930, which was sent to her, chez Humpus, at 188b Cromwell Road, London SW5. It included a personal letter from her headmistress:

> My dear Ursula,
> I am very glad that you have done well in the School Certificate examination. It is delightful that you should have distinction in both English and French. You are also first in the school in Latin. You are fifth on the whole school list for your total marks. The details are as follows:

Scripture	Pass with credit
English	Distinction (second in school)
History	Good
Geography	Pass with credit
Latin	Good (first in school)
Greek	Fail
French	Distinction
Spoken French	Good
Arithmetic	Weak pass
Art	Pass with credit

> You can now go straight ahead and specialise in Classics.
>
> I hope you have had a good holiday.
> Yours affectionately,
> E.M. Tanner

Humpus, with her modern attitudes, was the very antithesis of Lady Maude. She saw Doris already separated from John and sadly recognised that reconciliation would be impossible, so she urged Doris to divorce him. She knew how much Doris still adored the errant John – and what a terrible scandal it would be if they divorced (so ghastly a social stigma was divorce at that time that, as a divorcee, Doris would be barred from such social gatherings such as Ascot), but she could not watch as John's drinking tore them apart. Doris would never have divorced John had her mother not pushed her.

John Bower retired from the Navy in 1929 and he and Doris were finally divorced in 1932, when Ursula was eighteen – a split which left Doris and Humpus quite broke. John, as financially disadvantaged as the Bower ladies, went to live with his parents in Droxford. This was no easy home-coming, as Lady Maude disapproved of most things he did, including his drinking. John's letters to Ursula were peppered with phrases such as 'Her Ladyship won't stand…' and he cheerfully made a joke of his trying domestic situation.

Eventually John left Droxford and married his literary friend, Barbara Euphen Todd (best known for her Worzel Gummidge books for children). Ursula always got on well with her step-mother and liked her very much – as, strangely enough, did Doris. Although happier, John didn't give up drinking, and this took its toll on his health. The divorce coincided with the general financial depression of the early thirties, so Doris had no option but to work. Only thirty-eight when they divorced, she was still a very striking and attractive woman, so to make ends meet, she took positions as companion to elderly ladies on cruises. Far from being depressed at her situation, she made the best of it and enjoyed the shipboard life.

Ursula reflected on her own situation with the benefit of hindsight:

> I was at Roedean – I wanted to go to Oxford for choice, but anyhow somewhere to read archaeology, which was my passion. Then I happened to get to the sixth form just in the middle of the early nineteen thirties' financial crisis. There was my younger brother to consider, and I was just told that I had to leave Roedean before I was through the sixth. The money had to be devoted to getting my brother through Cambridge.

Lady Maude would probably have had her ten cents' worth about girls going to university – she would not have approved and would certainly have made her feelings known to Humpus. Educationally speaking, Ursula's fate was sealed.

3

The Reluctant Debutante

Whether it was down to failing finances or Lady Maude's disapproval, Ursula had to leave Roedean before she could complete her school certificate. As such a promising student, Ursula's removal mystified her headmistress. An additional problem was that Ursula was told that she must not divulge her reason for leaving. It would have been too humiliating for such a prestigious family to own up to money troubles – so she would just have to bluff it out:

> My grandmother thought the most disgraceful thing that could happen to a Victorian was to lose your money, and she absolutely forbade me when she removed me from the school to tell people that it was because we were short of money. And the school took it – because I take it I was showing promise – that it was my own lack of character and laziness. Nothing could have been more hurtful. I was so afraid of my grandmother, who was a most formidable lady, that I never dared say anything. I knew there'd be the most awful row.

As Ursula had predicted, her headmistress assumed that Ursula simply couldn't be bothered to finish her education and was in a hurry to get out into the world, so tore her off a strip. 'I got what we would call a "pie-jaw", which reduced me to floods of tears, because I dared not tell her that the one thing I wanted to do was to stay on and go to university.' Miss Tanner hoped to persuade her to stay and see her qualifications through – bandying words such as 'wasting your talents' and 'a great future in front of you', but Ursula did as she was told. Ursula was so upset she refused to go on with her classical studies, and so was also berated by her classics teacher, whom she liked very much. She too thought that Ursula was simply 'dropping out'. In abject misery, Ursula retired to the art studio, and perhaps guessing what the problem was, the art mistress lent a sympathetic ear. Ursula remembered, 'She just let me do nothing. I hadn't the heart to go on with it. What was the use? It was real heartbreak, absolute heartbreak.'

Many years later she met Miss Tanner and confessed the reasons for her removal – only to be informed, 'If you'd told us, you could have gone for a scholarship'. She was sufficiently good for the school to have paid, not only to finish her school certificate, but to put her through university too. Ursula's life could have followed quite a different course, but for an outdated Victorian taboo.

In an interview recorded in her sixties, Ursula summed up the situation at the time, the general view of women's lot in the 1930s, and the sad conflict with her much envied – and much loved – brother:

> He wanted to go into the Navy, but there was so much cutting of defence spending at that time that my father was bitterly against it – he said there was no career in it, that he would never get through and get the full promotion, and he'd better go into a civilian occupation. My brother didn't see that at all, and he eventually took the bit between his teeth in 1939 and went into the Marines, in which he served for quite a reasonable career. However, I was stranded – very unhappy for about five years...

It was Ursula's great misfortune to be born a girl,

> I heard it said that girls always marry. It was no good spending money on me because I wouldn't want a career – while my brother would ... but of course that isn't so. It was purely the social attitude of the time, that women didn't have careers. Women didn't take jobs – not in the service families at any rate.

Crushed in her hopes of pursuing her passion for archaeology and the career she would so have loved, there was an even worse indictment inherent in the end to her education, 'The thought that I wasn't worth spending money on was a most dreadful thing. It was a very unhappy time.'

What was more, the financial sums didn't add up. There *was* money available to educate Graham – and after Ursula had been dragged from Roedean, the family paid for her to go to finishing school in Switzerland for six months – perhaps on Lady Maude's recommendation. Ursula enjoyed Switzerland and learnt to speak beautiful French – but returning to England, her linguistic abilities and newly acquired social sophistication were no antidote to the disappointment of life in London. Ursula was expected to live with and look after Humpus – but adoring her as she did, she set about it with as good a will as she could muster.

As etiquette required, there was no public acknowledgement that the Bower ladies were short of money – if they really were. Ursula 'did the season' and spent a year going to balls and social gatherings. Unlike her mother, this was not her idea of a good time. She was no longer the violet-cream-eating podge of her childhood, but she was still a generously proportioned girl and disliked having to dress up and do the rounds, making small talk. Digging up pottery shards or old bones somewhere in the country would have been more her style.

Society magazines carried photos of white-clad debutantes, engaging the camera with a confident eye. Ursula's 'coming out' portraits, however, show a pretty but wistful girl, staring away from the lens, looking uncomfortable in her elaborate debutante dress. 'The season' was an upper-class family's way of launching their daughters on society and getting them to all the right parties to meet eligible young men, so Ursula complied to oblige her mother and grandmother. London society was a rich hunting ground for girls with marriage in mind, and Ursula (despite having nothing further from her thoughts than matrimony) certainly met some interesting people, including James Robertson Justice, with whom she later recalled sitting on a park bench. Given Ursula's candid and matter-of-fact character, that wouldn't have been a euphemism for anything more intimate.

The society parties of the mid 1930s did nothing to boost the confidence of a girl much in the shadow of her glamorous mother. Ursula was now a tall, 'well-covered' young woman, and living with the ever-indulgent Humpus, dieting would have been out of the question. In any case, feeling rejected by her mother and thwarted in her wish for an academic career, Ursula was hardly a vain girl. Bound up in the duty of being a companion to Humpus, she got on with the job in hand, finding interests and hobbies with which to pass her time. She studied archaeology from books, and found outlets for her artistic talents in theatre and costume-design. Related to costume design, Ursula also enjoyed textiles, embroidery and calligraphy, and far from sitting and feeling sorry for herself, she kept busy. Humpus either failed to notice her grand-daughter's discontentment with London life or, with the best will in the world, turned a blind eye. The die had been cast and there was nothing she could do to compensate Ursula for the university education she had longed for – or to cure the frustration she felt at the lack of real, Bower-standard excitement in her life.

On her occasional visits to London, Doris would take Ursula out – although this maternal attention stopped short of going clothes shopping with her unfashionable daughter. Arriving one day at Humpus's house, svelte and immaculately dressed, Doris Bower watched with disbelief as her daughter, in her late teens, came downstairs wearing a suit more appropriate for a fifty-year-old. 'What ARE you wearing?' she demanded – and irrevocable damage was done. The hurt must have gone very deep, as Ursula later remembered the incident vividly to her own daughter, Catriona. She recalled, 'Mummy was completely devastated, because no-one had ever come with her to buy her nice clothes or to think of how she was dressed.'

Looking back, many years later, Ursula assessed her relationship with her mother,

> It's a rather painful affair, but I think it's got to go down. My mother, who was a most charming, intelligent and very, very attractive woman – a wonderful woman with a surprisingly strong character – or rather a strong moral character – great determination. What she wanted was a really attractive debutante daughter, which was a desirable thing for her generation – who would make an extremely good marriage. Careers didn't enter into it. Career women were dull. Well, the last thing I was, was an attractive debutante. She wanted a very, very pretty girl who could dance and play tennis and golf and ride well – and what she got was me. So I'm afraid she just honestly didn't take any trouble. She had got her own problems with her marriage.

Even so, Ursula nursed no great rancour against Humpus – for whom she felt enormous respect and affection. As for Doris, the sense of rejection still didn't stop Ursula from wanting her mother's approval and trying to be as good a daughter to her as she could.

Doris spent holidays with Ursula and Graham, and she would often take them to the West Highlands. Here Ursula discovered the beauty of Scotland, the love of which would stay with her all her life. Scotland brought out the psychic instincts in Ursula – certainly Doris and Humpus both had a sixth sense, which had been passed on to Ursula. On one occasion Ursula and Doris were camping in the western highlands. Graham was not with them, so the two of them were touring in a car, and as dusk fell they planned to make camp. They found a gate leading into a field on the side of a hill at the top of which were the remains of a *broch* – a vitrified fort. It was a very ancient,

Bronze Age site, and as was the custom in those days, the defenders built walls of stone then, to make them extra strong, lit fires around the edges so that the minerals in the stone melted and turned into strong glass.

Although the gateway into the site was quite wide, it was badly rutted and they had trouble getting the car through and into the field. Closing the gate they unloaded their kit and started to pitch their tent. Ursula began to feel uncomfortable and both of them found themselves instinctively looking over their shoulders to the top of the hill. Doris wasn't happy, 'I don't like this place. It doesn't feel good,' and at this point Ursula looked up and saw a strange, twisted shape – a contorted figure – looming down towards them from the *broch* above. 'Quick! Let's get out of here!' They threw their kit into the car, jumped in and drove off. Going in the other direction the car fairly flew through the gate like a cork from a bottle. Neither questioned in the least what they had both seen and felt – they had both experienced the same sense of terror and they simply drove away and found somewhere else to camp.

Ursula's special solace was her car 'Aggie', a hugely expensive Aston Martin. For a girl whose education had had to be curtailed due to lack of funds, this sounds an unlikely purchase, but Ursula eventually got to the bottom of the family finances:

> It turned out when it was too late that my grandmother had provided savings for me which would have sent me to university – but nobody told me about those, and they were never used. I think they matured when I was about twenty-one. They were never drawn on when I really needed them, which was when I was seventeen. So when eventually I got them, I regret to say I blewed them on an extremely nice sporting car which was the joy of my life.

Ursula's idea of a good time was to take her beloved Aggie up to the highlands and to tramp the wild country in search of archaeological relics, or to look for hill-fort remains in Dorset:

> I used to go off whenever I could get away. I wasn't awfully popular because it meant they had to pay somebody to come in and live with my grandmother and housekeep for her. I used to go off to Skye and do hill-walking all by myself in the mountains. It was lovely being back in Scotland – the Scottish feeling is very, very strong – still is. I loved that. Sometimes I used to have old school friends with me, but quite a lot of the time I was alone. I loved hill-walking. To start with I found I suffered from a certain amount of vertigo, but I didn't like this because it interfered with my walking. So, I simply made myself go up steep slopes and risk it – and I cured myself.

Ursula found another way in which she and Aggie could escape. It was not unusual in the thirties for young women with a taste for speed and excitement to take part in car rallies. Certainly, not all of them would have had their own cars and many would have been navigators rather than drivers, but Ursula enjoyed the sport and, particularly as many of her rally partners were also women, she made sure she could deal with engine problems by taking a course in mechanics. John Bower was quite happy with Ursula rally driving – it was typical family behaviour. His only objection was raised when he found out that her current navigator was a man. This racing partnership was certainly no romance – in mentioning her new navigator to her father she referred to him as 'the Gloomy Dane' – but while he could deal with his little girl hunting, shooting, fishing, engine-fixing and rushing around the country in a fast car, he could not countenance her doing the latter closely closeted with a man, and they had an enormous row. Ursula protested the innocence of the partnership, and John, having a man's instincts about the 'GD's' possible ulterior motives, was furious. This caused a serious disagreement and a rift between them, and they didn't speak for a long time – in fact it was probably the last time that Ursula saw him.

Doris, meanwhile, grew tired of globetrotting in the company of elderly ladies and married an old – and, fortuitously, extremely wealthy – family friend, Eric Patterson. This wasn't a marriage of convenience – Patterson was a charming, kind and gentle man – and as Doris never expected to recapture the breathless passion of her first romance, she entered into her second marriage with a more measured idea of love and what made a working partnership, and this proved a recipe for lasting happiness.

With both parents resettled, Ursula remained with Humpus in London. With no prospect of her life changing, Ursula grabbed every opportunity to escape, especially loving her trips to Skye: 'That was bliss. Every year I used to go and stay in a farmhouse near Bla Bheinn at Torrin on Loch Slapin – go up for about six weeks every summer.'

On her holiday to Skye in 1937 Ursula met Alexa Macdonald – the only other guest at the small family bed-and-breakfast. She, like Ursula, loved the highlands and the great outdoors, and both jumped at the opportunity to go out with the local crofters on a night-fishing trip on Loch Flavin. Wrapped up against the summer evening chill, they sat in the small Hebridean fishing boat and watched the spreading wakes ripple the moonlit surface of the bay as they cast off. Ursula always remembered that night, the huge black mountains of the Barlam Range towering over them, the enormous full yellow harvest moon and the water like black glass, without a breeze to disturb it. Between hauling in bucketfuls of mackerel until after midnight, the girls got talking and, hitting it off at once, they spent the rest of their holiday hill-walking together. Their walks and picnics afforded plenty of opportunities to discuss their hopes and aspirations, and Ursula confessed her longing to travel. She wanted to go somewhere wild and untouched, and explore for herself a different culture, rich in history and tradition. It was a wistful notion – as things were, Ursula could envisage no turn of events which could break the routine of her life in London.

Ursula's photos from the holiday show more of the wide-open spaces and local landmarks than people and faces, but there are some snaps of their hosts at the farm. To them these two young ladies must have painted an unconventional picture of modern femininity – but judging by their warm smiles in Ursula's album, they were won over by the townies' unaffected manners and their enjoyment of their island home. By the end of the holiday a great friendship had been cemented. The girls exchanged addresses and promised to stay in touch.

4

From Kensington to India

Ursula settled back into her household routine with Humpus, where the immediate prospect was of autumn, then winter in London, with little chance of escape. As she acknowledged, 'Kensington is not what I would call a terribly exciting area for a young woman of rather adventurous tendencies.' Then in autumn, a letter arrived from Alexa inviting her to India. It was a gift from heaven. Alexa was going out to housekeep for her brother who was in the Indian Civil Service, and she wondered if Ursula would like to keep her company through the winter.

Ursula admitted she had no idea what she was going to. 'Of course, I jumped at this, and I may say I thought of India entirely in terms of the Taj Mahal and Delhi.' It was an opportunity not to be missed, and surprisingly, even the family responded with enthusiasm to the idea, despite the fact that alternative arrangements would have to be made to look after Humpus. The cause for this soon became clear as one of her mother's friends pointed out gleefully, 'My dear, you never buy a girl a return ticket to India'. Girls were shipped out to India with a view to finding a husband, and Ursula was under no illusions as to the reason for her mother's enthusiastic support. 'By this time I was pretty well on the shelf. I think my mother saw me off with the light of hope in her eye.'

Ursula set about gathering together suitable clothing for the trip and, methodical and inclined to make lists, she jotted down items she thought would be essential:

> 3 pants, 2 evening frocks and coats, 1 slip, 1 nightdress, 1 pyjamas, 1 pyjama belt, 4 scarves, 2 belts (elastic), 2 bras, 1 bed-jacket, 2 shirts, 2 frocks, 1 pant, 3 handkerchiefs, 1 face towel, 2 shorts, 2 silk frocks [this latter was struck through on better consideration]

Eventually the day came for Ursula to leave London, and wanting to preserve every memory of the forthcoming adventure, she started a diary:

> Saturday 25 September
> Breakfasted 8.30 and finished packing. Mother and Graham came round about 10.45, found me still busy. Feel rather awful about going. Set off in rain for Euston. Taxi took long way round, but caught train. Aunt Mary came to see me off, brought proof of Yiewsley photo. Baby in carriage – would spit. *City of Marseilles* not bad boat, quite clean, but native cabin boys. Mother left before boat sailed to catch 5.20 train. Felt very miserable at final parting. Cabin mate elderly Mrs Whitehouse. Quite friendly so far. Unpacked while boat sailed; dinner and early bed.

Ursula brightened up the evenings aboard ship by fortune-telling for her fellow travellers, using a deck of cards. Ursula had known for some time that she shared the sixth sense which ran in her mother's side of the family – so it was just an extension of this to pick up fortune-telling with cards under the instruction of Humpus' housemaid back at home. Ursula was blasé about her talent, and regaled her fellow passengers with whatever predictions came naturally to her. On one occasion she foresaw a windfall of money – which the would-be recipient pooh-poohed as impossible, and the groundswell of opinion was that Ursula was picking ideas from the air and saying what she thought people would like to hear. Convinced of the accuracy of her predictions, she gave up the card sessions – partly due to her co-passengers' reaction – but also in case she foresaw anything more sinister. Her confidence in her predictions was entirely vindicated when the girl wrote to her later, confirming a surprise legacy.

For a British woman travelling alone, and speaking no Hindustani, the journey by a series of trains and boats to the railhead at Dimapur was a daunting one, but at last, in late October, she arrived. As the crowds dispersed and the dust of the station cleared, Ursula looked around her – and with a surge of relief spotted Alexa. Ursula's impressions of that first journey into the unknown were to stay with her all her life:

> The car hummed on, round steeper bends, between bamboos, through lighter, drier forest – the hazy plain falling lower and lower behind – and up the feet and knees of the great Barail Range itself.
>
> A group of hill men scattered before us and stood on the roadside, staring. They were not the slim-built Assamese of the low ground. The sight of them was a shock. Here were the Philippines and Indonesia. Bead necklaces drooped on their bare, brown chests, black kilts with three lines of cowries wrapped their hips, and plaids edged with vivid colours hung on their coppery shoulders. Tall, solid, muscular, Mongolian, they stood, a little startled as we shot by.

Many years later, in 1985, her wonder and enchantment were undimmed by time:

> I must have sat there like a fool, gaping. Illumination so plain, so known and obvious, that I was speechless at my own stupidity in not remembering sooner. And suddenly, in the split second before it reached full consciousness, the knowledge was gone. It vanished as cleanly and completely as writing wiped off a slate. The car swept on up the twisty road, and I sat there dumb in the back seat, trying to snatch from the edge of my mind the vital, the intensely important thing which a few seconds earlier had been so clear. I never did.

Later, with better knowledge of the region and the local tribes, she could have identified the men as Nagas of the Angami tribe – but at the time she saw only the four distinctive tribesmen. She recalled the vivid colours of their woven plaid cloths – a sudden flash of something timeless and intriguing:

> Just one look and they were gone – and I was left with my head fairly going round, wondering what on earth had happened to me. I knew Nagas – I was certain I knew Nagas. I just didn't know where I was.

En route for Imphal to the south, Ursula and Lexie paused for refreshment at Kohima, the administrative capital of the Naga territory – but her memories of this are sketchy. She stared away to the mountain ranges beyond the town to the east, to unmapped lands, accessible only by bridle-roads, winding down the bare spurs in big, looping folds. Hills stretched away into the hazy distance – an ocean of peaks with wild forests covering steep clefts and gulfs. 'That landscape drew me as I had never known anything do before, with a power transcending the body – a force not of this world at all…'

The next morning Ursula surveyed her surroundings. Imphal was the main town of Manipur State, which occupied the plain and some of the mountainous region between Assam and Burma. What she saw was a pleasant backwater, whose one long road to the railhead effectively cut it off from the rest of the province, and where a single mule-track opened up the route to Burma to the east. Imphal was a comfortable little British garrison with a company of military police – the Assam Rifles – along with two civil service officers, the Political Agent and Alexa's brother, Ranald Macdonald, who was the junior, with an engineer and a doctor – and that was it.

In true British Raj style, the flavour of suburban England had been painstakingly recreated with tiled bungalows and gardens full of snapdragons and lupins among the native bougainvillea bushes. Beyond the European settlement the crumbling and dusty bazaar sprawled away towards the locals' domain – a huge area of bamboo huts forming a mass of villages among the lush, dank greenery and many ponds across the plain.

For the British, life in Imphal ticked by at a leisurely pace and the local amenities provided sedate entertainment. There were shady lawns, golf at the 'Club', tennis at the Residency, and the men went shooting duck on the lakes to the south. Although Ursula was a proficient shot, it was not expected that she would join them, so she accompanied the memsahibs instead. 'We womenfolk idled comfortably. We shopped at the Canteen, we dined, we visited the Arts and Crafts showroom, and twice a week we went to watch the polo.'

The high spot was the Golden Market, held in the bazaar, when the local colour emerged after the heat of the day. Traders in their dazzling clothing wended their way past the polo ground bearing their produce. Not Nagas, but Assamese, the men sported turbans and mainly white garments with brightly coloured wraps of green and blue to keep out the evening chill, while the women wore more sombre colours – black and gold, black and purple – their dark hair sleeked back in shining knots. Hill men came in too – dishevelled and naked – all mixed among the press of humanity heading for the bazaar in a cloud of golden dust.

The market assembled as dusk fell, with every kind of local produce on sale – pottery, coconuts, dried fish (stinking to high heaven, Ursula observed), gold jewellery, fragrant spices and local snacks, all laid out on plantain leaves. Among the seething mass of people, lorries nosed their way through to the buzzing centre of local commerce, and away in the distance, the hills of the horizon stood velvety and black against the darkening sky.

Ursula soaked up the atmosphere and, apart from a hankering to explore the distant hills, had no problem just going with the flow. Although no outsiders ever came through the surrounding highlands to the plain, there were occasional visits by officers and officials – people whose work centred around the distant hills and their inhabitants. One such was the Civil Surgeon, Colonel Taylor, who along with his wife, was about to set out on a dispensary tour among the Tangkhul Nagas of the Ukhrul area to the north-east. Confident of Ursula's hardiness for the long march, he invited her to join them.

Almost before Ursula had finished unpacking from her sea voyage, she was gathering together the essentials for camping on the march, and packing them into a *jappa* – the tall carrying basket used for hill transport:

> 10 November
> Got up at six, finished packing jappa. Coolies came at 7.30. Colonel Taylor arrived a few minutes later. Shumshu came out of back premises at last minute, minus jappa. Taxed, he said he had private arrangement with coolie who would take S's bedding loose, so fifth coolie only had others' bedding and my camp bed, which refused to go into the bedding jappa. … Left at 2.45 in Fergus' car, with Shumshu in back. Left my socks behind and Marguerite and Ranald came haring after with them. Long, dusty drive to Yaingangpokpi, and very tight fit in front seat. Road vile, and Fergus found petrol-tank lid missing when he arrived. Tea at bungalow, and then Fergus and Lex went off fourteen miles back. Only two rooms in bungalow, so dined and sat in my bedroom. Sanitation by long drop – v. interesting.

She recounts in her diary, that the next day the navigable road dwindled to a mere bridle-track, then there was no choice but to go on foot to the nearest village. The path took them through dry, barren slopes with deep red gullies where thick grass held the heat, then as they ascended, they marched through cooler woods and green open spaces. Ursula looked out on a majestic open landscape with views stretching miles and miles toward the distant horizon. The sky was blue and the air crisp in the higher woods – Ursula could almost have been back in an English forest in winter. As the track plunged down again, they re-entered steamy, dank jungle with lush banana trees and densely tangled creepers.

News had travelled ahead of the dispensary tour, and at points along the track Naga people had gathered to wait for treatment. Many of them naked and all sweaty and smelling of wood-smoke, they squatted in the heat with their offerings of eggs and fruit in return for their medicine. Children peered curiously at the outsiders from behind the legs of their parents and, the doctor's visit being something of an event, the headmen came out too, tall and solemn in black and red togas, decked in all their silver and bone jewellery. Typical of the Tangkhul Nagas, they wore their hair in a stiff cockscomb with the sides of the head clean shaven, giving the impression of a classic Greek or Roman helmet. By the end of the day, despite the fascination of the Naga people, Ursula had to own up to a certain weariness:

> Hell of a long march (fourteen and a half miles) climbing through woods, but once or twice through jungle. Reached Songphel about 3.30 and damn glad to see it. Blisters developing.

The second evening gave Ursula her first taste of ad hoc Naga entertainment. A party called and offered to dance for them – and at 8.30 the dancers came back, evidently 'pretty ginned up (or rather zu-ed up, from the local rice beer)'. Their first offering was a choral effort, 'one man giving the words, like a psalm in an old Scots kirk, one man singing it solo and the rest joining in the chorus in harmony.' They went on to a song and dance, skipping about in the light of the veranda lamp, followed by 'a sort of Nuts-in-May dance, formed in two lines'. The finale was a war-dance, with much spear-shaking and mock fighting. One man 'leapt about with an imaginary spear, then dashed off and came back with a hedge-stake, with which he did the most marvellous war-dance. It was really thrilling and he acted marvellously'. Two men bounded about with stakes in a very fair imitation of the real thing, and the headman got between them at an early stage, waving his outstretched arms. Apparently the bucks sometimes got so worked up in these dances that they would go for each other in earnest.

The next day they set out with an escort of headmen and some of the previous night's chorus. In spite of painful feet, 'hellish sore, and badly blistered, but well greased and plastered up', Ursula joined in as the party returned the compliment from the night before and gave a rendition of some English songs. Ursula noted, 'We sang a good bit of the way. Hope the Nagas enjoyed it. It sounded pretty bloody to me.' More cases for Colonel Taylor were waiting en route:

> Awful sweat for four solid miles uphill, but jungle magnificent. Crossed pass, then four miles down and up again – mostly up – to Ukhrul. Gosh, what a sweat! Stopped on road to attend to woman with apoplexy, so Col T went off with headmen. Lumbus (village dignitaries) had already met us with zu and chickens at foot of pass, and had a couch of banana leaves ready and spread with red blanket. Couch beautifully made. Went on and Col T had no sooner joined us than we came on a man lying by the roadside, half-dead with pleurisy and pneumonia. Col T attended to him, watched by all the reception committee, lumbus, hoi-polloi and what have you, while Mrs T and I sat on miraculously produced stools and sank more zu. If it hadn't been for the zu I should never have got up the hill.

Having been a squeamish girl whom her cousin Joan remembered as being 'hopeless at anything messy – if the dog was sick she would run screaming from the room and get someone else to clear it up', Ursula had become an effective assistant nurse with a necessarily strong stomach. She was quick to learn on the job – most of the dispensary stuff was common sense. Fourteen miles on they arrived in Ukhrul and joined Sub-Divisional Officer Duncan and his wife.

Next morning, Ursula went out alone to photograph the buffaloes going up to the watercourse. At the bridge she halted and realised she had drawn an audience of locals, fascinated at this white woman and her unaccountable interest in their everyday surroundings. Preserving a dignified detachment, she turned back along the Tuinem Road and found herself followed, at a respectful distance, by about thirty small boys and a couple of youths. Much to the interest of her retinue, she paused at the roadside to change a film, spreading out a handkerchief to protect the camera – which she supposed they saw as some advanced form of *puja* or magic. Alone and surrounded by strangers with no common language, Ursula was unnerved and embarrassed by the scrutiny of a gaggle of children and she was grateful for the timely arrival of Mrs Duncan's servant who accompanied them to inspect the old Ukhrul fort.

Five days into the tour, Ursula awoke feeling 'distinctly seedy'. However, she couldn't afford to be lily-livered, as a local *bundobast* – a festival – was scheduled for 10.30. This might be the only chance she would get to photograph the ceremony, so she made the best of it, headache and all. She passed the rest of the morning photographing chief Michivam's memorial cairns, where a woman came and made rice offerings. Exchanging nods and smiles in greeting, the chief invited her into his house to show her his collection of heads – relics of a time not long past when head-taking was the custom. Undeterred, Ursula went in and accepted zu – and found herself speculating about how the splendid Michivam would look in full war-paint. It wasn't just anthropology or the chance of using her photos lucratively on her return – there was something about these dignified primitive people which spoke to Ursula, and she threw all caution and concern for convention to the winds to understand them better. However, gastric disorders are no respecters of anthropology or photography, and Ursula recalled:

> Whether zu or internal disturbance of intimate nature, felt bloody all day and was sick as a dog after tea. Col T dosed me when they came back from their walk – internal disturbance had resolved itself by that time and I felt better. Empty as Hades and ate good dinner at Duncans'. Slept like dead under new Naga blankets.

The next day there were groups along the way who wanted treatment, so with intermittent stops they made just four miles in two and a half hours. It took them five hours to reach Thoubal, but once fed and refreshed, they left the clutch of cases to Pongse and joined the Colonel to fish at the river. The chaprassi – messenger or bearer – came up with a spare rod for Mrs T, and something resembling a small tree trunk for Ursula:

> I fished with the beanpole for a while, watched by an entranced bunch of coolies who were waiting for me to fall in. I didn't think they'd be disappointed, but I kept upright for the honour of the white Raj. Thirteen Nagas, five Kabuis, two servants, two memsahibs and one chowkidar, and we didn't catch one single ruddy fish.
>
> Time was running out and it was the last night of the tour, so despite a severe shortage of chairs at dinner, the evening was very convivial – all retired pleasantly merry to sleep.

On the final morning the tour party walked down in drizzle to a village near to Yaingangpokpi, where a car arrived through the mud to pick them up. Totally enchanted by the people and their land, Ursula returned reluctantly with Alexa to Imphal.

To a less intrepid spirit the tour might have been an exquisite form of torture, with its unpredictable accommodation, dirty, sweaty Nagas with revolting ailments, and relentless foot-slogging marches – but for Ursula a fire had been lit. Reflecting on the tour some fifty years later, she summed up the sudden, but then enduring, fascination. 'Off we went towards Ukhrul, and the further I went, and the more I saw of Nagas, well, frankly, the more hooked I got. This is my place, and I belong here.'

5

Nagaland

Nagaland is a small and little-known country, situated to the far north-east of India, on the border with Burma, with the Indian states of Manipur and Assam to the south and west respectively. Since the first records were kept, the area was inhabited not by Indians, but by Naga tribespeople, whose proud boast it was that they had historically held out against all attempts by invading powers to colonise or subdue them. Only the British succeeded in conquering some twelve Naga tribes, and ruled them from 1880 – but the remaining fifty-four tribes never came under British rule. Indeed, it was a matter of some frustration to the British that even in these so-called 'British-administered areas', they still failed to impose full rule over the Nagas, despite punitive expeditions, fines and even public hangings.

The fiercely independent and proud nature of the Naga people set them apart from their Asian neighbours who, over the course of centuries, succumbed to relentless colonisation by the British. The British joined the Portuguese and Dutch in staking claims to areas of India in 1612, and continued expanding her colonies and promoting trade.

The Industrial Revolution in Europe, from the late eighteenth century to the middle of the next, kept the colonists supplied with new technology – not least superior weaponry with which to subdue the sword- and bow-wielding Indian peoples. The European colonists rushed to bag India's natural resources, so that by the end of the nineteenth century, the plunder of Asia was almost complete. Britain had seized most of India, and with newly-constructed railways and the establishment of new sea routes, Indian cotton, silk and spices were flooding out of the country to the West.

Britain soon secured trading and extra-territorial rights to the remaining sovereign nation's resources, this 'conquest' being made possible almost entirely by Britain's superior military technology. Burma and Assam fell to the British, who then set their sights on Nepal which, despite courageous resistance, finally succumbed. Bhutan was conquered and subdued in 1864, followed by Sikkim, Tibet and Afghanistan.

Only Nagaland resisted this onslaught. Nagaland is about 400 miles long and at most 200 miles wide – a wild land of range upon range of craggy hills, crumpled and twisted as they rise and plunge in steep gorges through dense, humid jungle in the low areas and fresh, European-style forests on the heights.

The Naga people, of Mongolian origin, comprised some twenty tribes with many more sub-tribes, speaking almost as many Tibeto-Burman dialects. They were muscular, well-built and, due largely to the relative scarcity of textile fibres, mainly naked – the name 'Naga' is almost certainly a corruption of the Assamese 'nuga' or 'naked'.

Significantly, the Naga people were, and remain, a race apart from their neighbouring Indians, Chinese, Tibetans and Burmese.

The British had only been in control of Assam for a short time when warlike tribes from the surrounding hills started causing trouble. The tribes to the south, including the Nagas, posed the greatest threat, as their village units were larger and they had a close-knit social system which enabled them to stage large-scale raids. They were known to be head-hunters – not an enemy to tangle with.

The British administrators managed to bring the majority of northern tribes under control by building a system of forts, at which were garrisoned forces adequate to the task of suppressing any uprising, and they also operated a system of Danegeld (simplistically, a payment to pay off the would-be attackers). However, the Nagas were a different kettle of fish, and there was no question of them accepting any rule other than their own. During the first twenty-five or so years of British rule in Assam the British had to make repeated punitive expeditions to suppress Naga uprisings. The Nagas responded robustly to any attempts to take over their lands and subjugate them, and by 1850 it was apparent to the British that they would have to do something more drastic and considerably more costly – in funds and lives – to assert their supremacy. A strong expedition entered the Angami country and stormed and burned the fortress of the dominant group, Khonoma, then retired, but then it was not until 1874 that the British finally took over the Angami country and then the Lhota area to its north-east.

Throughout the nineteenth century the British took over province after province in the main Indian continent and eventually, on 1 January 1877, Queen Victoria was proclaimed Empress of India. Conquest was complete – at least in India proper. Even so, the Nagas continued to rebel against British rule, but all this resentment still did nothing to make the British question their rightness in remaining, subjugating the indigenous people to suit their own convenience, and plundering the area of its natural resources. It did, however, bring about a change in policy. It was easier to prevent trouble than to contain it once it had broken out, so the British devised an administrative system which retained and respected Naga law and existing institutions, so that the villages continued to operate almost unaltered. Only this 'hands-off' policy allowed the gradual annexation of more Naga territory into the administered zone.

An era of successful Anglo-Naga relations began, due entirely to the administration of a new dynasty of sympathetic and sensitive Deputy Commissioners – Dr J.H. Hutton, J.P. Mills and Sir Charles Pawsey – all experts on the Naga tribes, having spent most of their service lives in the region. Keen anthropologists, all these men had come to understand the Naga people and felt a duty of care and responsibility for them. Their interpretation of the new British policy was exactly what the Nagas needed – and they responded as positively to this light-handed administration as they had reacted against the former suppression and punitive expeditions. Hutton, Mills and Pawsey found the Nagas intelligent, loyal, hospitable, witty and dignified. It is a mark of their relationship with the Nagas that the Naga Hills were ruled for more than sixty years by a skeleton staff of two British officers at a time – one senior and one junior – a little used battalion of military police (the 3rd Assam Rifles) and no civil police except for a small armed guard on the Kohima Treasury.

This informal regime, run on mutual trust and genuine affection, made the Naga Hills administration one of the most successfully run, albeit least known, of British territories. If there was a downside to the policy, it was that the Nagas remained very isolated, both culturally and politically. With the inexorable march of progress, the outside world must inevitably knock on their door at some point, causing a massive and unpalatable culture shock, but this was in the distant future. Naga loyalty to their fatherly administrators was such that several thousand volunteered for overseas service in 1917. Men who had never before left the Naga Hills were shipped out to the trenches of the Western Front and no small number lost their lives.

At this time James Philip Mills was serving in North East India. He had graduated from Oxford in 1913, gone straight to India to work with the Indian Civil Service, and his life-long relationship with the Naga people began in 1916 when he was posted to the Naga Hills as Sub-Divisional Officer at Mokokchung. His colleague, Dr J.H. Hutton, based in Kohima, was Deputy Commissioner in charge of the whole area.

Only part of the Naga Hills was directly administered – an 'inner line' defined the Naga Hills administration, and as a protective measure to prevent the exploitation of the people, their culture and their resources by outsiders, admission to the region was strictly by special permit, issued by the Deputy Commissioner. The Naga people themselves could move freely in and out of the area, and a good many of them worked in the tea gardens of Assam.

Mills was witness to a period of gradual change after the Great War. There had been an American Baptist Mission in Ao Naga country for some time, and through their work Christianity – and literacy – spread though the administered area. (The distinctly un-Christian habit of head-taking had long been proscribed by the British Government, although it remained part of the culture in more far-flung areas.) For the Nagas, their standpoint scarcely needed to be reinforced. The British alone had conquered them, so if they were to withdraw from India and Nagaland, they, the Nagas, intended to revert to political independence and self-determination. They were not even of the same race as the people of the adjoining plains, and would certainly not be willing to be absorbed into what they felt to be militarily inferior and socially and religiously alien communities.

The Simon Commission of 1927 acknowledged the chalk-and-cheese nature of these two peoples – along with the difficulties in melding the tribal areas into any future independent Indian constitution. The response was to introduce a series of reforms throughout the 1930s, and eventually, in 1937, the Assam frontier districts, including the Naga Hills were declared 'Excluded Areas', lying outside the remit of the Central and Provincial Legislatures. Acts passed by this body would apply to the Nagas only if the Governor of Assam and his special adviser felt it appropriate. While this satisfied the Nagas' insistence on independence from all things Indian, it rankled with the Indians, who felt it was a slight to their administrative abilities. However, this strategy had proved good for any problem area since the British took over Assam in 1826, and fortuitously, all but a very few truly vocational Indian personnel wanted to work in the hill districts. This was the situation, with J.P. Mills in office as Deputy Commissioner, which prevailed when Ursula first set foot in the Naga Hills.

6

The Fascination of the Hills

> There is no describing the fascination of the hills. Neither heat, sweat, dirt nor discomfort could break their hold. It was as though I had rediscovered a world to which I had belonged the whole time; from which, by some accident, I had been estranged.

After Ursula's first short tour among the Nagas, her view of life had changed irrevocably. She recognised that she was 'not yet of the hills, but already divorced a fraction from my own race' and now, looking at the life of ex-pats in colonial India, she felt noticeably less in common with her own compatriots. Her only aim was to go back to the mountains and jungles of the Nagas.

It was arranged for Ursula and Alexa to accompany Mr Jeffery, the State Engineer for Manipur, on his next tour of bridge inspection. The hills of Manipur were divided into eastern and western sectors – Ukhrul was the main town of the eastern region, with Tamenglong its counterpart in the west. Both areas stretched from the border of the Naga Hills to the Chin and Lushai Hills to the south, and in both areas there were tribes of two groups – the Nagas and the Kukis. Of these, the Kukis were the more recent migratory arrivals, and while they had established a few large communities, their smaller groups tended to drift and relocate wherever they could find fresh farming land. The Nagas, on the other hand, had been long settled in their territories – the Tangkhuls around Ukhrul to the east, with some Angami groups in the Naga Hills proper. Then to the west, at Tamenglong, were the group known as the Kacha Nagas, comprising the Kabui, Zemi and Lyeng.

Ursula's foray to the Barak River was to last three weeks. Far from a pleasure cruise, however, there would be hard marching over native paths and overnight lodgings of the most primitive kind. The Sahibs and Memsahibs of Imphal were unanimous in their condemnation of two young ladies going on such a tour – words such as, 'You'll never stand the marching' were bandied about, and there hung, like Damocles' sword above Ursula, the threat of being taken sick en route and having to be carried back. She reflected many years later,

> We were practically back to about 1900 in the social taboos – the social mores – and it was firmly stated that women could not stand the marching. You could almost *hear* the capitals.

Jeffery, however, had faith in the hardiness of his two female companions and, despite foul weather, the tour party was ready to leave on 1 December 1937:

> We left Imphal on a wet, foggy December afternoon, preceded by eighteen depressed Kuki coolies and enveloped by premature Christmas rains. The rest of the party – 'Uncle Jeff', three black labradors, Shumshu the bearer, Jenap the cook, Kharran Din the paniwallah [water-carrier], Hamja and Umaid the shikaris [hunters], and a skewbald pony with a syce – were already gathered in the small bazaar at the foot of the hill, and in a few minutes we got going and began the cold, wet, slippery climb to Kangchupkhul, invisible in the mist above us.

Climbing in long zigzags accompanied by the melancholy clanging of the coolies' kerosene cans, they arrived in Kangchupkhul about an hour and a half later. Their accommodation was incredibly dark and desolate, set in a misty pinewood:

> Bungalow dreary in the extreme and very cold. Fire smoked out nest of white ants in chimney and nearly smoked us out too. Clothes and bedding in jappas damp, so slung line and hung them to dry.

The evening was spent ducking between strings of drying underclothes and killing white ants with bits of damp firewood.

The weather continued wet and misty the next day – 'we were hustled over the pass by a lashing rain which would have done credit to Scotland'. Ten miles later, over slimy tracks, they finally reached Haochong. 'Bungalow earth floored, tin-roofed, three-roomed.' In fact the place was remarkable chiefly for its dank cold, and the fact that the girls' bedroom curtain fell down, much to the joy of the coolies who had gathered on the veranda.

As 3 December dawned, it was still raining heavily, but when visibility cleared, Ursula was presented with quite a different prospect from the eastern Ukhrul landscape. Where the Ukhrul hills had been dry and grassy with very European pine forests, the area to the west was humid and lush, and covered in dense rainforest.

It became unexpectedly hot and as they sweated on, Alexa fell on a slippery wet clay bank and cut her knee and Ursula twisted her ankle, but both pressed on until they reached the bridge near the village.

> From the bridge we had a long, zigzag climb through dense bamboos, and on the spur below the summit, the bungalow chowkidar met us with a bottle of zu, some oranges and a hen.

This put them in better spirits and as they set off, Ursula and Alexa joined in the coolies' chanting – much to their amusement. The last quarter mile was downhill and it became almost impossible to stand up. As they lurched and scrambled down the ditch, they met a large Naga wedding party with its best beads and berries on, and they lined up on the opposite bank and watched the girls' impromptu skating display with great interest.

The Nagas were equally fascinated by the phenomenon of Ursula's legs and she recalled 'an incident' on the march to Lukhambi:

> I do a certain amount of walking in Scotland and had just then come back from the Ukhrul trip – both conducive to muscular development, and I had shorts on.

> As we passed the coolies on the hill, I noticed that every man's eyes were glued to the back of my legs and exactly the same thing happened with the reception committee. Their gaze came round to my legs and thereafter never shifted. I asked Jeffery about it and he broke it to me that it was my legs' marriage-price and mithan value that was causing the excitement, and that as he was gadding about the hills with two young women, the Kabuis must think they'd got hold of a real pukka sahib at last, and were probably computing what we cost him for the pair. Anyhow, the interest continued unabated all down the Barak, and I had got quite used to it when we reached Dinomlong, and Lexie and I went up the village without Jeffery and with only the lumbu.
>
> I stopped to photograph an old lady winding thread and had just taken her when I felt a fluttering and clucking going on round my calves, and looking down, I found a perfectly respectable Kabui lady sitting in front of me, crooning a little song of admiration and raptly patting my legs. Round in an admiring ring stood fifty per cent of the male population. I blushed, sputtered, shook her off and flew out of the yard, but instead of bolting down the village, I bolted up and gave the populace, who followed looking more admiring than ever, a perfect view of my legs in rapid action up the street. When we got to the top I recovered my wits and took a picture, which is an uncommonly funny study in expressions, but when we and the story got back to Imphal, Mills and Gimson insisted on fixing my official marriage-price in case there were any inquiries or exchange offers from influential headmen.

On 5 December Ursula recorded, 'Began climb. Frightful sweat, higher and higher, range after range, rising into view. Stopped at beginning of zigzags for tea and oranges.' The climb continued in burning heat, until at last a group of lumbus met them with bottles of zu. 'Fell on them and had tiffin on corner.' Now that the trees had petered out, they looked down over Tamenglong. The British settlement was laid out on a series of small peaks – the Sub-Divisional Officer's bungalow on one, the resthouse below it on another and, a little further away on a third, an ancient stone fort.

Shaw, the SDO, escorted them to his bungalow for tea, which they took in the bandstand – a summerhouse commanding good views all round, which had been built long ago by forced labour. Settled in their own bungalow, Shaw joined them for drinks on the veranda, and they looked out on a glorious sunset, which even the heavily smoking fire could not spoil.

On the eighth day the main activity around their camp was the construction by the Nagas of two rafts for their river journey – the girls christened theirs HMS *Barak* and Jeffery's HMS *Naga*. The craft were long triangular structures made of bundles of bamboo, secured at the bow and braced with more ties amidships. As the bases of these rafts were always awash, a low platform was built on each to keep the passengers dry.

> We fished our way downstream, Alexa and I seated in a ladylike manner on bamboo rafts, on little cane stools, and from time to time, if we happened to get into difficulties in the rapids, the rafts would disappear underwater and we'd be left sitting on our cane stools, looking like all that's left of Noah's ark.

The journey settled into a new pattern, with overnight camps being struck in tiny clearings cut from the marginal woods. A far cry from wintry London, extraordinary scenery slipped past them – thick borders of jungle, arches of bamboo in every imaginable shade of green, with the way punctuated by grey rocks, occasional rapids and huge pools. Jungle fauna came and went – tiger tracks appeared overnight, barking deer called in the darkness and otters slipped into the water as the rafts slid past. Incongruously and much to the amusement of the boatmen, the girls occupied themselves by knitting.

A couple of days on, a new crew took over the boatmen's duties,

> …one dumb, furry, complete savage, but wearing singlet (Pong) and the other lean-faced, high-cheekboned, intelligent, humorous, sly and starko except for loincloth, dao and cloth worn round the shoulders, carried or hung on jappa (Ping).

Pong proved 'very jungly' and not keen on Ursula's camera, while Ping was unworried by it. The day unfolded full of excitement when they spotted an animal believed to be a tiger, moving on the bank. 'Great thrill, Ping and Pong squeaked; sensation among crew generally; Humja grinned'. With every day, Ursula found she communicated with the locals with a growing easiness and enjoyment.

A 'rest day' followed, while new rafts were built, so Ursula and Alexa were free to explore and they climbed back towards the falls to bathe, accompanied by Umaid and the tiffin-coolie. The Nagas' gentle respect and dignity inspired confidence, and the girls had no qualms about emerging in bathing dresses to swim – although the sight of so much pale European flesh made a novel spectacle for the onlookers. 'Nagas' eyes nearly fell out at sight of Lex in bathing dress; her skin is very white.' Both girls enjoyed the warm, green water and swam for some while, returning only when they heard a lot of noise in the jungle across the pool. It proved to be a group of monkeys crashing around in the trees – this was a very different world from Kensington. The evening provided more enduring images. 'Camp very lovely in dark. Mist hung over trees above, moon shining through, glow of fire and white-wrapped Nagas standing about like ghosts.'

On 14 December the new rafts were ready and HMS *Barak II* pushed off into strong currents to cross the river. Some 200 miles later, having passed the three great falls of the Barak, the expedition came ashore for the last time.

> It was the end of a dream. Already the outer world was near us – Silchar and Imphal, where Nagas were an obscene joke, and the incredible beauty of the jungle meant nothing. There was this last camp, with the Kabuis of Kambiron, who, old friends of Jeffery's, had moved down in a body seven miles and taken us to their hearts in a family picnic, but every moment was sharpened by its impermanence.

By Christmas they were back in Imphal. Ursula was desolate, 'Things would never be the same for me wherever I went. What Ukhrul had begun, the Barak had clinched.'

Ursula was not due to return to England until April, but no other tours were planned, so she and Alexa had to content themselves with ex-pat life. Apart from the usual social round – golf, tennis, shopping, duck-shooting, polo to watch and the high spot of the evening bazaars – there was little to distinguish one day from another. However, in late January the Imphal community was sent into a flurry of social fervour over the visit to Manipur of Sir Robert Reid, the Governor of Assam. The Maharajah of Manipur laid on a programme of events to which the ex-pats of Imphal were invited with proper formality and ceremony. Individual invitations were issued for every event:

> His Highness the Maharajah of Manipur requests the pleasure of
> The company of Miss Bower to the State Banquet and to witness the Manipuri Dance at the Palace on the 24th January 1938 at 8.15 pm (local)

Ursula would have preferred to decline, but with little else to pass the time and aware that to do so would be seen as unpardonably rude, she accepted. The welcome banquet in the Governor's honour was a major social event and the Palace chefs pulled out all the stops:

Manipur State Banquet
To His Excellency, Sir Robert N Reid,
KCSI, KCIE, ICS
24th January 1938

Menu

Potage
Crème St Germain .... Flor de Jerez Sherry, William Humbert's Bristol Cream

Poisson
Filet de Nga-mu Porrong à la crème

Entrée
Becassine à la Manipur .... Veuve Clicquot 1928

Roti
Longe de Mouton roti .... Imperial Bual Madeira

Entremets
Ponding à la Meite .... 1819 Grande Champagne; Liqueur Cognac

Savoury
Anges dos de Cheval

Liqueurs
Dessert
Café

Prior to this there was some sporting entertainment, and Ursula's company was requested for

> Tea and to witness the Boat-Race at the Palace Moat on the 23rd January 1938 at 3.30pm, and Manipuri and Naga athletics on the Polo ground 24th January 1938 from 11.15am to 12.45pm (local).

The hospitality and entertainment were relentless – one day later their presence was requested to attend a further sporting spectacle – a Manipuri Polo Match on the Polo ground on 25 January 1938 at 4pm (local). Although Ursula made no comment on the banquet or the boat race, she recalled the polo vividly:

> Manipuri polo is quite remarkable. There are no rules whatsoever and if you can't hit the ball, you hit everything else, including the opposing rider. There was one moment when the ball shot up the pavilion steps and clean between His Highness the Maharajah and His Excellency the Governor, hotly pursued by two players, up the steps on their ponies – which is a thing I had never seen at Hurlingham!

At last, as the finale of the state visit, the native entertainment offered something Ursula could really enjoy:

> His Highness the Maharajah of Manipur requests the pleasure of
> The company of Miss Bower to witness the Kabui Nagas dance on the Residency lawn on the 29th January 1938 at 6pm (local)

The Imphal residents' attitude to the Nagas was a mixture of condescension and mild distaste – this would have been their least favourite entertainment laid on during the visit. To Ursula, however, it was to be the highlight. Yet, having been so captivated by the Naga people in their own environment, she felt embarrassed at being party to an event where they had unashamedly been recruited for their novelty value – a controlled opportunity to see some sanitised savages. To Ursula their dancing was more than a colourful turn laid on for the British – however, faced with the prospect that she might never see Nagas again, she succumbed to temptation and made free with her camera:

> There were very fine Naga tribal dancers – whom I'm afraid I photographed. They must have thought I was mad. They were so picturesque – magnificent dance steps. Eventually I managed to buy one of the costumes. I went up to a young man with the aid of an interpreter and said that it was a beautiful costume, and I would so much like to take it back to England … and with the greatest good humour he let me trade some cigarettes for it.

With a case full of Naga artefacts and many rolls of film, Ursula prepared to leave. Far from being physically beaten by the heat, tortuous terrain and unfamiliar food, she had relished the challenge and grown in confidence – and as for feeling intimidated by the strange, savage people, she had been entranced by them from the very first sight. She reflected, enraptured, 'We did two hundred miles on our hind legs and never got so much as a sore toe – and we loved it. It was marvellous.'

In April Ursula was at sea, bound for London, with no idea that she would ever see India and the Nagas again.

7

Ursula – the Anthropologist

Back with Humpus in London in the summer of 1938, Ursula was short of cash and, with no likelihood of returning to India, had to consider her winter visit as a wonderful but never-to-be-repeated adventure. She sent her films to be developed – and much to her surprise, the photos were no mere holiday snaps – they were of a professional standard, and of considerable anthropological interest. A family friend took Ursula and her photos to the Royal Geographical and the Royal Central Asian Societies and introduced her to some independent anthropologists. All enthused about her photos and asked if she would be going back – it would be a waste of her evident talent and unquestionable passion not to follow up this promising start. As a boost to her confidence, the Royal Geographical Society put on an exhibition of her photos and eminent anthropologists were generous in their praise.

Even so, Ursula still had no-one to back her and no way of getting back into Manipur – then she received a letter from Jeffery. He was planning one last trip to the Barak River before retiring – if she and a suitably hardy chaperone would like to accompany him, they would be very welcome. Ursula needed no second bidding.

> Here was my chance, and it was up to me to use it. I should be going through country where very few people went and there was no point in travelling aimlessly and wasting time and films on casual pictures. I must concentrate on something, and as I was interested in the tribes, the obvious field was anthropology. I knew nothing at all about it and I had no training, but I felt that there might be some worthwhile work simple enough for a layman to tackle.

Feeling presumptuous in daring to approach established anthropological experts, and risking rejection, Ursula wrote to Professor J.H. Hutton and Professor Hodson of Cambridge, asking for advice.

She explained what she had learned en route and how she was desperate to return. She concluded:

> In spite of all the mistakes, I have a considerable collection of pictures – about 850 – covering nearly every tribe in Manipur, as well as some outside it. The Secretary of the Royal Central Asian Society, hearing that I had been asked to join a party going through the Barak gorges below the Cachar road, suggested that as I was really interested in the Nagas, I should ask advice from those who knew most about them…

She was delighted to learn that there was plenty of work she could do. Very little photography had been done in the Manipur Hills and although trained observers had made written records of technical processes such as weaving, pottery-making, brass-casting and building, they had not captured them on film. Good quality stills or, even better, cine films, would be very welcome.

Ursula was invited to lecture to several anthropological societies – with gratifying success, albeit not much remuneration.

> I had found I could lecture, I thought I could write, I could sometimes take good pictures; I knew I wanted adventure. There wasn't a scrap of certainty that I should ever make anything of it, but I saw – which matters more at twenty-four – unlimited possibilities.

Ursula spent all her savings on a Bell and Howell model E cine camera and films, prepared a list of subjects, and by late September she was ready to go.

World events took an alarming turn in late 1938 as Germany embarked on an aggressively expansionist policy under the National Socialist regime of the Chancellor, Adolf Hitler. When Neville Chamberlain returned from the Munich Conference in September with a promise that there would be no war over Czechoslovakia and that there would be 'peace for our time' – whatever that really meant – the nation heaved sighs of relief. Desperate not to be drawn into another war like that of 1914–18, people in Britain read into Chamberlain's pronouncement what they wanted, and on that basis, international tension relaxed. All the same, the British authorities began to prepare for war and Ursula volunteered for the London Ambulance Service.

There was still no war, so travel was no problem, and Ursula was much encouraged by a letter from Professor Hodson of Cambridge:

> A line to wish you good luck and complete success in your enterprise. You know what to do, what to wear, what to take, from past experience. It is a lovely country – those deep gorges, great trees and the swirling river. There are mahseer to be had – huge fellows. But for me the great interest is still in the people. They are very human, quite friendly to those who want and are seen to want to be friendly with them... Anyway, let them talk, get them interested, and out of the fullness of their hearts you will surely get information of real scientific value... We look forward to a visit from you here when you come home again, and if there is anything else I can do for you, I am only too ready.

By November, Ursula was back in India. The tour was down the Barak River, but this time going further downstream towards the Lushai border. This area was further away from the Naga Hills and the people and villages Ursula most wanted to photograph, but even so, the area wasn't without interest. Just being out in wild country and among the local tribes was enough. The serious photography could wait while Ursula regained her 'jungle legs'. The route covered some 200 miles, part on foot and part by river, passing through the territory of a number of different tribes, including the Kuki. It might not be the Naga Hills proper, but it was new ground with old friends.

While Jeffery still had Hamja and Umaid as his regular staff, Ursula's companion and 'chaperone' was to be Celia, wife of SDO Duncan.

The first port of call was Lakhimpur, where one of her photographic subjects from the previous tour, an old man from Kambirong, arrived carrying the photo which she had sent to him via Jeffery.

> He was tickled cock-eyed. Gave him big copy out of exhibition and delighted him beyond all belief. The world's biggest thrill. He compared it with himself and told the story four times over before they finally cleared off for the night.

The next day more visitors came in from Kambirong and Ursula entertained them with the previous year's photos. This was an enormous success and soon the visitors were recognising men they knew from Oinomlong and Okoklong – which as she observed, was quite clever, as they were not used to photos. Meeting white Europeans was a novelty in itself, but to be presented with photos, and to see the technical equipment was little short of miraculous. A young buck explored the cine camera and tripod with awe and fascination, and worked out how to work the tripod – 'much erecting and collapsing of same by all parties'.

By the campfire that night, the men from Kambirong invited Ursula and Celia to see a song and dance party – a filming opportunity not to be missed. The girls set off in the early morning, and having got past the obligatory welcome committee with zu and oranges ('we drank zu for the honour of Britain'), they went on to the village where a considerable welcome committee awaited them at the headman's house:

> Were received by assorted elders, and parked on morahs on spread matting with hens and zu laid in huge quantities before us. Village then gathered in a body, most of it in a rag and a bead, and beamed and stared and giggled. Bucks appeared in fragments of costume. Babies invaded the matting in all stages of nakedness … More partially dressed performers appeared and giggled. Crowd thickened, so did atmosphere.

Their visit was a real event, and Ursula explained many years later:

> Long after I had left India and was back in England in the 50s, 60s and 70s, I met grown men – Nagas visiting England – who remembered seeing me when they were small children.

The downriver journey continued, sometimes negotiating between steep cliffs and gorges, and disembarking to avoid rapids, where the coolies lowered the rafts down on ropes to the next level of the river. The descent on foot was often steep and tortuous, and the girls scrambled clumsily down slippery, moss-covered boulders and sheer rockfaces. On one very rugged passage, the only route down was through dense jungle, so Ursula instructed one, 'Cuthbert,' by sign language, to go ahead and hack away. Twenty minutes later they reached steep descending rocks, which Ursula slid down, 'largely on my tail', clasping the only handhold available – a banana-trunk swarming with ants. While Cuthbert tried to dust the ants off Ursula, Celia slid down behind her in the same way, so that she too was covered with ants. 'One ant started up her shorts. Gentleman in blue jacket gave a seraphic smile and pursued and captured it.' But the locals had no hidden agenda. They were unashamedly entertained by these Western women's antics – in a gentle and childlike way. Ursula had no great love for social niceties, and far from finding this familiarity menacing or inappropriate, she was in her element.

At Longphailum, she and Celia 'chatted' in sign language with the local grandmothers who brought babies to show them, before tackling a rush of stomach-churningly revolting casualties:

> First, boy with festering dao cut on wrist. Then man came up, peeled off his shirt and revealed hole two inches long, one inch wide and half an inch deep over left shoulder-blade, apparently full of maggots. Washed it for half an hour in strong Dettol and water solution, hot. Succeeded in loosening matter, which we had taken for maggots.

Ursula had high hopes of the next camp offering some modest creature comforts, and at first sight, it looked promising. Once again, however, the 'H of P' let the camp down. 'Most insanitary on record. Smell nearly gassed us out of camp. Guessed someone else had been using it before us.'

All the same, they stayed put the next day, Ursula and Celia

> held a super washday and disposed of enormous arrears, including the shorts covered with mud. Heard loud wallowing just after we had hung things up to dry; suspected elephants. Went back to bank (in pyjamas) to see. Saw elephant swimming, lathi-wallah up and baby swimming alongside and round. Elephant landed near port. Man called he would come to camp. Ran up to camp, elephant wallowing after in slow time. Man parked elephant in mid-camp, among the washing; baby still wobbly on legs and absolute comic turn.

The next day on the river Jeffery had dropped some distance behind them when they reached the first stopping place, so they waited on the sandbank:

> The entire party, by ones and twos, took off its clothes and bathed in *puris naturalibus* all round the shore. Some very good figures revealed by this process, all with a much lighter band where the loincloth went. Regular sculptor's model among the later bathers.

The locals watched with interest while the girls swam – but it was two-way traffic, and Ursula was fascinated by the display of bronzed Naga physiques.

With all this marching and exercise, Ursula lost weight steadily, despite the hearty meals and regular stops for zu and oranges. On 1 December Ursula logged a trek of between five and seven miles, with a bumper thirteen-miler the next day – 'more off the waistline we hope'. This was a perfect lifestyle where she could work up an appetite and eat to her heart's content, knowing that she'd need every bit of energy to deal with the next day's march.

The next port of call was Talbung where, once again the locals gathered to spectate:

> Huge crowd of people, mainly babies and all very dirty. Inquired after weaving and went up village with forest Chowkidar who would speak English I couldn't understand, and filmed and photographed plain tension loom in house, enormously hampered by large crowd and almost total lack of light. House had sliding door and shutters. On our arrival, window opened to admit light, door closed. Lady previously weaving in almost total darkness. Large skull, presumably buffalo, by wall near loom, also thapus full of raw cotton, into all of which I backed periodically. Filming not easy, and goodness knows what results are.

Desperate to do well, Ursula could only wait and see.

The party carried on to Pherjol, a Christian village where the camp proved to be shabby, full of borer beetles, bugs and accompanying showers of sawdust, and tastefully situated near a graveyard full of standing stones. These Christian faithful lacked the charm of their pagan neighbours – 'Locals plain, missionised and generally pretty awful. Society for Preservation of Paganism has received a smart fillip from them'.

That evening Ursula recorded:

> Had a large curry dinner backed by Jeff's most ferocious cocktails, and all went to bed delightfully tight and quite riotous. Had lengthy and gin-flavoured discussion on theology round the fire.

Ursula's impression of the locals remained unimproved by the gathering the next morning:

> Locals swarmed round basha rails like crowd round lion's cage and watched us breakfast. Disliked them more than ever. Much giggling, and unpleasant atmosphere after pagan villages. Nasty, unco-operative feel about them.

It was with relief they reached Thalon, where the welcome was comfortingly pagan and bibulous: 'At long last, reached reception committee of one zu-nosed Kuki with bottle of the usual.'

The tour passed through an extravaganza of flora, fauna and scenery, and Ursula waxed lyrical:

> Long, very zigzag climb, towards crater; lovely moss-grown rocks, magnificent views towards Lushai territory. At last reached timber-line and edge of crater. Jeff had the gun and fired two shots, and echoes went rolling away like a thunder-clap all round crater. Tremendous gulfs and gullies down below, and trees clinging to face of sheer sandstone cliff. Climbed on, and got into lovely high timber, tall trees sixty feet or more, with no branches for forty feet of it. Beautiful march through this forest – orchids, tree ferns, dwarf bamboo – till woods and secondary jungle began and we reached camp near fields.

All too soon the tour was at an end and Ursula and Celia were back at the resthouse. 'Had excellent dinner, and so to bed, not really sorry to be in comfort and a solid building for once, but regretting bitterly our hills, which Celia loves as much as I do.' Back in 'civilisation', Ursula reflected on the last twenty-five days – time seemed to have been playing tricks: 'It felt as though I hadn't been away a day. And I could not believe I'd been in England six months; it was like another world.'

8

Going it Alone

Even before this last tour, Ursula had been captivated – but now she was totally enthralled. She admitted, 'I really had got the bug', so as soon as she got back from the Barak trip, she applied to the Political Agent, Gimson, for permission to go out on her own, with her own camp with a small staff and coolies, to continue with her photography. This would be the acid test. She had proved she could deal with the rigours of marching and roughing it – but running the trip herself, exercising her own authority and earning the respect of the Naga people without any supervising authority would be another matter.

To Ursula's surprise, permission was granted. Ladies were not in the habit of setting out unchaperoned into Naga country with only native staff, and 'there was a great deal of tut-tutting and firm belief that at the end of about three days I should be borne home in a fainting condition.' With all this negative opinion, even Ursula had to admit, as the time got nearer for her to depart, that it was all rather alarming. She had no backing, so had no money except for her allowance from England, and her camp set-up was sketchy in the extreme. She eventually scraped together a camp bed, chair, table and bath, some cutlery, a set of cooking pots and a plastic picnic set, and as far as her wardrobe went, she had some cheap cotton shirts, a few pairs of cotton drill shorts, one warm sweater and a golf jacket. This vision of hill-walking sartorial elegance was finished off with Pathan-style open sandals called chapplis, and British Army socks. These bare essentials would have to see her through – what was going to be important was how successful she was with her photography. She'd invested in good-quality equipment – if she didn't have the skill to get good results with these cameras, then no amount of fancy camping kit would make any difference.

The trip to a Kabui village, which Ursula would later see as a 'preliminary canter' but which at the time was pretty hair-raising, kicked off on 7 January 1939. Jeffery accompanied Ursula to the Bishenpur inspection bungalow, where she met her 'staff'. One was Abung, who so closely resembled a baleful-looking wombat that Ursula couldn't help referring to him in her diary as such. The other, a Kuki student boy who would be her interpreter, bristled with efficiency – he seemed intelligent and had a reasonable grasp of English which, Ursula predicted, would become a good deal more fluent than her Hindustani over the next few days.

Although reasonably confident with her staff, Ursula confessed to feeling very cold and small as she climbed into the truck, her baggage stacked on the back with the servants piled on top. 'We rolled off towards the foot of the hills and I was alone with my abilities.'

At the very first village the coolies started 'trying it on', saying that they wanted to change over there and then – meaning Ursula would have to take on new carriers. Starting as she meant to go on, Ursula put her foot down and with Student Boy Efficiency translating, the coolies were persuaded to carry on.

The next stop was a large, unspoilt Chiru village, just downhill from Kakadang where she would be staying. A welcome committee escorted them to the village, where a large crowd of mixed Nagas had gathered:

> Was presented with two goats, seven dozen bananas, some oranges and three bottles of zu, which I don't want. Handed out ten rupees for basha, 3/8 for coolies plus one baksheesh and about twenty packets of cigarettes.

This established cordial relations, and Ursula knuckled down to some dispensary work:

> By way of opening gambit, picked out Chiru with bandaged foot. Found it a healed burn, but applied Tannafax for the good of the advertisement. Immediately scored a damaged knee, sore eyes, baby with boils and skin eruptions – wriggly patient and yelled like hell; took four, mother, headman, Efficiency and self to cope. Followed two failing sight, one rheumatism, two (alas!) suspected syphilis and a Chiru who arrived at dusk with the hell of a damaged and suppurating foot, got by falling off a bridge... other patients boy with sore ear from earring and gent with inflamed eye.

Ursula recorded her first solo day's events in minute detail, from what the village looked like, to what the locals wore and what she had to eat:

> Abung not a bad cook. Had sausage, soup, carrots and biscuits for post-surgery lunch – 3.30pm. Soup, sausage and two fried eggs for dinner, also tinned (very sweet) raspberries, remainder of which I have postponed till breakfast.

It was an adventure she wanted to remember forever.

The highlight of the next day was a feast in neighbouring Majuron:

> Arrived in village and found party assembled outside decorated house. They built a huge fire at my feet and so roasted me. My almost healed scratches began to bleed! They danced with great enthusiasm, but moderate skill, all the old women joining in the songs, including one permanently drunk old hen from Kakadan, who refused to leave me alone. Had to drink zu out of a brass bowl polished first on somebody's cloth, then on SB's handkerchief. Then mine. (God help us!) Dance went on. I got hotter. At last, during interval for refreshments, I managed to move my chair. Found myself all among the firewood and the girls. Stood by the fire and laughed and ragged with them; gave them two hairpins, which caused much merriment.

Back to the village and Abung by 10.30 – 'faithful Wombat, looking faintly reproachful, produced dinner'. The villagers threw themselves with gusto into providing hospitality. The Chirus carried on the previous evening's party and Kakadan was quick to offer their support, arriving en masse in full dress, carrying a large drum slung on a pole. The Chirus' orchestra included a string fiddle, a gourd bagpipe, and mithan horns used for percussion and their music was unlike anything Ursula had heard before – but unfortunately she had no sound-recording facility. The villages vied enthusiastically to put on the best entertainment, and again Ursula handed out baksheesh of cigarettes – it was as well that she had sent a man with a chit to Jeffery for more cigarettes.

Later Ursula opened the dispensary, but was interrupted by the return of the coolie from Jeffery along with another 'bearer' – Gaipuiga from Kambirong, and they fell on each other's necks like old friends. With great sang froid, Ursula instructed two Chiru coolies to kill one of the goats she'd been given. They were to save a hind leg for her, the rest was to be divided between Gaipuiga and headman Atongba, and for this they would be rewarded with the head and stomach. Ursula knew she would have to muck in and not turn squeamish – and the hard part would be getting used to the more gory aspects of village life.

Old Gaipuiga and his two kinsmen left the following day, and Ursula tackled the growing queue waiting for her at the dispensary. One case seriously tested her fortitude – if this one didn't reduce her to 'fainting condition' anticipated by the ex-pats in Imphal, nothing would:

> A woman from neighbouring village turned up with the worst case I have yet seen. Her baby's hand and left ear was a seething mass of black scab and pus, with heads of pus dotted all over the neck and body. It is the first case I have really jibbed at, but there was nobody to wish it on, so I got down to it with Dettol. Oh my God! The more matter came away, the more there seemed to be. Got most of the scabs off with swabs, hot Dettol and lint, the baby shrieking the place down all the time – I bet it hurt, too. Eventually gave up exhausted and bandaged the sores with wadges of cotton wool and lint in the hope of getting matter away.

Away from the safety net of hospitals and doctors, people just got on with being ill and, if not cured by local medicine man or getting better of their own accord, they simply died. The baby was brought in again the next day, 'bleeding this time and looking an awful mess', and after tightening the bandage, Ursula sent mother and baby away until the next day – 'the ordeal is too much'.

Ursula fitted photographic forays in between the dispensaries, methodically ticking the subjects off her list as she captured them: inside of houses, spear-throwing and sports, weaving, dancing, pottery – and she never failed to be delighted at the presents brought in for her or to give appropriate baksheesh. Ursula was utterly captivated by the people, and if her attitude towards them sometimes seemed patronising, it was because they were often disarmingly childlike.

Night was falling on the eve of Ursula's last full day. Patients treated, more photos in the bag and she was ready for an early night:

> Student Boy and Abung made the deuce of a noise in the cookhouse when I'd gone to bed, Student Boy yodelling interminable hymns. Stood it for a while and then got out of bed, went to door with torch and yelled, 'Stop that noise!' Instant silence.

> Someone came to the cookhouse door. I shone the torch on them, but couldn't see who it was. I went in again. Door unslammable, but I would have if I could.

Eventually, on 16 January, baggage packed, it was time to go. Before she left, however, there was bad news – a boy, one of the dancers from the party a few days back had died in the night. Ursula had not even known he was ill, and it was a salutary reminder of the tenuous hold the hill people had on life, and an insight into why, when any opportunity for fun arose, they never failed to make the most of it.

Recalling the solo trip during an interview in 1985, she summed it up:

> They couldn't have been more delighted to be honoured with the presence of an unescorted young lady. They did me proud. And the neighbouring villages came in and danced – we had a gorgeous time. It was ten days, and far from coming home with shattered nerves, I returned in triumph in the lorry, as happy as a sandboy, clutching specimens and being the best of friends with the Kabui village. I brought back a very nice young man's cloth, and a very beautiful cane basket of the kind that young men use to keep their ornaments in. At the present moment it acts as my work basket … I wouldn't part with it for anything.

In her own words, her ten days away had been 'riotous', and although her sojourn among the Kabui Nagas might not be everyone's idea of a good time, to her it was heaven. 'I came home after passionate and affectionate farewells with the village, laden with specimens, photographs and information. After that there was no holding me.'

Ursula was now ready to go unaccompanied for as long as could possibly be managed. Her success with the Nagas was largely down to respect – and genuine liking:

> They were a most marvellously civil and courteous people – very shy. They didn't know anything about Europeans. They didn't want to give any offence. We certainly had some rather amusing episodes, but they were simply charming. The more I saw of them, the more I liked them.

Even the language was becoming less of a barrier. Ursula was mastering Hindustani quickly, and using that as a common language, and with a fair smattering of English on the part of the interpreter, communication was no problem. Ursula simply relaxed and enjoyed herself – and the Nagas, having fun with this strange Englishwoman in their midst, were delighted to help her.

With confidence high, Ursula prepared to go out again – this time to Tangkhul country to the north and east of Imphal. Apart from the coolies, Ursula would have just two companions – her servant, Abung, and a Manipuri compounder. The former, 'small, faithful, furry and no cook', had become an important member of Ursula's household at Imphal and it was only some time later that she realised how many difficulties he smoothed over for her. The latter was a gentle, kindly soul who would deal with the lion's share of dispensary duties.

In the drought of February, Ursula set out in a pillar of dust across the plain towards Ukhrul. The land is mountainous, with river valleys etched out between the ridges, which run in a roughly north-south direction, and Ukhrul is situated on one of these ridges, some 6,000 feet above sea level. At the Sub-Divisional Officer (SDO)'s bungalow, Duncan awaited them, and the dark bungalow had been made available for Ursula, who took a day to refit and reorganise it. Celia Duncan had considered accompanying them, but was unable to, so on 13 February Ursula, Abung, the compounder and ten Ukhrul coolies set out in the cold, the threat of rain in the air. She admitted to feeling very forlorn at the head of her little cavalcade. Ursula's particular aim was to photograph native pottery-making, and the two Nungbi villages, Khulen and Khunao, being situated near a bed of clay, had something of a local monopoly in this field. The route took them through pinewoods where red needles carpeted the forest floor, and they headed into the hills, bright green, blue and brown in the rain-clear air. At Khunao, relays of reception committees welcomed them to a very satisfactory basha – although a bitter wind had blown up which swept through it and the grass-and-matting huts all around.

By now Ursula was an old hand at entertaining the locals, and soon after arriving she produced her camera tripod, typewriter and a clutch of photos. In no time the crowds were filling the veranda. One young buck, Luikai, stood out particularly – for one thing he had a face like Mickey Rooney, Ursula observed. For another, he was nursing a case of scabies. He knew some Hindustani and was familiar with English characters, so they had some fun with the typewriter and the tripod, as ever, proved a source of endless amusement.

Ursula found out that Luikai, 'a small, grimy, snub-nosed Tangkhul', had run himself into debt over his wife's funeral. For whatever reason, ignorance or sheer perversity, he had given the prescribed parts of the sacrifice to the wrong people and had therefore had to pay for the whole ceremony to be performed again. He was desperate to earn the money and, his wife being dead, he had no reason to stay put – he wanted to join Ursula's staff on a permanent basis. Wearing just his tattered cloth, he stood shivering and anxious as Ursula and the compounder considered the appointment. She decided to take him on – 'scabies and all, as he seems intelligent and is admirably decorative for a foreground figure' – as she further commented in her later book, *Naga Path*, 'he had the itch, unfortunately – but then most Tangkhuls had'.

The next day Ursula headed north:

> Down from Nungbi we went, to the hills I had looked at so longingly the year before. It was like a dream now to be walking their rise and fall; the air of morning in one's face, the mist clearing, the file of porters in front, the pad-pad of barefooted followers behind. Never had I known such exhilaration, such passionate happiness; your loads up, your porters off, the mountains round you and the world ahead – can anyone twenty-four and adventurous ask for more?

A daily routine soon developed. With the first gleam of daylight through the walls of Ursula's hut, Abung would arrive with tea. All available hands packed the kit and got the porters off on the road while Ursula and the compounder held a final dispensary. The tour took them well off the beaten track to bring medicine to out-of-the-way settlements where undoubtedly there was an urgent need for treatment. Ursula and the compounder were generally on the road by eight o'clock, but even with only a short march to their next scheduled stop, there would be halts en route. These would seldom last under an hour, after which, having gained the locals' confidence, Ursula took photographs:

> sometimes posed, grave headmen against their house-fronts, to show the sweep of the Tangkhul haircut, the fine features; sometimes unstudied, snatched at the right moment, a quick portrait of a laughing boy.

Then it was back on the road to arrive at the camp where, she hoped, the porters had set things up for the night. There would be a short rest and a bite to eat, then another long evening dispensary.

Although the cases arrived marshalled along by a headman, there was still an unpleasant press as the jostling circle of bare, brown, unwashed bodies wriggled in ever more tightly around them, chivvying to be seen. Scabies, worms and malaria were the most common problems, but coughs and bronchitis came a close second, followed by a range of sceptic wounds, abscesses and ulcers, with the occasional tooth extraction. Sometimes there was no building in which to conduct the dispensary so they set the medicines out on a bench or on the ground, and they had their work cut out to keep the dust and flies off. The British administration provided good medical facilities – however, the hill-dwellers were naturally nervous of travelling to a 'big town' such as Imphal, and when ill, preferred to stay at home. The people were happier if the treatment came to them, so when a dispensary tour reached them, they flocked to it. As Ursula recognised, 'used in this way, a few plain drugs could relieve a disproportionate amount of suffering'.

At her next camp, Ursula's accommodation was a large, plank-walled building, surrounded in the clearing by the men's shelters – all very well laid out and reasonably comfortable. As night fell, Ursula came to lock up and found that the crude wooden door had no latch or bar to hold it shut, and as it wouldn't wedge closed, she just had to leave it swinging open. Looking out, the fire was down to a few embers, everything was quiet and there was not a breath of wind to carry sounds from the village. All Ursula could hear was the breathing of the men in the nearest huts, and in this peaceful atmosphere she left the door open, went to bed and slept soundly.

In the morning the camp was in uproar. The coolies said they had heard a tiger, prowling among the huts and growling – and now they were desperate to get away. Abung was positively pop-eyed with fear and the compounder was distinctly uneasy. Ursula expressed her doubts – tigers were not common at that altitude in cold weather, and it would be even rarer for a tiger to venture among buildings and near to fires. If there was a man-eating tiger in the area they would have heard about it. Only later, as she recalled the incident to Duncan on her way back, did she learn that legend had it there was a 'were-tiger' in Luchai, and this was generally accepted locally. Given this circumstance, it was the Nagas' immediate conclusion that it was this were-tiger that had visited them. The original man-tiger was apparently dead, but his son was still at large, although Duncan said he could not get the villagers to reveal who it was. Certainly not silly or superstitious, but awake to the possibility of an uncharted world of the paranormal, Ursula was not going to pooh-pooh local lore. Given the evil reputation of the were-tiger she thought back with a shiver to her 'un-shuttable' door.

Much to the relief of the compounder, they were soon en route for Chingjaroi, where a terrific crowd gathered for the first dispensary, and Ursula wondered if they were all genuinely ill or just curious. Again, a crowd of unwashed bodies pressed around her – her photos, tripod, knitting and zip fasteners attracted the usual interest and when she produced the typewriter, the veranda creaked with a crowd which Ursula owned 'nearly gassed me. God knows what I've caught, both germs and lice'.

Luikai was proving invaluable, and Ursula thought about the new addition to the household. It was odd to think that he was already a widower – he didn't look more than twenty-two or twenty-five – and although shivering in mere rags, he was trying very hard to please:

> After some heartburning I told Abung to call him, and gave him my best Tangkhul cloth. He made a hasty sort of salaaming motion and said, 'H'zoor!' and went out of the door like a bullet. I saw him legging it hard with a broad grin.

Next morning Ursula set out to climb Chingjui Hill which rose up 7,000 feet high behind Chingjaroi, with Khullakpa and two other elders and Luikai carrying the camera, along with a party of twelve strong bucks equipped with daos.

This was a major excursion via a vertical path which had not been used for some time, and although an advance party had been out to hack back the overgrowth, the bucks were there in case more cutting was needed. The weather had been generally cold during the tour, but on this day a steamy heat hung over the cliff-face as they toiled upwards in a cloud of mosquitoes. Making regular stops to catch her breath, Ursula confessed 'my form not very good', but it gave her a chance to enjoy the wonderful views, only slightly spoiled by the smoke rising from the jhum burning of stubble below. At the top of the first ridge they paused – the grey of the horizon melted into a lowering sky and just one feature stood out in a blaze of white – the snow-covered peak of Saramati.

> Had sudden vision, just below summit, of snow-covered hills miles away into the unadministered country. Sun was on the snow and it looked glorious. The vision was short lived. There was just the one glimpse of it, bright, unearthly; and then the sun went and the greyness swallowed it up.

As the party toiled back to camp, Ursula was suddenly stricken by the onset of fever and aching all over. However, there was nothing to be gained by taking to her camp bed, so after a late tiffin she had a fire lit outside in the evening, sent zu down to the cookhouse and watched while Luikai and a young Kuki Naga competed at acrobatics until they were exhausted.

The next day, feeling little better, Ursula marched for Khunao proper. As she opened the dispensary, Ursula realised with alarm that there were lepers among the cases. There was a leper asylum not far away in Kangpokpi, and she had refused to go there – now there was nothing she could do but send them away. The persistence of this almost biblical condition gave Ursula pause for thought, but there was little time to brood over it, as what appeared to be a ladies' glee club arrived and serenaded them with a repertoire of specially composed songs, mainly about her and the compounder, and another about her as a *maibi*, or priestess – and how pleased they were to have them there. Lyrics were on the lines of 'she came from far off, yet she was here now and they were much pleased with her behaviour'. They considered it to be a good show and much appreciation was shown for the medicines dispensed.

Arriving shortly after the compounder at the next village, Ursula found a huge throng awaiting treatment:

> Awful jam of people, germs, etc. Felt half dead. They gave me a lovely cloth, but I was too tired to see it till later. Crawled up the hill to Huining after camping at bridge and collecting reception committee, hunting party etc. Had to sit down and rest and panted at every corner. Oh, disgrace! Had a grand whisky, tea and two aspirins and perked up no end.

Thus fortified she turned out for the evening dispensary, where spirit attack seemed to be the order of the day. Among them 'one old boy had been "severely attacked by a vampire", so prescribed Carter's Little Liver Pills, with complicated directions. Calomel good specific against spirits.' Ursula was respectful enough of the Nagas' culture to see that the old man's faith in her ability to cure him was paramount, so a good panacea such as Carter's might be just the thing. Gratifyingly, he arrived in the morning much improved, 'full of beans and demanding more!'

Just thirteen days after she left, Ursula was back in Ukhrul. For the first time she was in charge of the money, so she checked over her accounts. 'Found I only have 20 rupees – barely enough for coolies. Cast up accounts and found all accounted for except a chip or two – well within the margin of error.' Ursula was not going to let a small matter of money foil her plans, and the following morning, eight house coolies in tow, she was on the march again, towards a camp outside Tuinem, a village high on her list of photographic subjects.

In other Naga tribes the women wove cloths for their own households, while only the particularly skilled workers made cloths for sale, but among the Tangkhul Nagas there were just half a dozen villages whose weavers supplied the whole tribal area. With her particular interest in textiles, Ursula was especially looking forward to seeing the weavers in action. The spectacle didn't disappoint:

> Nowhere have I seen such a concentration of textiles as there was at Tuinem – racks of blue and crimson cloths were airing outside every house; skeins of dyed thread, red, white, black, orange, green and gold, were stretched to dry or lay beside the women as they worked. In every porch was a loom, with a cloth on it at one stage or another.

The patterns, the intricacy of the work and the wonderful colours were intoxicating – Ursula hurried around with her cameras in a state of euphoria, the only disappointment being that she had only twelve rupees left to spend. But what riches could be bought with twelve rupees! After much deliberation, Ursula found a large men's cloth for six rupees for Luikai and a smaller one for herself at just five. He pronounced himself very happy with his gift – although he felt she'd been sold a pup in the case of her cloth as it suffered from a 'kamti' – some sort of defect. However, kamti or not, it was just the colour Ursula wanted. With no more money, Ursula put temptation behind her and returned to the camp.

With the end of the tour drawing uncomfortably near, Ursula began to feel that familiar depression:

> Another page turned. Oh God, how little I want to go! From Shongphel we marched down to the plain, the waiting lorry and Imphal; and every step away from the hills was a separate pain. For the first time I had known responsibility, loneliness, worry and exhaustion. I'd been revolted by wounds and filth, hampered by lack of the language, but nevertheless, I was going back to it if it killed me. And I couldn't have given a sane reason why.

9

Black Magic

Ursula was back in Imphal by 2 March, and a week later she had arranged to go out again. She had ticked every item on her list for photographing and filming – so on this trip anthropology was going to take second place. She'd seen the need for medical help in the more remote areas, so this was the purpose of her tour. As she had reassured Humpus in a letter, she had booked a passage back to England on the *Strathearn* on 11 March, but there was just enough time to go out again.

Abung was already established as camp cook, but Luikai's position was less certain – however, two days before setting off, he particularly asked Ursula if he could stay on. The compounder, however, had not volunteered for another tour, so a replacement had to be found at short notice. With apologies, the Civil Surgeon introduced the best he could find – a tall, sullen Kuki Naga called Jangsang who, he warned, was a trouble-maker and not to be trusted. Ursula would have to keep an eye on him and guard the key to the medicine chest closely.

Ursula headed north-east out of Imphal, and the first day's march took them seventeen miles over a very steep route to Lambui. Luikai chose his moment outside the village to announce that he would like to quit and go home. Ursula was getting the measure of compounder Mark II and was quite prepared to believe that he had put Luikai up to this – his resignation could not have come at a more inconvenient time. Two days earlier she could have engaged someone else in Imphal, but now there was no saying what sort of specimen she could recruit at short notice and in a small village:

> I reached Lambui in the blue, shadowy dusk, so furious that it startled even myself, Luikai (whom I had well and truly sworn at) trotting meekly after me. In the basha I couldn't trust myself within reach of him, so stayed in the veranda while he made beds etc, as a peace offering. Eventually his scared face and anxious patting of sheets were so funny I couldn't help grinning, and went in to look. Abung came and I told him. He jollied Luikai in a fatherly way, Luikai clutched a sheet to his bosom and said in a terrified voice he wouldn't go till the memsahib gave him leave.

The household was unchanged as they pushed on to their old camp at Nungbi Khunao, but already a blight had been cast over the start of the tour.

Two days later, on their last morning at the camp, Abung arrived with tea as the first light slanted through the flimsy walls. Ursula got out of bed and, shivering in the draught, took off her pyjamas. She was about to dress when the door flew open.

The figure of a man was silhouetted in the doorway, and he walked straight in. It was Jangsang. Grabbing a towel and wrapping herself up she shouted out, 'I'm not dressed yet. Please go away!' But he took no notice and, averting his gaze from Ursula as his only concession, proceeded to open and unpack the medicine jappa. Ursula watched, amazed, as he was followed in by a stream of dispensary cases who had no reason to suppose it was not all right to enter.

Only later did Ursula realise what was going on. 'I didn't grasp it – I thought he hadn't heard. "What is it, please? Is it urgent? I want to dress – I'd rather you came back later".' Unnoticed until then by the growing crowd of ailing Tangkhuls, Ursula's voice drew their attention and, shocked and embarrassed, they stopped in their tracks. Frozen, they watched as Jangsang toyed sullenly with the medicines. His movements were slow and his voice was groggy; a cigarette hung on his lip as he snapped, 'I want medicine'.

Then Ursula realised the enormity – the malice – of it:

> Sitting there on my bed, half-covered, the Tangkhuls shuffling uncomfortably and looking the other way, I understood. It was deliberate; and quite deliberately he had brought in the Tangkhuls, to shame me just that much more. I found myself shaking. I jumped up and ran over to him. I told him, over and over again, to go. He rose and walked out slowly. The Tangkhuls had gone. I slammed the door. Trembling, nearly crying, I crammed my clothes on. The camp was quiet outside. I sat on the bed till I felt better, then I went out.

Outside, in front of the door, was a heap of baggage and squatting next to it was Jangsang. Without looking her in the eye, he announced triumphantly that she had offended him by her rudeness and he intended to return immediately to Imphal. It might have been her outburst at his intrusion – or perhaps because the day before she had ticked him off in the basha for talking to her with his back turned and a cigarette in his mouth.

So here would be an end to the trip. He had engineered the whole situation, knowing that no other compounder would be available. There would be no exploration of the more distant villages, no photography, no film – and no medical treatment for those who so badly needed it and who, by bush telegraph, had been led to hope it would soon arrive:

> At one stroke he had freed himself and ruined my enterprise, and that with as much humiliation and indecency as he could contrive in so short a space of time. And then I saw why he turned his face away. He couldn't suppress, in his moment of victory, a triumphant grin.

Something more powerful than Ursula's resentment at her lost dignity and more focussed than Jangsang's malice took over. The ill-disguised grin was the last straw and Ursula was prepared to go to any lengths to save her enterprise:

> All my personal considerations went like smoke. Come hell and high water, that compounder was going on, and the hill men would get their medicine. If it was

> the last thing I did, I was going to win this battle. There was one stroke on which I knew he was not counting. He had complained of my rudeness, therefore he required an apology. I let him have it – an exquisitely polite apology. It took the ground from under him like a trap. He tried to recover, but it was no use. I had him. My daemon had taken charge. My other self, small at a distance, heard my own voice talking rings round him with alien fluency. When, half an hour later, we left for Chingngai, I felt as though I had been wrung out like a dishcloth, but a black-sulky and disgruntled compounder was with us.

Ursula wanted to get to areas not previously reached by medical help, so their route took them north and east, through a range parallel to, but one east of, the last one. This took them within one ridge of the Burma border and here the people were less accustomed to travellers. The locals proved wild and shy, running superstitiously from Ursula's camera. Luikai and the coolies got wind of a rumour that the Tangkhuls of Somra village, just over the border, had recently killed two Manipuri traders and, in keeping with ancient tradition, had taken their heads. This was never confirmed, but it was something for Ursula to bear in mind.

Head-taking was the time-honoured custom in the unadministered area, and no outside influence had infiltrated the region to prevent it. Mills had made a punitive expedition to Pangsha in 1936 to put an end to this aggressive village's predatory habit of raiding smaller villages to take prisoners – destined for human sacrifice. On this extremely risky foray into unadministered country, he'd been taunted, threatened and goaded by the arrogant, warlike Pangshas until, when British sabre-rattling was no longer enough to make his point, he was forced to torch the village, along with its gruesome head-tree. He felt he was lucky to escape with his life – he knew that to show a glimmer of weakness would be to invite an attack, and that decisive, forceful action was the only thing the tribes would understand. And, in the tradition of 'the noble savage', after the torching of the village and a pitched battle in which Mills's Assam Rifles killed a number of Pangsha men, the village headman approached Mills with the respect demanded of a warrior for his conqueror.

The Pangsha episode had been brought to a satisfactory conclusion – all without loss to the expedition, and bringing considerable prestige to Mills for his courageous stance against the bullyboys of Pangsha. But the fact remained that Naga tribes could be unpredictable and, given their internecine squabbles, could suddenly become hostile to anyone who befriended their 'enemies'. This was not an area to be visited without a strong back-up of men and guns.

Ursula recognised that there was a brutal logic to their tradition:

> They'd always been head-hunters. As warriors, if you come home with a head, the rest of the person is not looking for you. There is also in Tangkhul a religious feel to it, that the soul is supposed to reside in the head, and the power is transferred through various ceremonies to the taker of the head. There is another point, that it proves a man is a warrior, and in the unadministered villages, in the old days, no man could marry who had not taken a head or taken part in a head-hunting.

Old habits die hard, and Ursula could not afford to be nonchalant about safety.

At the next stop, Ursula gained another member for her household – a tall Tangkhul Naga called Chinaorang, who was an excellent porter and inherited the medicine jappa. Strong and athletic, he toted the sixty-pound load effortlessly, striding ahead of Ursula to reach each new camp a good three-quarters of an hour before her. Like Luikai, he had a tale to tell – of an unexpectedly romantic nature. A poor man, he had inappropriately fallen in love with the daughter of a rich family, and disapproving of the match, her parents had married her off to a well-to-do youth in another village. The couple didn't get on and the bride sent for Chinaorang, asking him to rescue her. He rushed to her aid – only to find himself on a charge of wife-stealing, for which a fine of one hundred rupees was levied. He'd studiously ignored demands for this sum, but the wronged husband had threatened to take the case to the SDO, so Chinaorang, like Luikai, joined up for the money.

The outpost made a good operational base, and after a couple of days' work, Ursula called a rest. The camp was festooned with washing and the coolies had gone into Kharasom village when a deputation of headmen arrived from Chingjaroi. There was a desperately urgent case in the village – would Ursula come at once? It was a straight march of eight miles along a ridge, and Ursula and party half ran, half walked the distance to arrive in early dusk. The sick woman was in the Christian settlement, and Chinaorang and Jangsang accompanied Ursula, reaching the village in near darkness.

The headman met them at the door and ushered them into an oblong room where a fire burned in the middle of the floor. By it sat a man nursing a bundle of whimpering rags, and a woman, dishevelled and dirty, tended a pot of rice. Filthy, soot-covered pots and baskets littered the floor and in the unspeakable heat Ursula could hardly breathe for the smell of food, smoke, sweat, stale clothes, dung and a sickening sweet odour. The patient levered herself up from a bed of rags – her face was greyish yellow and her face and body were terribly swollen. It was full-blown septicaemia following a difficult labour. With the best of intentions, the village midwives with their filthy nails and fingers caked with dirt had delivered the baby by hand. While the child, although weak from lack of proper food, had a chance of survival, prospects for the mother looked bleak.

In flickering firelight and using a torch, Ursula and Jangsang cleaned the woman up with Dettol. After an hour, the heady mixture of smells and heat began to affect Ursula and, faint and sweating, she dashed outside. As she gulped down cold air, one of the headmen – the woman's cousin – asked if she would pull through. She answered optimistically, but knew there was little hope.

Back inside, she and Jangsang applied bandages, gave an injection and helped the woman back to the bed. Ursula was racked with pity:

> She was quite exhausted and pitiably ill, but she tried hard to give us no trouble. She turned her head, her face so swollen it was hardly human, and said something in thanks. Her thick black hair splayed out on the rag pillow. I had felt it over my arm – it was wet with sweat and harsh as a horse's tail and as full of tangles. I watched the other woman pull up the covers. We turned to go. The husband, nursing the baby, stared after us. His thin Mongol face was sharp with misery.

Choked for words, Ursula resorted to crisp professionalism, 'That's all for now – we'll come in the morning. Just a day or two now and she'll be better.'

They felt their way out of the dark, foetid atmosphere into the cool moonlight, and Jangsang disappeared into the night. Outside, Chinaorang sat waiting, reassuring and reliable. Then a headman appeared, carrying a bundle of flaming torches and as he distributed them among the villagers, the street was lit up. The bobbing lights struck out along the steep path to the camp and led them back, and the squalor and despair of the evening was left behind:

> There is no magic, no beauty, like that of pine-torches at night. The spirit-fed fakes at military tattoos are a mockery. We moved in a red cave of light, black darkness receding ahead and closing behind… The torches burned with a rich, deep, smoky glare. The scent of burning resin came from them, pungent and nostril-tingling. They dropped fat sparks and gobbets of fire on the road, the needles caught and smouldered till the men following stamped them out. Now lit, now silhouetted, the file moved; the patter, the ripe, red-orange luxuriance of colour, changing, deepening, shifting always – with every change a new picture, an aesthetic experience so deep as to make one catch the breath; so, in an hour's journey we reached the camp – and the transcendent gave place to the mundane, to chairs and lamps and an anxious Abung.

Jangsang returned at noon the following day, exhausted and haggard. He had given the woman a further injection – she was getting better and might now pull through. He'd been on call all through the night to attend cases of infant diarrhoea and had had no sleep – he disappeared off to his hut for the rest of the day.

There was so much work to be done in Chingjaroi that Ursula felt they should stay on, so she postponed her passage until 29 April. Two days later the woman seemed to be out of danger and Ursula wanted to continue the tour, but Jangsang pointed out that they were almost out of drugs, and suggested that he return to Imphal to stock up. While this seemed sensible, and Ursula agreed, she doubted very much if he would ever reappear.

The next stop was the village of Jessami. Although Ursula had already had some brushes with Naga superstition, events here called on all her powers of persuasion and common sense to maintain order.

After a fourteen-mile march, Ursula's party arrived on a steep rocky descent into a green oak wood where the road ran through the village's graveyard. Here the gaonbura and village lumbu waited to welcome them, bearing the mandatory chicken and zu. 'My thirst made courtesy easier than usual and it was a good brew, smooth, white and mild, with a taste like smoky cider. I did it justice.'

Jessami's hospitality was very generous – Ursula's cook and coolies had arrived in an advance party and had taken receipt of enormous quantities of rice and gallons of zu. Ursula came into camp just in time to see a huge black pig carried in shrieking before being tied up.

Next morning, after a long dispensary, Ursula was looking forward to a rest when Abung appeared. Ursula had seen his expression before – it was the one he wore for domestic crises of the very first order – and he launched into an only partly intelligible tale, the salient features of which were magic, poison, zu, and Jessami. After several repetitions, Ursula finally gathered that the people of Chingjaroi and Kharasom – their last two halts – had told the Tangkhul Nagas that Jessami was a very bad place, full of witches who put 'jadu' in the zu so that strangers would die. As a result of this intelligence, the six were all in mortal terror and were drinking only water – a horrible hardship for any Naga. The six Chingjaroi coolies had been so spooked that they had taken their money the night before and had turned back home at dawn.

Ursula sent for Luikai and explained through him that all this was silly superstition – Jessami would never take any action against a sahib's party – and besides, there was no jadu in the village. Luikai, green around the gills and 'pop-eyed as Eddie Cantor' was beside himself, and dragging Ursula up to the village gate insisted, 'There is! There is! Come and look!' On the bank opposite the cookhouse was an egg, placed in a bamboo basket, with a thread round the basket and a piece of boric lint smeared with Antipeol ointment on top of it. The latter had been taken straight off a boil that Ursula had treated that morning.

With Ursula present, Abung and the remaining Tangkhuls became bolder and gathered behind her. The staff had gathered

> like a crowd at a street accident, all of them wide-eyed with fright. Jessami were massing behind the fence in an uncomfortable silence, and there at my feet was the egg, white, scrubbed and clean, with that absurd bit of pink lint on top.

Ursula owned that at first she didn't know whether to laugh or be angry – but the situation needed defusing:

> My seven obviously thought it was jadu of the blackest description, directed against us; but they had been stuffed up with these stories for some days and now that they were on the spot, their imaginations might have run away with them. This might be an innocent piece of sick man's magic with a bit of my lint thrown in for extra efficacy.

Realising that she had to act quickly and incisively, she took the plunge:

> Looking like the Statue of Liberty in shorts, I addressed my seven in atrocious Hindustani and assured them that Jessami's magic was not good against Sahibs or their servants, so they were all safe, and as I was the dickens of a good sorceress myself, they were doubly safe and Jessami might as well keep their egg. I said all three times, with variations for good measure, and my unfortunate seven stood there with eyes on stalks and drank in every word. Then I took off the boric lint, which seemed to come within my jurisdiction, retired with it to the basha and burnt it in spirits of wine with some hearty swearing and Luikai as audience. The others were gathered in the veranda, still looking very green, and some further gesture was indicated, so I hitched up my courage, marched back to the bank and took up the egg and basket. That seemed to be what everyone was waiting for and my seven began to look better at once.

There was still the egg to dispose of, so Ursula took Abung aside and was discussing what to do with it when the younger headman wandered into the camp. Ursula sent Abung to call him and he went across to her at once. Before Ursula could get a word in, Abung let fly with a tirade in Manipuri. The lambu was unaware of anything untoward and blinked in amazement when Ursula showed him the basket. By his reaction, he had had no idea of any magic directed against Ursula's party, and was shocked by what he saw.

The only connection Ursula could make was that in Chingjaroi the locals had made up a song calling her a 'maibi' – priestess – and perhaps word had travelled via the Chingjaroi coolies that she was a powerful sorceress – which had rattled the local practitioner. Even if the lambu had been taken by surprise by the egg, he clearly knew what it was all about. It was obviously a hot potato – so Ursula thrust it at him. He shied away until she lost patience and simply put it into his hand. There followed an undignified pass-the-parcel interlude – until it ended up with a small boy who had no-one else to give it to. He carried it away in great haste at arm's length as if it were a live bomb. Ursula explained to the lambu, through Abung, what she thought of all this and then withdrew with proper dignity. She watched through a crack in the wall as the lambu turned away and the rest of the crowd followed him … and the party was over.

Later Ursula learned that the lambu had wept for shame – they had tried so hard to lay on a proper welcome – then some unknown witch ruined it all. Ursula had told the gaonbura that she would make house calls for the most serious cases, so she resolutely prepared to go. As she saw it, 'I was not going to truckle to a mere egg, so I collected my team – Chinaorang and Saknio – and set off through the fateful gate.'

Ursula held the dispensary in the morning, then retired to her basha, only to find that she had visitors. Apparently unembarrassed by the tricky diplomatic situation, all the village women had arrived to see her and invited themselves in. In no time they were rifling, fascinated, through her possessions, while Ursula sat 'like an island of concentration in the middle'. Describing the visit to her mother she commented ruefully,

> I wouldn't mind if they didn't smell so much and spit so liberally. There is a refreshing lack of conventions among the ladies of Jessami. A girl has just spat on the floor, I have roared with rage, and they have all fled. They all spit furiously in their own houses, but I object to the custom in mine.

Ursula had accepted zu from the village, refusing to be rattled by silly superstition, but the cookhouse had resolutely turned down their share and it was piling up in Ursula's basha so it looked like a wine cellar. Jessami had lent them an interpreter for the duration – Zahilo – and in the afternoon he took Ursula and team around the village to see the sights. Just as they were going back to camp, Ursula saw Zahilo running after Luikai and Saknio with a gourd of zu and urging them to have a drink:

> With the air of those wining with the Borgias, the two young Tangkhuls looked around for me, and finding me in sight and looking pretty well after a course of the stuff, gulped down a mouthful each and scurried after me as though they were afraid they might drop down before they reached the camp.

Later that evening, Luikai hung about, scratching his calf with his toes in an awkward way. 'May we have some of the zu?' he ventured. 'I thought you wouldn't drink it.' He continued, 'Oh, it's all right if you're there, and besides, it's been in your basha some time now, and I think it'll be all right.'

Ursula noted,

> He left my disinfectant presence with his arms full of bottles, and was relieved of half his load by a shadowy figure waiting in the veranda to hurry them across to the three days' drought in the cookhouse.

Mortified by the incident, village headmen arrived during the evening laden with peace-offerings – hens, eggs, zu, rice and pumpkins – and were at great pains to dissociate themselves from the egg. This was the work of one malevolent individual, not the village as a whole. By general consent, the matter was dropped, but even if Ursula and team had put it behind them, Jessami had not. News reached Ursula some time later that they had held a public cursing ceremony to cause the culprit's death. They were then assured that the guilty party would die within six months – which Ursula accepted without demur, 'Nagas being what they are, it almost certainly did.'

Ursula later explained the power of black magic for the Nagas,

> I didn't like these practices in the least. Black magic is very, very firmly believed in, and can cause a most awful lot of trouble. It's something to be avoided at all costs, and it's used by a lot of the tribes – by those who have a reputation for it – to scare and blackmail other villages into doing what ever they want. One had to take a very firm line about that.

Much to Ursula's surprise, Jangsang turned up with fresh supplies, along with some essential stores and a letter to Ursula from Jeffery, with news of the outside world. Totally absorbed by her own surroundings and blissfully cut off from events outside, Ursula suddenly realised that the matters in Europe were reaching crisis point. On 15 March Hitler and his army had marched into Czechoslovakia and taken over Prague, and despite all the reassurances with which Chamberlain had returned from Munich the previous year, Hitler's aims were now clear. Ursula wrote in her diary,

> Europe in mess again. Hitler's been and gone and done it. God knows what's going to happen, and there's not much I can do about it for the moment, so I might as well carry on while I can.

An outbreak of smallpox in Lai-yi now scotched her planned itinerary. Ursula sent messengers to summon medical relief from Imphal, but in the meantime the safest course of action was to go south through the villages west of Paowi where they needed dispensary visits but where they would still be within call if the relief party needed them. Nothing closed down an area like an epidemic, so if they waited any longer they might find they could get no coolies. This route took them back through Chingjaroi where Ursula asked after the woman who had been at death's door. Word was that she was better, so they went to call. The door was opened by a young woman who appeared confused by the sight of so many visitors – and a memsahib to boot. She was holding the baby – Ursula assumed she was the mother's help – so she asked after the patient and went to go inside. The girl was even more confused, especially when they asked after the patient. There ensued a moment of chaos when everyone talked at once in four different languages, but the situation was resolved by the arrival of one of the headmen. 'This is the only one', he explained. Ursula and the compounder were stunned – in ten days the improvement had been staggering, and where they had left a shapeless, swollen figure, barely conscious, there was now a robust young woman in rude good health, looking as if she'd never been ill at all – let alone almost dead. In a rare moment of humility, Jangsang opined, 'I think it is with the help of God', and for once, Ursula thought he must be right.

With the satisfaction of a miraculous cure affected, they went back to their old camp at Paowi, where Saknio arrived with the 'dak' – a system of mail delivery by relays of bearers. Humpus had written to say that as of 23 March Britain was not at war, but it was only a matter of time. Still, there was nothing to do but finish the tour.

At Kachai Jangsang arrived looking worried and waving a note. Apparently two of his children were seriously ill, so he rushed away with promises that he did not expect to be too long. Enter Abung, an hour later to say that before he left, Jangsang had told the village Kullakpa (headman) that Ursula was not a servant of the Sirkar (British government), so he was not to give free rice to her servants. She had only one servant and the rest were coolies – but he had impressed on the Kullakpa that he, Jansang, was a servant of the Sirkar, so he could be allowed any amount of free food. Ursula was incandescent with rage – Jangsang had struck again:

> If true, this was one of the meanest tricks I ever heard of. I told Wombat not to make trouble, but that I would pay for everything they wanted. Now hens and zu are pouring in, in a way which makes me hot all over.

Ursula went alone to the Kuki Christian village outside Kachai, and all went well until a small child covered in an angry rash was pushed forward. It had to be measles, and Ursula immediately suggested they isolate him. The father replied that they already had it – but then another 'much-measled' girl came forward. It was evidently too late to contain it, and later in her diary, Ursula contemplated the probability of it spreading further:

> Gosh, I am angry about those measles. I shall be angrier still if I get it, and I shall be vastly surprised if I don't. Gargled wildly on return, and set staff gargling. Abung set the boys washing, so Lysoled their clothes and mine – no doubt a hygienic measure.

Despite plans to go further south and west, Chinaorang had become ill, so they decided instead to turn back. In Tuinem, Jansang rolled up tired and angry, and celebrated his arrival with a row over pay with the coolie, but Ursula was too tired to care. She made him pay the coolie what he owed. 'What with the marching, and the long dispensaries, and the unending struggle with him – he never left an unpleasant remark unsaid – I was worn out.'

With some relief Ursula arrived in Imphal and the party disbanded. She reflected on the long trek:

> Six weeks is a long time to be out, and we were all tired; but oh, I don't want to leave the hills and my Nagas. I would go straight back again if only I could, rain, cold, wind, dirt, smells, hot marches, leaky bashas, bad water and all. It is a comfort to have some clothes – for the last week I have had to mend my one shirt every night in order to have something to put on in the morning! I shall miss my gang of Nagas; they were good fellows and good company. I was alone, up there at Jessami for four days with them, and over a week without anyone to whom I could speak at all fluently. In the 'magic' trouble they stuck to me although they were scared stiff, when it would have been only too easy to desert – and they really believed their lives were in danger.

She had established an extraordinary relationship; as she reluctantly boarded the ship sailing for England, Ursula reflected, 'My three months of paradise were over'.

10

The World at War

Back in England, Ursula found the nation preparing for war. Plans were being put in place to evacuate children, air-raid shelters were being built and the armed forces were recruiting against the inevitable start of hostilities.

When she got her photos developed, Ursula was delighted with the results – it was her best ever work. She couldn't wait to get back to the Naga Hills, and immediately started making plans for winter. 'It looked as though I might really be able to achieve something, even if it did mean a big outlay in film-stock, fares and camp equipment.' But as her equipment stacked up, so her hopes of ever getting to use it shrank. Before war was even declared, by the end of August sailings were being cancelled, and the booking Ursula had made was switched twice.

Ursula needed something constructive to do with her time, and as she had volunteered back in 1938, she was called up to the London Ambulance Service. Alexa offered her services too, so from when the war began on 3 September 1939, the two were at their station, ready for duty, reporting at four in the morning then sitting it out, waiting for something to happen and knitting interminable jumpers.

Ursula was convinced she could be of more use in the Naga Hills and managed to get a berth on a sailing for India – however, at dawn on departure day, she and Alexa were called to ambulance stations and, utterly despondent, Ursula cancelled her place. 'I sat down to wait for the blitz, quite certain that I had seen the last of Assam and the Naga Hills'.

After two months, Ursula and Alexa were tired of knitting and waiting for the siren that never came. Ursula decided that, come what may, she'd get back to her proper place, and Alexa had an offer of a job in Delhi, and was ready to go as soon as possible. Doris and Humpus had originally been appalled by what they saw as the unmitigated madness of Ursula's passion for the Nagas, but now they were sadly resigned. 'They put up no objection that time – they had just decided I'd gone clean off my rocker and it was no good. I was going to go. I was going anyway.' All Doris's hopes of matrimony had come to nothing – Ursula was still defiantly single, and she detected a frisson of disappointment in her mother – 'a rather sad look' – at her return.

Sailing in December on the *City of Benares*, Ursula left behind the uncertainty of the Phoney War, and set out better equipped than ever to continue her work among the Nagas – and the nearer she got to India the more unlikely seemed her luck.

On 17 December Ursula reached Imphal and travelled on to the familiar rest-house. 'I walked on air up the path. It was unbelievable, it was true – I was there'. Ursula was still in a state of euphoria as, halfway up the path to the bungalow, a watchman met her with a letter. It was from the Political Agent, Gimson, and the gist of it hit Ursula like a brickbat. He regretted that this time it would not be possible for her to tour the hills. One of the tribes in the Manipur district was threatening trouble – they had done the same in around 1917, and it would be most unwise, he insisted, for her to be out in the hills without military protection.

Ursula was so stunned that she remembered almost nothing of the next twenty-four hours. She unpacked, spent a sleepless night and then set off the next day back to Imphal to see the Political Agent. He received her courteously and was not unkind – but he would not change his mind.

It was evening by the time she left the Residency and with no heart to return to the resthouse, Ursula walked and walked through the dusk and into the darkness. She trudged round the cantonments, passing the bungalows – 'the homes of lucky people with careers laid down'. Only when she was too tired to think did she finally go back to her quarters. She resolved, 'Tomorrow was another day. I'd worry about it when it came'.

Ursula, physically strong, mentally so steady, went into a decline – a breakdown lasting a couple of weeks. After all the uncertainty of the summer – then the relief at getting away from London and the joy of being back in India – this blow had a worse effect than she dared confess:

> I had just enough sense left to keep control. I put away or locked up anything which could be of danger in a fit of depression. I rented the small Forest Bungalow, I shopped, I furnished it; collected a staff, learned Manipuri, clung to anything, everything, all the small, fussy chores of daily life. It was a giddy path. The holds were so small; one clung by a hand – a finger. I kept away from the rest of the station. They didn't know and, at the worst time the least rough touch would have meant disaster.

As the rest of the European community celebrated Christmas, Ursula kept to herself, seeing only her household staff. Luikai was back, delighted to see her and, sensing her depression, he arrived one day with a Tangkhul friend who was selling dogs – would Ursula like one? She said she didn't need a dog, but he returned with one all the same. Dogs had always been part of Ursula's home life and this one was irresistible – Luikai had hand-picked him for her. 'At the end of a chewed string, rolled a fat, soft, fubsy, solemn toy – black-and-white like a giant panda. It fell over its own feet and sat down; and it was mine for a rupee.' With this puppy, named Khamba, a personality had entered the household, and his arrival did much to lift Ursula's spirits. The Christmas period passed as Ursula got to know her Naga hound, who assumed a place in the household second only to her own.

By the beginning of 1940, Ursula felt optimistic enough to tackle the authorities again. By this time James Philip Mills – the scourge of the rebellious Pangsha Nagas in 1936 – was the Governor's Secretary and Director of Ethnography in Assam, and Ursula arranged to visit him in Shillong on 1 January.

Mills, himself captivated by the lure of the hills and the charm of the Naga people, was extremely helpful. He came up with a number of alternative areas Ursula could visit – there was hope after all. Her heart was set on being with the Nagas and the place that caught her eye was the Zemi Naga area, North Cachar, immediately west of Manipur. All of a sudden there was hope.

North Cachar it would be – and Mills was very pleased. There had been some interesting political trouble among the Zemi about ten years before, and no-one had got to the bottom of it. Well-administered Nagas were a stable bunch and not prone to embracing new religions or to violent rebellion. He could fill Ursula in with the facts as he knew them – his hope was that she could discover what the troubles of 1931 were really about.

As with most inter-tribal troubles, a shortage of land seemed to have been at the root of the unrest. Throughout the previous century there had been power struggles among the tribes, but there was also considerable hostility against the British Government. The Kuki Nagas had rebelled against the British in 1918 and while they were at it they took the opportunity to settle some old scores against their Naga neighbours – namely the Kacha tribes. Since this time, the Kachas had nursed a justifiable grudge and ten years later were only prevented from an all-out massacre of the Kukis by the British administration. The roles had been reversed since 1918, when the Kachas had assisted the British troops against the Kukis – but now the Kukis needed British protection from the Kachas. Now, to the Kachas, the British had become 'the enemy'.

In 1931 the Kukis, saved from massacre by the British, appeared loyal to the administration, and were lending their support to any action to suppress the Kachas. The three Kacha tribes were still smouldering against British intervention in 1931, and it was not without reason that British officers toured only under armed escort.

The Kacha Naga movement had begun at Kambirong – a village Ursula had visited with Jeffery. Ever since the British had ruled India and taken over the administration of Assam and the Naga Hills, there had been a prophesy that one day a Naga king would rise up, drive out the British and rule over 'all who eat from the wooden platter' – in other words, all Naga tribes. In 1929, a seer from Kambirong, Jadonang, proclaimed himself the new messiah and founded a new religion which was a heady mix of paganism, Hinduism and Christianity and, as Ursula recorded, 'a sacred python just to top everything off'.

Jadonang pronounced that they should make human sacrifices, and the newly converted villagers, in zealous obedience, managed to capture four Manipuri traders. The men disappeared without trace. A year passed with no clue as to their fate, then some bucks from Kambirong went to a feast in the Kabui village of Kekru. In the middle of the feast there was a drunken quarrel with some of the Kekru men, one of whom shook his scarlet cloth in a rage and threatened, 'If you don't shut up I'll do to you what I did to the Manipuris'. There happened to be a government official within earshot, and he noticed that the scarlet cloth was tufted with human hair. He reported this to the authorities and the Political Agent – with full armed escort – arrived in Kambirong and set about finding the boasting buck.

Sober and chastened, the buck had burned the tell-tale cloth, but they discovered a concealed temple and unearthed the remains of bodies. Even if these were not the Manipuris, this was evidence enough of foul play. Suspicions were further confirmed when they searched the village and found cloths, pots and relics which had belonged to the traders. Jadonang was arrested, tried for murder and hanged. All the same, the religion lived on in the person of a fifteen-year-old priestess called Gaidiliu. The Political Officer had thought her harmless and too young to arrest, so they gave her a good ticking off, sent her back to her parents, shot the python and left.

Over the previous two years, Jadonang and Gaidiliu had amassed a huge amount of tribute. They had proclaimed a Naga Kingdom and anyone who didn't conform was forced to pay up – or be cast out. The vision they offered had been an attractive one – a Naga heaven where the faithful were to spend everything in one stupendous feast, massacre the Kukis and live in plenty ever after on the miraculous bounty of their gods. Cash rolled in and so did every profiteering gangster from the Kacha tribes, and the girl priestess who faced the Political Officer was not the innocent teenager she pretended to be.

Not only did she lead the religion, but was also the figurehead of what Ursula summed up as, 'as pretty a mob as ever graced Chicago' – the hub of 'a money-spinning god-racket'. Released, Gaidiliu realised, only until the Political Officer got better intelligence on her, she lit out for the north piloted by her right-hand man, Masang of Kepelo. As she went she spread Jadonang's gospel and roused the Naga tribes against the Kukis and the British. Not every village welcomed her, and some communities were split – among these the Zemi. Some were appalled by the new religion, but a few embraced it and worshipped Gaidiliu as a goddess.

Having let her slip through their hands once, the British launched a manhunt, but it was unfriendly terrain, and although some of the Zemi were not on her side, they were too afraid to give her away. Supporting villages lit warning beacons and Gaidiliu used back entrances, secret hideouts and tunnels to come and go like a ghost. Villagers convinced of her powers would be dancing and worshipping before an empty throne when armed sepoys, acting on the most reliable information, rushed in to arrest her.

Audaciously, she remained concealed for three months, right under the noses of the Gurkhas in the outpost at Hangrum. So entirely did the village put their faith in her that when she told them that she had put a powerful magic on the rifles of the local garrison and that the Gurkhas there would be powerless to harm them – they believed her. She ordered them to attack and eliminate the enemy. Ursula summed up the disaster,

> She said their bullets were water and would hurt nobody. The Gurhkas, very sensibly, had taken away all the firearms in the village, so Hangrum charged them at fifty yards' range, armed only with bamboo spikes – and the Gurkhas opened fire with the sort of results you might expect. How they only killed eleven of them, heaven only knows. Anyhow, it was an unmitigated disaster, and it left a legacy in the hills of dissension and fear. Half of them were anti Gaidiliu, and the other half continued to worship her, right up to my arrival.

To exacerbate the disaster, the whole village fled into the jungle and remained there for three days with next to no food – and the sepoys went into the deserted village, destroyed all the grain stocks, killed the animals and even torched some areas. Eventually the villagers were so cold and hungry that they lit a fire to cook some food. In an overzealous moment, the sepoys, seeing the light, rushed into the jungle, rounded them all up and marched them back to the village. They left the women and children there without food and marched the men forty miles via Asalu to Haflong, where the SDO used them as forced labour.

Rumours of this reached government officials in Shillong and questions were asked, so the SDO acted quickly to cover his tracks and bundled the Hangrum men on the forty-mile march back to their wrecked and foodless village. Tragically, weakened by hunger, illness and exhaustion, many of them simply gave in and staggered into the jungle grass to die. One selfish, greedy and callous official had effectively destroyed Hangrum – it was small wonder that the village nursed a grievance against the British.

Gaidiliu's thugs would collect tribute and take their commission, so it was to their advantage for her to stay at large, and they protected her. The ordinary villagers, bullied and financially drained by Gaidiliu's henchmen and harried by the pursuing British, grew tired of it, but Gaidiliu's men took care of the dissenters, and once a few bodies had been discovered it became harder than ever for British officers to illicit information as to Gaidiliu's whereabouts.

Gaidiliu did little for her own popularity by telling the villagers that they should destroy their grain so the British could not take it. They were not to worry, because plenty would arrive from heaven and they would be fed. Predictably, this manna from heaven failed to materialise and the people were in grave danger of starving. Many wished fervently they'd never set eyes on her – but remained too frightened to betray her. Her crusade, however, could only last so long.

Gaidiliu was heading north to Angami country when the Kuki caretaker of the resthouse at Lakema heard that she was in the area. He sent word to Mills, who instigated a plan to round her up. After launching a feint attack, the real arresting group arrived to find Gaidiliu's sentries drunk, having celebrated the 'duping' of the authorities. Sepoys swarmed over the palisades and surrounded her house, eventually finding their quarry shrieking spells and urging her bodyguard to resist. Gaidiliu was pulled out, kicking, screaming and biting, and inflicting the only casualty of the expedition – a nasty bite on the thumb of one of the naiks.

Hours later she was in front of Mills with a sob story – it was tough being a goddess. People wanted to worship her day and night and she never even had time for a bath. This comfort was accorded her in the resthouse, surrounded by sentries, and at last the elusive sorceress, evasive divinity and terror of the Kacha Nagas was in captivity. The following day she was found guilty of aiding and abetting Jadonang to murder, and was sentenced to fourteen years behind bars.

Nine years later, only one sidekick, Dikheo, was still at large. Masang, having served six months in jail, had been released. These men still had cause to believe in their priestess. Before her capture she had told them that even if she were caught, it would not matter, as they would only take a simulacrum into captivity. Her true, divine self would be kept safe elsewhere. She would stay in hiding until her chosen time, when she would return in a shape in which her enemies would not recognise her, and which only the faithful would identify.

Ursula had a brief from Mills which further validated her visit to North Cachar – she was to monitor the level of support for the still incarcerated Gaidiliu – and her ideal cover was her established occupation as an anthropological observer. Ursula returned from Shillong to her bungalow with a revived spring in her step.

In Imphal Ursula assessed her budget – she would have £450 a year to keep herself, her camp staff and Khamba – and for her own sanity she would reserve £50 of this for an annual holiday in Calcutta to remember her English. A further £50 would be needed to buy medicines for a very basic dispensary – the best way to get acquainted with the villagers. There would be no compounder to help her – but with the basic Red Cross training she had received in the London Ambulance service, the crash course in minor operations (boil-lancing, wound-dressing, tooth extraction, etc) her previous tours had afforded her, and a tropical dispensary handbook, she was confident she could provide the help the hill people so desperately needed.

Ursula outlined her staff for Doris,

> I have a fat Mohammedan cook called Gulap – or the Indian Rose (believe it or not); an infant paniwallah, who fell ill within a week of joining and is now crawling about so thin you can't see him sideways, a hunchbacked sweeper; and Luikai – only he's gone home on a week's leave. He turned up on Christmas morning, looking relatively clean and free of scabies.
>
> I have, in an extraordinarily rash moment, bought a Naga dog pup. It looks like a small bear just now; I don't know what I'm going to do with it, but it is extremely engaging! The breed must come of the same stock as chows, but are much huskier and tougher and are generally black or black and white. I asked Luikai to suggest a Tangkhul name and he cast his eyes up to Heaven and whispered to himself as if he was saying grace, and then suggested 'Wakhamva' or 'White Throat'. The 'KH' is pronounced with a guttural gurgle like 'CH' in 'loch'. The poor pup is full of worms. Could you get Mrs C and P James of Cheltenham to send me some worm powders for it? It's around three-and-a-half-months old now, and will be about the size of a chow.

Ursula knew her family thought she had taken leave of her senses, and enjoyed relating her doings with humour and sang froid, anticipating her mother and grandmother's expressions as they read her letters. This new life of hers was infinitely more dirty, smelly, risky, cold, uncomfortable and unpredictable than anything she portrayed in sanitised form for them, and she could never hope to make them understand how much she loved it.

11

Mixed Receptions

Before setting out to North Cachar, Ursula got a glimpse of some Zemi Nagas from the Barail area who had just arrived in Imphal. One of them, Gumtuing of Nenglo, made a splendid impression as he walked round the corner of Ursula's bungalow, a tall, imposing figure with a bottle of zu in one hand, a chicken in the other, a hibiscus flower stuck jauntily behind his ear and his headman's scarlet blanket wrapped around him. If he was typical of the Zemi Nagas she was to work among, Ursula would be very happy indeed.

The second Zemi was Masang of Kepelo – Gaidiliu's right-hand man. He cut a very imposing figure:

> Where Gumtuing was tall, Masang was short and deep-chested. His thick black hair was cut in a page-boy bob. His little sharp eyes were never still – they flickered ceaselessly, alert and wary – he missed nothing. In front of strangers he wore a silly grin and clowned continually. It was a clever disguise. He was a cunning devil, was Masang, as clever a ruffian as they come – and yet I never quite made him out, right to the end. There was something in him that was not wholly the villain.

Masang joined the household and Ursula set out for North Cachar. The Nagas she had stayed among to date had been flattered by her interest, respect and friendship, but now these people presented a completely different challenge. The North Cachar Nagas were disaffected with the government, still unsettled and volatile – and if Masang was anything to go by, the people were not going to welcome her or confide in her easily. She suspected that they might see any man as being a government agent, but hoped 'there was a sporting chance that a lady on her own – a young woman with sympathetic feelings towards the Nagas – might possibly get to the bottom of it.'

The first stop was the Mahur Bungalow, where Ursula soon realised that the temporary interpreter, Gailung, whom Booth had found for her in Haflong really didn't have a clue, and an opportunity arose to replace him with an ex-government servant, a Zemi called Namkiabuing – Namkia for short:

> Gailung (long, would-be handsome, but sags at the knees and has less gumption than a dead eel) – was sent home and his red cloth given to Namkia of Impoi – ex-dobashi [interpreter], now attached to my staff.

Namkia, although only in his thirties, had recently resigned his government post and lived just a mile from Asalu. To Ursula he seemed well suited – fit, muscular, well-built and tall for a Zemi, he looked intelligent and capable. Despite the honour that the likes of Luikai felt to be attached to a post with the memsahib, Namkia didn't seem particularly keen on the job, but he would obey the SDO's orders without question. He took on the red cloth of office and went home to collect his things.

A government resthouse had been built outside the main settlement of Laisong, but Ursula wanted to integrate with the locals, so they were to camp in the village itself. Laisong stood high on a spur which sloped away from the main range, its main street a rocky track which widened into a something that was not quite a village square. This was important as the water-drawing centre, and two huge water troughs fed by bamboo pipelines running from springs further up the hillside dominated the area. Nearby, a reminder of the customs of the area, was the hazoa – the sacred jumping stone – beside which the heads taken in war were traditionally buried.

Beyond the lower morung, the street dropped steeply and the houses petered out where the path forked. One branch led through a stone-walled gateway and down the cliff and the other turned upwards again and round the hummock at the end of the spur. Here, still within the village limits, was the little thatched camp, built specially for Ursula's party. Perched on a cliff in the giant landscape, the camp was like an eagle's nest above the steep cliffs to the south and east, from which Ursula could just see the shining ribbon of the Jenam River in the distant valley.

Some basic practicalities needed sorting out. The main hut needed adjustment as with the existing layout Ursula's 'H of P' was opposite the cookhouse door. Ursula got the necessary alterations under way before turning in early, feeling chilled and shivery. This condition persisted the following morning, but there was work which couldn't be put off. Booth had suggested that they host a feast for the surrounding villages so that they could meet Ursula. The promise of such largesse, a share of the mithan meat and lashings of free zu would draw people in numbers – all in a warmly receptive mood. Among the guests would be those who had organised the rebellion – to hold a big official feast to prove there were no ill feelings would be a springboard to establishing cordial relations with them too.

It was down to Ursula to provide the mithan bull which would be killed for the event. 'Woke feeling rotten – diarrhoea, tummy well upset. Only one mithan in village – owner wants 60 rupees.' In her letter to Doris she described the bull mithan – 'a huge brute like a black Altamira bison':

> We got our mithan after a fearful hunt, and it was brought into the village by all the bucks, ho-ho-ing and whooping, and tied up opposite the bachelors' house. The villagers' buffalo was also tied up there. The bull stood as high as my shoulder, and the horns spanned forty inches on the head, tip to tip.

Ursula recognised that a good many Naga customs would be hard for her to stomach, especially as an animal-lover – and this was one of them. It took a number of men to throw the bull over, left side uppermost, and then Gumtuing made an initial stab over the heart, followed by more little probing stabs until the blood flowed. At this point Ursula recorded, 'I did not look any more than I could help'. Then it was Luikai's turn to spear the buffalo – which was left tethered on a platform a little way away so it did not smell the blood and panic. 'He lunged with the spear and I think plunged it among the logs to the side – and then somehow he stabbed again. I don't know how, because I didn't look.' When the meat was eventually served up Ursula couldn't bring herself to eat any, leaving it to Booth to 'eat for the honour of the party'.

Invitations had gone out to five villages, but word had travelled fast, and deputations of headmen and performers streamed in from at least nine settlements. The guests made a fabulous spectacle,

> ...young bucks in their most gorgeous full dress, green beetle earrings, huge orange, blue and black feathers, ear ornaments, scarlet-edged cloths with black embroidery, blue kilts, white belts and pipe-clayed legs. The little girls all had embroidered skirts and dark blue cloths round their top halves and masses of necklaces. The young men were all about twenty to twenty-five – their girls seven to fourteen. I think the older girls were shy and a little scared.

The Zemi tribes were renowned for their feasts and celebrations, but even by their standards, this was a massive festival – Ursula was assured that there had never been such a gathering. With extraordinary speed, the mithan and buffalo carcases were butchered and the meat made into a massive, hot, rich, well-chillied stew. Meanwhile, the dancing began, each village performing in turn, and as darkness began to fall, the drums started – first singly, then joining together. It was a fantastic spectacle, the lights of torches guiding the dancers up the street and trailing in orange streams against the deep blue of the sky. An area had been levelled some forty yards long and the spectators gathered around the edges. Huge bamboo torches set around the field shed light on the enormous feast, which was like an initiation – and it fulfilled all her hopes and expectations. It was a magic, enchanted occasion – intoxicating and unforgettable.

> Dance followed dance; torches burned to stubs and were renewed and the bamboo-ash blew about the bare ground like tufts of grey hair. Stars rose over the far hills, climbed over us and dipped away, and still the wild music shook the spur, still the torches flickered in the night wind, and still the kaleidoscope of dancers melted, changed, and swung leaping on, on, on.

There were over a hundred dancers, and some 500 people wined and dined with food left to spare – as Ursula summed up the evening, 'It was a terrific binge'.

Booth returned to Haflong, while Ursula went on to Bara Nenglo. They parted at the village boundary, and the party was over. It was the end of the honeymoon and Ursula was well and truly out on her own. This wasn't just a short tour, but how life was going to be for the foreseeable future.

The Zemi populace seemed divided into two very polarised factions. 'One, which included Namkia, regarded me with dislike and suspicion. The other fell on me with a hospitality which was frightening.' Ursula was fascinated by the Zemi – and because of their strangely divided behaviour, she could only assume that 'fully half of them were mad. That at least, was the only explanation which occurred to me at the time. By no possible conception was their conduct rational.'

At Bara Nenglo Ursula noticed that the drinking water tasted odd, and on making inquiries from a well-zued Luikai, Ursula discovered that it hadn't been boiled. In fact, it hadn't been boiled since leaving Haflong:

> No wonder I felt like death and had diarrhoea! I blew up in a rage, and feeling worn out and in expectation of death by something bugsome, drafted a farewell letter, tore it up and so wearily, wearily to bed.

Still feeling ropy next day, Ursula set out in pouring rain for Hangrum. Remembering the village's disastrous attack against the local British fort, carried out at Gaidiliu's instigation, Ursula was surprised to find a reception committee awaiting them outside the village. They escorted her to a settlement high on a saddle backed up by a high peak, commanding the most wonderful aspects all around. The reception committee augured well – but as soon as Ursula entered the village she felt the latent hostility. It was incumbent on the headmen to extend an official welcome so as not to fall foul of the administration, but the villagers could choose how they behaved.

> There wasn't a woman in sight – which is always a very bad sign. All the men were arranged on the house platforms in silent rows, two deep, looking down on me. I walked up there just waiting for the first stone.

Mills had been right, and there was much disaffection among the Zemi villages. It was nine years since the ill-fated charge against the sepoys' rifles, but most of the men of the village had suffered injury during the attack or in the reprisals that followed. Their fellow tribesmen had been killed and wounded and their village had been burned – the whole community had been punished – so it was not surprising that there was still a smouldering grudge. Having survived running the gauntlet of the village, she set about winning their confidence with determined good humour.

Two days later, Hangrum was mellowing, and apart from a large crowd gathered for the morning dispensary, there was a special request for her to bring her gramophone. The crowd was too big for the dekachang (morung), so Ursula took it outside:

> The whole village turned up! Small boys under the platform, everyone who could conveniently fit there on it, and me and the dobashis and the HMV in the middle! Found the hot sun was warping the records.

In the afternoon the village staged a spear-throwing competition and young people danced – all this was very convivial, but none of the individuals seemed inclined to extend any personal welcome. Hangrum was not going to fall for a few gramophone records and a dispensary.

A very different welcome awaited Ursula at Hajaichak where, despite pouring rain, an enthusiastic reception party awaited them outside the village. Much strong drink was proffered and as she walked under escort into the straggling main street, elder after elder fell at her feet, calling her 'Mai' or 'Apui' – 'mother'. It took some time to fight through to the perao, which with the usual lack of foresight had been built next to the local wash-hole and was full of flies and mithan. The H of P, too, was in its accustomed place, opposite the cookhouse, with an additional screen of wandering mithan and their dung.

Ursula tackled Namkia about the 'Apui' greeting. In personal address it did indeed mean 'mother', while the longer 'Herapui' meant a 'goddess'. She was mystified as to why one village should be so effusive and another so aloof.

Masang was expecting her the next day in Kepelo, and after much puffing and blowing on the uphill march, Ursula and entourage arrived at a very satisfactory camp and were welcomed with the traditional offering of eggs and zu at Masang's own house. Mrs Masang put on a warm welcome and took the opportunity of presenting all the little Masangs for Ursula's admiration.

All was good-humoured hospitality in Masang's home village, however, the next dispensary was to be held in Guilong. This village had suffered badly in the Gaidiliu troubles and Ursula fully expected the same chilliness she had met in Hangrum – but not a bit of it. As she arrived with the traditional welcome escort, the villagers – men and women – swarmed around her, pressing cup on cup of zu on her. If anything there was an excess of hospitality:

> They caught hold of me, pulled me by the wrist, tugged at my clothes, and even prised my hand open to make me accept, in person, the gifts they offered. In fact, they behaved as I had never known a Naga village do before, with raving insanity. I hadn't a second's privacy the whole time I was there. No matter what I was doing, sleeping, eating, resting or even bathing, the hut was invaded regardless by somebody crying parrot-phrases: 'Oh my mother! Oh Queen, Oh Goddess! You are our mother, you are a goddess. There is none greater, there is none better than you!'

Gaidiliu had complained that she couldn't even take a bath without someone wanting to worship her – and Ursula realised just how trying this could be:

> I was having a bath and in strolled a very elderly gentleman holding a chicken in a basket. I at that moment was standing up in a canvas tub. I hadn't even got a bath towel. My only weapon was a cake of soap, and I threw it at him and scored a direct hit. My yell of rage brought my interpreter running, by which time I'd got a towel. The old gentleman was hustled out in no uncertain fashion and I went out and retrieved the soap, because I hadn't finished.

This adulation carried on so that Ursula had no hope of privacy – even barred doors made no difference. Barricade it as she would, an arm would work its way through and remove the bar. The villagers were genuinely offended if Ursula shut them out, so eventually, she realised resistance was useless. Despite her initial denials about being a goddess, Guilong was ecstatic to have her among them and couldn't do enough to welcome her.

> Guilong then wound up the whole lunacy with a dance; and never have I seen such a three-ring circus – the drums and choir each doing something different and the dancers wildly at variance with each other, even to having two dances going at once

> in opposition – a performance of stark, staring, undiluted anarchy. Next morning, thank goodness, we left.

Given this strange state of affairs, Ursula made a detour to see Mills. She suspected that this potentially inflammatory situation might be too dangerous to be allowed, but after she had explained, with some embarrassment, that she was being worshipped as a goddess, he looked at her with a twinkle in his eye. 'If they must have a goddess', he mused, 'they might as well have a government one'. Ursula went back, determined, all the same, that the nonsense had to stop.

Booth had seen enough of Ursula's relationship with the Zemi to approve her staying for a year. He suggested she base herself at Laisong, where a new camp would be built, laid out to Ursula's specifications. If she was to gain their trust and live among them within the perimeter of the village, she would have to agree to live by Zemi law and not stand on her status as a European – to which she readily agreed.

Continuing the dispensary tour, she wrote at length to her mother on 22 April from Nenglo to chart her party's bibulous progress through the Barail villages. Namkia was certainly one of the boys as far as the rest of the household were concerned, and did more than his fair share of chatting up the local talent as they moved from village to village. With Ursula, however, he still maintained a 'speak-when-you're-spoken-to' remoteness which bordered on distrust.

At last, on 1 May, Ursula caught sight of the newly thatched roofs of her Laisong camp. It was an incredibly welcome sight, perched solidly on a hilltop like a Rhine castle with the house-tops just visible above the low scrub jungle. Ursula negotiated the steep climb in burning heat and finally reached the village gateway, where a breeze cut through the sultriness of the day – and there was the new camp.

Ursula's bungalow was tall, cool and airy, made of matting on timber frames with a roof of thick grass thatch, affording the luxury of five rooms and two verandas. Behind it were the cookhouse and men's quarters in two long, low huts. New staff had been recruited – Ramgakpa as scullion, a new Manipuri cook and Degalong, the dog-boy from Impoi – and now this was home. Ursula oversaw the unpacking of the jappas, ate her first meal by her new hearth and retired for a siesta.

Less than an hour later, Ursula woke to utter darkness. A wind had whipped up and was banging the bungalow doors violently to and fro – the whole structure was creaking ominously. Black clouds turned the day to night and Ursula struggled to find the heavy veranda door which was flapping madly in the gale. She tried in vain to pull it shut, but instead it shook and lifted like a sail in the wind, and as she battled with it a sudden rattle hit the back wall. It was hail, and it looked as if the whole structure would capsize under the force.

> The whole bungalow leaned over, groaning. The groan was lost in the noise of the hail on the walls. It was not now a rattle but a roar – a continuous, shaking roar like an express train in a tunnel. Even though I was in the lee of the house, it took my full strength to force the door to, for the wind was flinging it about like a piece of paper. Inside the bungalow, small hailstones, twigs and shredded leaves were blowing in through the back eaves and up over the inner partitions and showering down over everything in the place. The half-grown dog Khamba, terrified, was

> dashing about. As I grappled the second door he broke out past me. I ran after him into the veranda. The whipping hail at the corner stung him; he doubled back. I caught him and dragged him in and shut the door on us both, and out of the open window I saw the hail outside.

What greeted her was the sight of hailstones the size of golf balls, slashing horizontally in the wind and spinning off the rocks of the spur. This barrage went on for ten minutes and Ursula could only sit it out. The bungalow might or might not remain standing, but it would be suicidal to go outside. Ursula and Khamba huddled together by the front wall until the roar subsided and the wind died down. Miraculously the bungalow creaked and returned to the upright and as a watery sunlight broke through, Ursula went out to inspect the damage.

Ramgakpa was sitting on a bamboo bench in the cookhouse in a lake of melting hailstones. The whole building had had been blown fifteen degrees from the upright but there was no serious damage. To the rear, a two-foot drift of hailstones had accumulated and an old hut from the previous camp had been ripped to ribbons. Ursula looked out on a scene of devastation. The exposed north side of the spur had been stripped of scrub jungle – every leaf had been torn off in a belt a mile wide and the banana trees looked as if they had been raked by machine-gun fire. Masang and the new caretaker came rushing over – they had survived unscathed, but the village had been terribly badly hit. The hail had battered the morungs so violently that the bucks had had to shelter under benches – but even then some had been injured. Outside, every pig, dog, goat and chicken had been killed outright.

The Nagas were philosophical about the damage. While to Ursula it had been the storm to end all storms, to the locals it was a bad setback, and while the loss of livestock would certainly cause hardship, it was nothing that time wouldn't mend. She hoped that, in time, she could help the Zemi overcome their setbacks and so be accepted more quickly. She set out to fetch the rest of her belongings, but had only reached the top of the pass on the way to Asalu when she came down with a fever. Feeling terrible, but determined to make it in under her own steam, she laboured on and, after 'a hideous march', she fell into bed in the Asalu camp and succumbed to her first serious illness since coming to the hills.

Ursula had been unaware before now quite how dependent her household were on her for direction, and with her *hors de combat*, they went into various states of decline. They were, she admitted ruefully, 'broken reeds'. The cook lost control and gave way to hysterics, stamping and raving in panic when Ursula declined to be carried in. Ursula had hoped that Namkia would provide some support and look after her, but he too was gripped with panic and sloped off and got drunk. On his return, Ursula whispered weakly that she really was very ill, and asked him to stay in earshot, but he replied shortly, 'Oh, take some medicine and get better,' and went home to Impoi. Incensed, Ursula was literally lying in wait when Namkia arrived in the morning.

> I rose on my pillows, launched what must have sounded like a dying curse, and then fell back in a semi-coma. It scared the daylight out of him. He nursed me loyally all the rest of the time.

Ursula couldn't help wondering if there was, after all, something in the Jessami 'jadu'. There seemed to be a jinx on her plans, as no sooner had they settled into the Laisong camp than Luikai went sick and couldn't work, and Ursula went down with malaria. She was languishing, feverish and shivering in bed when an interpreter arrived in a state of agitation. Booth had got news of a potential rising among the Zemi, so Ursula was to return to Haflong at once.

This was the final straw, and she toiled back, exhausted and despairing. To add insult to injury, it emerged that Luikai's illness was venereal disease – a condition he must have been concealing for weeks. He was hospitalised and would be out of the picture for a while. As for Ursula's year of study among the Zemi, her hopes were in tatters and she retreated, heartbroken and weakened by malaria, to the western plateau.

12

In Exile

Ursula was effectively in exile. There were some Zemi villages there, but they were small and disappointing, and their Naga character had been so diluted that the vibrant spark which so characterised the hill villages was all but totally absent. In addition, Ursula found the stifling heat of the plateau exhausting, but she was resigned to it for the time being. Even more depressed, however, was Namkia. He had dutifully agreed to take up the interpreter's red cloth – and despite some run-ins had served well and nursed Ursula through the worst of her fever – but he was finding those duties daily more untenable. He handed in his notice on a daily basis and even when persuaded to stay on, remained aloof.

Gradually, however, in the heat and dust of the plateau, Ursula could only attribute it to shared adversity that the ice at last began to melt and Namkia began to talk to her. Their talks revealed a man of many admirable qualities – a strong moral sense of right and wrong and an innate awareness of his identity as a Zemi. Namkia was a man Ursula could relate to and admire:

> His was an unusual character. A pagan humorist, a Zemi to the backbone, and with all the faults and virtues of his tribe and race, he still had an inner core, a moral citadel, which made of him a Hampden. He had an intense, a vivid, sense of right and wrong. They were to him a personal responsibility. He could no more compromise with wrong than he could stop breathing; not see a wrong done, nor an injustice, and not right it, at whatever cost to himself. It was not a quality to endear him to all masters, and neither was Namkia (whose intelligence, though it worked on different lines, equalled that of any European) the man to be a mere obedient instrument; and as a mere obedient instrument was, in most cases, all that the harassed district officer required, Namkia had recognised that he was not wholly suited to Government service and resigned. He was an honest man, an accurate interpreter, an organiser, and expert in tribal law, and a notable man among the Barail Zemi.

At the end of July Ursula returned to Haflong and discovered that her exile had been largely due to a false alarm. The situation had calmed down sufficiently for Booth to approve Ursula going back to Asalu – but not as far as Laisong. If there was any whiff of trouble, Ursula would be close enough to the railway to get back to Haflong.

Grateful for even this small concession, Ursula and entourage moved into the leaky bashas of Asalu. Luikai and Chinaorang rejoined her – the latter happy to be the only Tangkhul among the Zemis. However, syphilis had taken its toll on Luikai's brain and, previously an obedient and obliging servant, he was now so unmanageable that Ursula had no option but to send him home.

The Zemis derived a good deal of fun from good-naturedly teasing Chinaorang. He never minded the ragging, even when his tormentors nearly scared him out of his wits. On one occasion Namkia faked tiger-tracks around the water hole so that next morning Chinaorang spotted the pug-marks and giving a yell, dropped his buckets and ran like a deer for the camp.

It was quite common in the hot weather for tigers to move to higher ground to escape the heat. These solitary animals would roam the hills, killing livestock until they were either tracked down and shot, or the onset of colder weather drove them back to the plateau. One such beast had developed a routine beat from Laisong to Mahur, and rather than struggle through the thick wet jungle, chose to use the bridle-track, as Ursula said, 'as boldly as a taxpayer'. His route took him on a short cut over the Asalu spur, passing some mere thirty yards from the camp, and so regular was his patrol that he'd trodden a lasting track through the grass.

The tiger continued to patrol his beaten path, walking boldly down the road from Impoi punctually at six o'clock every morning. Namkia came from Impoi to bring Ursula her morning tea at this time, and it did occur to Ursula, given her previous experience of a were-tiger, that her interpreter might be a lycanthropist. This uneasy feeling was short-lived as the real tiger put in an appearance one evening when Ursula and Namkia were working late. An appalling bellow came from the village, followed quickly by much shouting and commotion, and the baying of the village dog pack. The tiger had taken one of the cattle from the copse, and the village was in uproar.

Gradually daily life returned to normal – although the nights still struck fear in the hearts of Chinaorang and the cook. Meanwhile, Ursula continued her dispensary duties, at last finding more time to write to her mother:

> Our 'there-song' lately has been 'Hans can't dance, he's got ants in his pants', played by Whoopsie Bower and her Hotcha Head-Hunters – that is, when it wasn't 'Tiger Rag', though nobody showed any enthusiasm for 'Hold that Tiger!' There is a plague of ants – black ones. We had a pogrom on the red ones a fortnight ago. The black ones are awful. They pursue the jam from place to place, cluster on the chutney, nest in my spare trousers, besiege the marmalade and fall into the drinking-water in their spare time. We have poured kettles of boiling water on them and killed them in scores, but still they come. 'How to do?' as Namkia so aptly remarks.
>
> Khamba has got rather heavier, and now the chokra simply cannot hold him! The dog-boy used to be called 'Khamba's Father', but now is known as 'Khamba's Flea'. Lesser livestock is still plentiful. I had a lizard in my pyjama trousers this morning and yesterday a snake fell out of the cookhouse roof in front of the chokra. He gave one 'Whoosh!' and leapt for the door, catching his foot a most almighty crack on the sill, while the snake left via wall with equal velocity.

But there were greater dangers to life than the local wildlife. Namkia's brother-in-law, Haichangnang – the mail-runner – was a simple, lovable, child-like soul and he was devastated to the point of self-destruction when his small daughter suffered a summer bout of diarrhoea then, after a sudden deterioration, died. The day after her death he tottered up to Ursula's hut and, his face contorted with tears and sobbing, threw himself at her feet. He was wailing incoherently in Zemi, so Ursula called in Namkia. He pulled himself together and asked quite rationally if she had any medicine which he could take as poison – he couldn't bear to let his little girl go on the long dark road of the dead on her own. It took all Ursula and Namkia's efforts to calm him – their most cogent argument being that he must stay alive for his surviving baby. He set out with the next mail delivery and eventually reached his home village – only to hear that an hour earlier the baby had also died. Lives hung by a very thin thread in the harsh environment of the hills.

Towards the end of July the threat of trouble subsided and Ursula moved back to Laisong and got her first opportunity to start to understand the Zemi – and the pieces began to fall into place:

> These people were not treacherous savages. They were honest, bullishly stubborn, farming people. They were not sophisticated, and lived by standards which, to Europeans, would have fallen far short of their own understanding of what was civilised, and as such were excitable and credulous. But that didn't mean they weren't decent folk – good citizens. Something had gone badly wrong for the relationship with the Government to break down so comprehensively. There now stood between the Zemi and the Government a wall of misunderstanding, fear, suspicion and mistrust, and behind it, cut off from the outside world, these decent people got on with their tribal life, following their traditions as they had always done.

It was fortunate that Ursula and Namkia had established such a warm rapport, as Ursula realised how very much an outsider she was in Laisong. She saw, too, that there was no 'quick fix' for the alienation from the British government, or for her to become integrated into the village. It was going to take time, patience and a gradual growth of mutual understanding to repair the rift. How it took place created a strange turnaround in Ursula's outlook:

> When I first reached Laisong, I was outside it. As their reserve melted, the wall dissolved, and I found myself on the far side and looking back at a familiar world seen topsy-turvy, as Alice passed through the looking glass and saw her own room reversed when she looked back. So seen, the world I had left did seem odd; there was foundation for the Zemi attitude. Civilisation had certain features which were only apparent to an outside view. Nevertheless, it was all wrong that so profound a misunderstanding should exist. I made up my mind to do what I could to right it.

Ursula would be bound by Zemi laws and customs, with no special treatment – but she could be present to record their ceremonies and, accorded the unprecedented privilege of being an honorary man, she was allowed into the men's dekachang, which was usually taboo for women, but Ursula came to an arrangement: 'They were very nice and they used to let me in – they counted me in on rather the Joan of Arc principle, but I wasn't entirely a lady, in both senses, so I was allowed in' – and she was always treated with the utmost courtesy by young and old alike.

Ursula drew the line at living in a Zemi house, but from her own camp within the village confines, she remained in close touch with events. Her basha had two big rooms – a bedroom and sitting room – with a veranda all round. Her bathroom was a section of the bedroom and there was a storeroom, a small back hall and a tiny office partitioned off the sitting room at the end of the veranda. Behind the basha was the servants' accommodation – and she finally settled with a team of seven, including herself – a cook, kitchen boy, an interpreter, a man to carry the post, a gardener and a dog-boy. As the Zemi are rather short in stature and Ursula was five foot nine, she couldn't help seeing a resemblance to Snow White and the seven dwarves.

Once the basics were catered for, Ursula needed some stores and provisions to offer a little variety – some flavours of home and creature comforts. While some luxury items – specially-made clothes, mosquito boots, and other essential memsahib's jungle gear – needed to be ordered from home, mainly from the Army and Navy Stores, it was possible to get British products sent up from 'the civilised world' in India. The ex-pat communities at Imphal and Kohima would have found it hard to maintain their British aplomb if forced to eat the local fare, so Ursula had access to the same provisions they did, albeit they cost rather more and could mysteriously disappear in transit. Ursula's cookhouse staff quickly adapted their culinary skills to serve up British-style food, to which end Ursula wrote lengthy lists to send down to the stores of Imphal. One such list ran as follows:

Kerosene oil
Matches 2
Soap 4
Tinned butter 4
Ryvita 6
Bisc-o-rye 2
Whisky 1
Chutney
Tomato sauce 1
Tinned sausages 3
Marmite 2
Bovril
Tinned fruit 3
Tin-opener
Tea 1lb
Klim 1
Akhbar Shahs 3
Lime juice
Salt
Pepper
Tinned fish
Tinned soup 3
Tinned peas 2
Bromo 1
Spare batteries 3

555 cigarettes
Kippers 2
K snacks 1
Lea and Perrins sauce
Lard

Ursula's purse-strings were tight and with her modest income from her allowance, it was a job to stay in the black, especially when she was constantly having to hand out baksheesh in the form of cash or cigarettes. An entry in one notebook gives an idea of the costs involved (in rupees):

Balancing the accounts		
Klim [milk, bought in powdered form]	1 lb	1/3
	2 and a quarter lb	3/4
Vita-wheat	2 lb	2/2
	1 lb	1/6
Ryvita	1/10	
Carr's assorted creams		1/4
Huntley and Palmers		
rich mixed	no.2	3/4
	no. 1	2/2
Spare torch battery – 6 volt		4/8

Dispensary needs	
Tincture of iodine	8 oz
Elastoplast	2 1/2 inch
	3 inch
	4 inch
Iodex	
Aspirin tablets	100
Burroughs Wellcome Chlorodyne	
Crookes' Lacto Calomine	
Dettol	
Dettolin	
Ellimans	
Minadex	
Protargol drops	

And if the opportunity arose for a visit to Mukerjee's in Calcutta:

Acid, boric	1 lb
Soda bicarb	1 lb packet
	1 lb bottle
Mag sulph	1 lb packet
Mandel's pigment	1 oz
Angier's emulsion	

Antipeol
Aspirin (B and W)
Aspirin (Boots')

B and W:	
Calomel	1/2 gr
Grey Powders	1 gr
Quinine hydrochloride	5 gr
Eucalyptus and menthol pastilles (Boots')	
Optrex	
PD Cocillana	4 oz and 16 oz
Kotex	

The provision of a water supply by bamboo pipes meant that Ursula could address the woeful condition of the kitchen garden, and regular manuring eventually turned the plot into something with potential to produce edible results, and Ursula set down a planting schedule in the well-thumbed notebook:

To go straight in:
Dwarf French beans
Beetroot
Cress (first sowing)
Peas (first sowing) – two kinds
Spinach
Mixed herbs
Parsley
Onions

Into boxes:
Capsicums – 3
Lettuces – first sowing
Cress

While fencing protected Ursula's kitchen garden from large predators, the local insect life proved more difficult to repel. She wrote feelingly to her mother of her problems with the resident beetles:

> We have been having a pogrom on the local beetles. They are foul beasts and live in holes in the ground. At night they come out shrilling like six cicadas and eat all the baby lettuces and radishes the mali and I planted with such loving care. They have to be dug out of their holes with a dao, thus affording quiet employment for the small boys. The mali has been dubbed the 'Baghicha Sheb' – or 'Tea-garden Sahib' (if you could but see him!), so the head beetle-catcher (who is simply dressed in two necklaces and a piece of sticking plaster on the left shin) has been called the 'Beetle Sahib'. He and the mali between them earned three annas this morning, at current rates of one farthing per beetle. The mali departed

> whooping to buy a bottle of zu for two annas of it, and gave the odd anna to the Beetle Sahib.

Ursula wrote at least every week to her mother, and the consistent factor in her correspondence was her unfailing cheerfulness, her genuine affection for her Zemi hosts and Naga staff – and gleeful relish at what she knew her mother would see as the utter lunacy of it all.

13

Tribal Law

Laisong was strongly autonomous and traditional, despite its closeness to rail communications and the fact that it had been under British administration since the early nineteenth century. The light-handed approach to 'administration' favoured by Mills had meant that the Zemis' tribal polity had persisted almost unaltered.

Their tribal structure and regulation were established from the time of the Zemis' first arrival in the area. Communities who had been driven from their home villages by Angami aggression drifted in search of a place to settle. Each of these had a leader, with a lieutenant, and these figureheads staked the village's claim to the land where they settled, and from their families were chosen the village headmen. In this way, the ownership of the land and control of the village itself were handed down through the families of these 'men of the soil' – the kadepeo. Through their hereditary right, these men wielded unchallenged authority – only in the very rare event of there not being a new male incumbent of suitable age would the leadership be given to an outsider. This system went on unchanged – the only difference was that under British administration the headmen wore the official red government blanket as a mark of their status.

Each Zemi village was run by a village council, over which the kadepeo presided. He, along with the village priest, chose elders to serve on the council and attend particular meetings – but there was no despotism. If the council felt that public opinion was against any of the kadepeo's policies, they would overrule him. Respect for the village councils was such that their rulings were accepted as irrevocable. Criminal cases were few and far between, and judgements were made according to long-standing tribal law, and where crimes were considered serious, banishment was the most likely sentence.

The more Ursula saw of the Zemi village administration, the more she respected and admired their common sense and practicality. The village was run by four secular and four religious officials. The chief in the village was the senior headman, followed by his junior headman and two assistants. On the religious side, there were the first and second priests – both very elderly – whose care was the religious life of the village. Although Christianity had been introduced to some Naga tribes by missionaries, the Christian communities tended to co-exist alongside the original pagan ones. The old priests (only the very aged could communicate with the gods without coming to harm) would have a younger factotum to deal with the heavy work, and a town-crier who broadcast around the village any pronouncements whispered to him by the elders.

The Zemi lived in a patriarchal community, and as pagans their religious life was regulated by seasons and the gods of nature. What was particular throughout the Naga tribes was the morung system. The morung buildings – great halls of which each village had at least two – were clubhouses for the young men with associated dormitories for the girls. As soon as a Zemi baby was born, a deputation would come from one of the morungs to claim then as a member of the club – the kienga – and this would dictate their club allegiance for life. Boys and girls would stay in their family home until the age of about eight, after which it was felt to be inappropriate for them to remain at night in the same house as their parents. Girls would spend their days at home, working with their mother, then retired to the morung dormitory at night. Here they would hold girls' get-togethers such as spinning bees, or stage musical entertainments. All above board and very proper, these entertainments might be visited by village headmen or elders, who took a purely fatherly interest. What was less above board, but seemed to go on with tacit acceptance, was the universal custom of the young men of the village creeping to the door of the dormitory after dark and slipping inside to seek out their particular girlfriend from the rows of sleeping benches inside.

For boys, the morung was a full-time, live-in school, run by a resident village leader. The boys' hall was a massive foyer which led to the master's home, and his wife would act as school matron. Once in the morung, the influence of a boy's father was replaced by that of the male community. It was a system designed to foster a sense of membership and belonging, and to inculcate responsibility, self-reliance and discipline. Right from the start, the youngest boys would 'fag' for the older ones, as in a public school, so they could begin to learn the ropes. If they misbehaved, the boys would be given a stern talking-to by their elders, and as this was the same for everyone and could not be avoided, it tended to create a sense of unity, fairness and loyalty. It smoothed off the rough corners without jeopardising individuality.

The next phase for a young man, from assuming the kilt of manhood to the time of getting married and setting up his own home, was largely devoid of duties or obligations. Naga bucks were excused all field work – this was left largely to the womenfolk – and days were whiled away drinking zu, chatting, playing music and occasionally making the odd basket before bathing and decking themselves out to look as impressive as possible in the evening. This latter was important – the bucks were not just permitted, but tacitly encouraged to spend their nights out courting, and they wanted to look their best. The philosophy was that the responsibilities of manhood would be loaded on the young men all too soon once they settled and married. The bucks might at any time be called upon to protect the village against attack, so youth was all too short. With a great openness of spirit, the Zemi indulged the bucks during their carefree youth before the harsh reality of manhood set in for keeps.

All the same, the young men's lives were not entirely gilded leisure. They still came under the strict discipline of the village elders, and all had to learn hunting, fishing, fighting, physical training and sports – but this all contributed to the sense of youthful rivalry and competition. Once married, the family man would set up his own home, returning to the morung merely as a clubhouse during the day. Only in the case of war did all the men gather and stay in the morung at night, so as to be ready to defend the village. But even solely as a clubhouse, the morung was an excellent institution.

There was a welcoming reception for visitors – dances, feasts and informal meetings were all held in the hall where the long wall-benches were laid out around the central fire. The blacksmith worked there too, and all the paraphernalia of hunting and war were stored there against any eventuality.

Ursula began to explore the role of women in Naga life. After the age of eight, girls made only brief formal appearances in public – and that under the aegis of their kienga – and married women had no part in public life at all. It was considered highly inappropriate and immodest for a woman to enter the main hall of a morung and it would be unclean and unnatural for a man to eat any meat of any animal that had been killed by a woman. These two taboos posed a particular problem for Ursula, however, she came to an agreement with the elders that she could be an honorary man for the purposes of entering the morung. With regard to women slaughtering animals for food, Ursula was once more acknowledged as an exception when she bought a shotgun. Although hunting might be a man's job, meat was scarce, and exigency sensibly took precedence over tradition.

Even if men did all the heavy work, the women's contribution had the most economic impact. Women cooked, brewed, eked out their meagre resources, carried wood and water, sowed, weeded and harvested, spun, dyed, wove and sewed, and managed the household and family. A hard-working and economical wife could provide a reasonably comfortable life for the whole family – whereas a man alone would literally be condemned to poverty. With this in mind, a young man wanting to marry would have to pay a large marriage price to the father of his intended as compensation for losing a most valuable asset.

The death of a wife or mother was an economic as well as a personal tragedy for a family, a harsh reality apparent to Ursula when she visited a village hit by an outbreak of smallpox. Some small children had been vaccinated and survived, and the stronger men were able to come through the illness alive – but by a freak of circumstance, the disease had claimed almost every woman from sixteen upwards. The economic life of the village had ground to a halt as the inadequate numbers of young men struggled to keep up with work in the fields and married men stayed home with the very young children. Ursula summed it up:

> The influence women wielded, aside from that which affection and sentiment would in any case have allowed – for family life is everything to a Zemi – was remarkable. Nor did the women take their responsibilities lightly. They were, behind the scenes, the real rulers of the community.

This was the structure of Zemi family life – and in a village there was no other sort. Ursula respected their system and saw much to admire in it – so it was no problem for her to cement her place, at first as a stranger and guest, then increasingly as a friend and sister, among the people of Laisong.

14

The World Beyond the Hills

While pursuing her anthropological studies Ursula was able to sound out what was causing anti-British feeling among the Kacha Nagas. Namkia kept Ursula abreast of events in the local villages, and he accompanied her on her trips to record, collect artefacts and make notes. Theirs had become a friendship based on mutual respect and genuine liking – an eventuality far from both their expectations when they first met – which was just as well, as visits by other British to Laisong were few and far between.

By September, Ursula had to admit that she felt just a little cut off from the Western world. There, as far as she knew, the war was still going on. She had received only one letter and two cables from Doris since June – and those revealed that none of her letters had reached their destination in the UK. As she wrote to Alexa,

> I have been writing the wittiest of letters, too, every week, and latterly by airmail. Either my accounts of the quaint old Naga customs were too much for the censor or a long, long trail of letters is still going round the Cape.

Ursula couldn't expect Namkia to abandon his own village entirely, and he spent his free time in Impoi, where his standing was enormously enhanced by his employment with Ursula. It was also a matter of considerable pride for Namkia to take Ursula to his village, and it was returning from one such foray in gathering dusk that the two walked through a winding path through tall jungle grass leading to a steep and rugged 'ladder' of rocky ledges leading up to the village. Two lads met them with torches below the camp and they paused, smoking furiously to keep the flies off. Namkia 'joyously loopy as usual, suddenly announced that this would be a splendid place for holding off the Angamis'. Old enmities had deep roots, and these warlike people had been wont to hunt heads on a twice-weekly basis in Namkia's grandfather's era. Time had done little to dull the edge of inter-tribal aggression and Namkia launched a spirited mock rear-guard action, hurling all the stones he could lay his hands on down on the imaginary enemy below. The lads joined in, whooping and yelling so that Ursula was genuinely concerned that Laisong might turn out in full battle order in response.

The warlike Angamis, who at anything up to six foot, were tall as a tribe, had so victimised the Zemi with raids and head-taking that a fair number had taken flight and, at the safety of three days' remove, had adopted quasi-Angami dress as a precaution. Ramgakpa's village, Gobin, was one of these, and Ramgakpa still sported Angami dress, despite being ragged about it by others in the camp:

> He stands about four foot ten inches, and has only to appear with a spear in his hand to be chaffed unmercifully about his warlike intentions. It has been rudely suggested that in case of a clash, he should hop into his opponent' clothes and bite him.

Ursula's presence among them lent the Zemis of Laisong a new sense of security – the British would scarcely allow a village where she was resident to be subjected to Angami aggression, and the longer she was there, the happier they were and the more inclined to make her feel at home.

In other areas, notably amorous ones, Naga custom persisted un-anglicised and Ursula simply got used to it. The mali, Samrangba, whom Namkia had deputised as 'body guard' while he went back to Impoi, appeared to enjoy a particularly active night life, drawn to Ursula's attention by the noise of his nocturnal comings and goings. Concerned only about getting a good night's sleep herself, Ursula took Samrangba aside and pointed out that 'if he wanted to steal out in the night to do a bit of boat-deck work in the girls' dormitory, he must go out of the right-hand window, because the shutter squeaks less.' This helpful advice was greeted with 'mahogany-red flush and juicy chortles'.

All this 'free love' in Laisong (and every other Naga village) went on under Ursula's non-judgemental nose – but she, alone among them, had no partner. In a letter to Doris she gave a hint of a shipboard romance on her passage to India a couple of years before, and her mother must have read it with a mixture of sympathy and impatience. At the start of November Ursula made a trip to Calcutta for ten days with Namkia – partly for practical purposes, but also to fulfil an obligation. She wrote:

> I went for all sorts of reasons, including a visit to the dentist, necessity of shopping, and so on – and also to see a boyfriend, a tea-planter, whom I met on the boat two years ago. He seemed very keen then, and since we got in touch again last year, he has proposed twice. He did on the boat, as a matter of fact, and I refused. However, he continued so keen I thought I'd see him again and think it over, but I'm no more in love with him than I was before, and I don't feel it would ever be a success like that. He's a very good sort – rather plain Scots – but very kind, dead straight honest and very much in love. I like him and I'm sorry for him, but one can hardly embark on matrimony on those grounds, and considering all the other difficulties – living out East (in the plains, too), question of brats (parking of), local social amenities and everything else, I think very definitely *not*. I wish you were here so that I could have your dear motherly advice, but I've thought it all over several times and it seems to me that it just *would not* work, and it would be better to decide that before than after the ceremony. Anyhow, we ran round together in Calcutta, I adequately chaperoned by Namkia, who slept in my room because it was deadly hot in the passage outside, and he liked the punka. Pat wanted me to stay on, but Calcutta is the most expensive place in the world bar none, so I went back at the end of a week, and Pat's face as the train pulled out haunts me yet. So that, as it were, was that.

Namkia had never been further from home than Silchar in one direction and Kohima in the other, and evinced no inclination to go further afield now. However, loyalty to Ursula dictated that he should accompany her to Calcutta. On the train journey, on a halt at Maibong, Ursula passed his compartment and found him sitting bolt upright, staring fixedly ahead of him, for all the world like a man facing execution. He appeared almost in tears as he said goodbye to some Naga fruit-sellers on the platform – and he studiously avoided looking back to his homeland in case the emotion became too much for him.

Their first change was at Lumding – and here Namkia was cheered to find a stall on the platform selling curry. The Lumding stop was as unnerving for Ursula as it was comforting to Namkia. In the refreshment room she found a party of Europeans – the first white people she had seen for four months, and at the risk of appearing rude, she couldn't help staring. Compared with the smooth Mongol faces of the Nagas, these Europeans looked oddly knobbly and craggy – and the women particularly were unnaturally pallid, like plants left in the dark. In retrospect, Ursula concluded that the first sight of one's own kind after a long separation was the greatest culture shock – after that the chasm didn't seem so wide and it became easier to make the transition between the two very different worlds.

Compartments for servants and sahibs were in different parts of the train, but as they waited to move off again, Ursula caught sight of Namkia standing in the doorway of his carriage, resplendent in his scarlet blanket, black kilt, golden-yellow necklaces and cane knee-rings – and before him was a growing audience. Between Namkia and the crowd was a small sepoy, and this busy little man was parading up and down, answering the crowd's questions about Namkia:

> Yes, he is an important person. He is of my own caste. He, too, is a Naga. We may eat from the same dish. Seller! Bring some soda-water for my Naga brother! Oh, there! Bring some cigarettes!

Both vendors were quick to respond and the sepoy continued, 'Nothing is too good. I will pay all!' and then to Namkia: 'Oh my brother! Take, please, some cigarettes as a present from me! It is so very long since I saw another Naga, and it has made me so very happy!'

Ursula watched as Namkia rose to the occasion.

> Namkia, the old sinner! – what he must have been as a buck – posed there, so statuesque and conscious of himself in the narrow doorway, the heavy scarlet drapery falling from his bare shoulders; under the bare lights and the black, barren, girdered roof, he was a magnificently barbaric figure.

Although he didn't actually catch Ursula's eye directly, he knew she saw his enjoyment. He relished that too – with what Ursula recognised as his own puckish humour. She watched as, with polite reluctance, he took a packet of cigarettes from the vendor, picked one out and lit it, and addressed the crowd.

'Yes, my brother, we are both Nagas. I thank you for your presents. Though you are an Ao and I am a Zemi, yet we are both of the same caste.' Fortunately the shrill whistle of the guard and a convulsive jerk forward by the train prevented him from milking the situation any further, and Ursula legged it down the platform for her own carriage.

Namkia's flagging morale was soaring – and ensuing events only served to boost it further. When they changed trains at Parbatipur there was no servants' compartment, so Namkia found himself squashed into a third-class carriage with some sixty other people. Seen as a very unusual novelty by his fellow passengers, he was closely questioned – so he answered with customary Zemi courtesy. Eventually the questions began to pall, and some inquirers overstepped the border of politeness to the point of fingering his clothes, asking for scraps of his blanket as souvenirs and prodding at him – at which his patience deserted him. Someone asked, in a hushed voice, if Nagas were really, as plainsmen believed, cannibals.

Namkia took a deep breath and replied. 'Oh yes. I couldn't tell you the number of times I've tasted human flesh.' As if by magic, a space grew up all around him and gratifyingly, his audience shrank away from him. Pleased with this effect he continued:

> In the last famine, my wife and I decided we should have to eat one of the children. We couldn't make up our minds (we had four, you know) whether to eat the eldest, who was about ten, because there would be more meat on him and we could smoke it down, or whether to take the youngest, which was quite a baby, because we shouldn't miss it so much, and we could easily have another. We argued for hours.

Seeing the effect this was having, he was unable to resist a final salvo:

> I decided at last against killing the eldest. He'd been such a trouble to rear. Unfortunately, my wife was fond of the baby. You never heard such a scene – eventually, though, I insisted on killing it; and it really was extremely good, most tender – boiled, with chillies. But my wife, poor woman, was most upset. She cried the whole time and couldn't touch a mouthful.

Namkia now had not only the bench to himself, but most of the carriage, as his audience had pressed itself into the far corners of the compartment. Smiling cheerfully he spread his bedding out and slept in spacious comfort the rest of the way to Calcutta. If anyone new entered the carriage and approached to ask him to move over, the rest out the carriage hissed, 'Look out! Man-eater!' and Namkia slept on in splendid isolation.

Namkia's triumph was short-lived – the swarming crowds and maze of streets terrified him, and although he could find his way through impenetrable jungle with no problems, he had no sense of direction on the streets. So bewildered was he that Ursula had to bribe one of the hotel bearers to keep an eye on him when she was elsewhere, and take him about with her for the rest of their stay. This led to some interesting situations, and Ursula was led to wonder if the Ladies' Department of the Army and Navy Store would ever really recover from his visit.

Pat still nursed hopes of his proposal being accepted, and accompanied Ursula on her domestic shopping trips. After calling at Hall and Anderson's to buy bedclothes, Ursula robustly thwarted all Pat's attempts to steer her into the furniture department. They must have made a strange trio touring the stores – an earnest Scotsman, a deeply tanned Englishwoman – and a colourful half-clad Naga.

The hotel alone posed all manner of problems for Namkia – he had never seen a three-storey building before and, assessing the Great Eastern Hotel, he reckoned you could fit around six Zemi villages into it and still have room for a morung in the dining room. On the first night he had been sleeping outside Ursula's room while she was out at dinner and on waking up, left his post to go down to the courtyard. Forgetting that he was on the second floor, he climbed up only one floor on the way back and wandered about in the semi-darkness – almost completely naked – peering down the corridors in search of his bedding. All round the first floor, servants sleeping outside the rooms woke to find a strange apparition looming over them. Worried that this alien savage might be a cannibal in search of food, they huddled in their blankets and resorted to desperate praying, as Namkia drifted aimlessly, frightened more than anything that people would suspect he was a thief and he would be arrested and thrown in jail.

Eventually some bright soul suggested going up one more floor, and he padded anxiously up the spiral stairs. He finally rounded a corner, saw his own bedding and sank on to it with enormous relief. He was still awake, in a state of nervous collapse when Ursula got back. After this, he insisted on sleeping in Ursula's room on the mat below the punkah. He claimed it was cooler, but more particularly, his elder sister, the She-Sahib, could keep an eye on him.

Touring around Calcutta, Namkia was fascinated by the zoo, the local Chevrolet taxis and the Metro cinema. This was the first chance Namkia had had to see colour movies, and when Ursula found a shop with a projector on which to show her own films, he was thrilled. Although some of them had been spoiled by heat, there was some good footage, and he was tickled pink to see himself on the screen.

Back in Laisong Namkia told his tales of the big city, and basked in the enhanced status of one who has travelled widely and experienced the unknown world beyond the hills.

15

Christmas and the Spirit World

As 1940 drew to a close Ursula faced the prospect of a lone Christmas at Laisong – followed by the Zemi New Year Feast of Hgangi, which started immediately after.

On 9 December Ursula received a cable, sent from Booth by runner. It brought the news she had long been fearing. Humpus, who had been struggling with ill health for some time, had died. It read, 'Our darling H passed quietly away December 4th. Much love, Paterson.' Ursula, miles from anywhere in the Naga Hills, too far from war-torn England to return to comfort Doris or say her own farewell to the grandmother who had brought her up, was devastated.

She wrote the next day to Doris and to Alexa. To Alexa she tried to be rational,

> I feel rather as if the bottom had dropped out of things, but it is for the best. You know how she hated being an invalid, and it must have been lonely there at Leigh, none of her friends able to see her as they used to do in London. Years of it would have been terrible.

To Doris, too, she had to admit that it was probably the best thing – but her thoughts were distracted:

> I feel singularly b------ awful. Last night when I wept, my large bodyguard sat down beside me and wept in sympathy, and then retired to the cookhouse and spilt boiling water over himself, providing a useful diversion.

The final dak arrived before Christmas, bringing three letters from Doris – the earliest of which, written in October, brought more bad news. Her father, never able to give up the drinking which had spoiled his first marriage, had died of cirrhosis of the liver. Although step-mother Barbara had remained in touch, even through Ursula's difference of opinion with her father over 'the gloomy Dane', and they had made things up at a distance, Ursula had never seen her father again. Now, only in his fifties, he was dead. Ursula wrote to her mother, who must have felt the loss of her first love very deeply:

> Poor old Daddy! I do feel sorry for Barbara. She was really fond of him, in spite of her throwing periodic temperaments. Quite a number of people were fond of Daddy in spite of everything and all. Poor old dear.

Aware of her father's declining condition, his death, like that of Humpus, was one Ursula had been expecting. It was fortunate that life afforded her few chances to sit and brood.

Ursula's letter to Doris of Christmas Eve filled in the latest instalment on Pat, who had very generously sent her a five-pound chest of tea, and followed that up with a pair of geese to fatten up for Christmas – which had already gone 'the way of all flesh'. Now he was importuning her for an answer to his proposal of marriage:

> Pat wrote me a letter asking for a final answer, and said that if I said 'No', he was going to cable a girl at home. I wrote him a lovely renunciatory letter, and was just about to order a nice set of silver-plated toast-racks when he wrote back to say he wasn't going to give up yet, and the lady would have to wait for her cable. So we are back where we were, more or less. He has been at it now for two years and two months. One might almost think the boy had serious intentions. I still don't think I should be at all a successful Mrs Pat.

Through considerable skimping and saving, Ursula had amassed twenty-two rupees – enough to buy a small mithan as a Christmas treat. The beast was slaughtered by the cook and the body left at the water-point for the village blacksmith to cut up. With her Christmas roast dinner at stake, Ursula had intended supervising the butchering in the hope of getting something approaching a recognisable joint, but when she arrived at the water-point the whole animal had been hacked into lumps weighing about a pound each. Even the hide, which Ursula had had her eye on as a bedside rug, was in pieces. She and the cook sorted through the gruesome and bloody mound of flesh and eventually found something which might, by a long stretch of the imagination, be treated as a roasting joint.

Namkia called Ursula at crack of Christmas dawn for a pig and mithan chase starting in the village. She saw two pigs caught – they scarcely had any lead before they were captured just a couple of yards from the start line. There remained a mithan to chase, and the bucks and young married men lined up at the lower bungalow to start the chase. It was some time later that Ursula got back for the scheduled dispensary – there was no change to Naga arrangements for Christmas, although the main concession to the day was to get affably drunk, and this they did with great application.

First thing that morning the cook had reported sick, however, he had given Paodekumba full instructions, and Ursula was not to spoil her Christmas holiday by slaving over a hot stove. When Ursula eventually got back for lunch, Namkia entered from the cookhouse bearing Ursula's Christmas feast. With a ceremonial flourish he laid it before her on the table – a piece of bone swimming in water, from which hung some sodden fibres most resembling wet, brown string. Paodekumba had warmed it through in some tepid fat early in the morning, transferred it to a large vat of water and had boiled it vigorously. Ursula opened a can of tongue.

The Zemi believed in an afterlife, and the dead were thought to linger in their homes until compelled to leave at the Hgangi festival. In one fell swoop, at the turn of the year, all the dead would be finally bidden farewell. All that they might need in the afterlife: clothes, tools, gourds, seeds – anything that had not been provided when they were originally buried – were offered now, and the senior priest conducted a ceremony at the top of the village. He would then move down the street, calling out for the ghosts to take their offerings and depart through the open gate at the lower end of the village. The unseen dead were allowed time to take their leave, then the priest would close the gate after them.

As Ursula arrived, the priests had started down the path and Namkia – who had halted by the big stone – called out to stop her from going higher up the path to film. If she went on she might meet the demon of sickness before the priests cast him out of the village. All the living kept well out of the way as the souls departed – there was always the danger that the souls of the living, being easily influenced, might be drawn along with those of the dead, and if the soul were to leave, the body would die. This was not a risk to take lightly, and only the priests remained in the street. The old priest had lost his own son in the last year, and as he recited the words of dismissal, his tone had a specially melancholy ring. 'Oh, all you dead, go to your own place and leave the living here. Oh, all you dead, it is time to depart. Let the living remain and let the dead go!' Repeating this litany, he passed down the street, the atmosphere chill in spite of the sun. Eventually he passed from view, although his voice could still be heard as he went towards the gate. Then he turned back. 'The dead have gone to their own place! The dead are separated from the living!' Life rushed back into the village and everyone was ready to enjoy the lighter part of the festival.

The next day there followed a sequence of events which Ursula wrote up later as 'Incident at Laisong' – and it was a vindication of the Naga axiom that a bad night means a bad day to follow. Ursula had not slept well, and Namkia woke her first thing in a very melancholy mood, having had disturbing dreams. Ill omens or not, it was a beautiful sunlit morning and as she smoked an after-breakfast cigarette on the veranda, she looked across to the village.

Down in the street there was more activity than there had been for a while, as the Hgangi festival meant that all work was taboo, but on this particular day a few vital jobs were permitted. Everyone was leaving the village to replenish their depleted larders and log piles. Admittedly, no-one was meant to leave until the main ceremony of the day was properly completed, but Laisong was known to be rather lax in its observation of rituals, and besides, the fields were a good long way away. None of the elders had turned out to prevent them leaving, so they were setting off in good time to get the chores done and be back for the feast later.

Ursula noticed a thin plume of wood smoke rising from the hollow near the water-point, so the village elders were evidently getting on with the day's ceremonies and sacrifices. She had been mugging up on local lore and knew that each of the fourteen spirits known to the Zemi had to be called on by name to join the feast. The ritual was a dangerous business, as the spirit gods were capricious and unpredictable, and lived on the souls of men. Once called, each of the fourteen gods had to receive a separate sacrifice, and if there was even the slightest deviation from the ritual, the sacrifice had to be repeated until the procedure was perfect. The most dangerous eventuality would be to call one of the spirits to the ceremony then cheat him of his offerings by making a mistake. The spirit would be there, angry and insulted within the confines of the village. Ursula noticed that the fire was out by noon, so she assumed that offerings had been made to everyone's satisfaction. The old priests finished off the remaining zu and made their way back into the village and a cluster of dogs and pigs were left squabbling over the remains of a feast from which the gods had absorbed the spiritual essence. Everything had apparently gone normally.

It was a man visiting Ursula's camp from a neighbouring village who first noticed that something was wrong in Laisong. It was not quite dusk, but the sun had dipped behind the surrounding range of hills and Ursula was just about to make up a fire. Through the open door she could see her three visitors strolling around the garden, as they waited for the evening meal. Suddenly they paused together and looked with evident concern towards Laisong. She picked out the word 'death' and she strained to make out what was being said. A sound drifted up from the village – a confused murmur which might have been sobbing. From a window overlooking the village she saw a man hurry past, and from his expression she could see that there was something serious afoot. She called for Namkia to find out what was happening, but by the time he arrived the distant crying had taken on the unmistakable moan of a death-bed lamentation, and the sound rose towards the camp through the perfect stillness of the air.

Namkia returned quickly with the explanation. There had been something wrong with the morning's offerings – perhaps the old men had been negligent, as they had been in letting the villagers out early to the fields. Maybe they had failed to spot an error and not repeated the ritual until they got it right. Whatever had gone wrong, a spirit had been angry and had chosen a victim in place of the sacrifice offered.

Samrangba's mother-in-law, an old but fit and robust woman, had been among those who left the village early. She had walked the few miles to the fields, carried back a full basket of vegetables, and all had been well until she reached the mound just outside the village gate, where the sacrifices had been made earlier. As she passed the mound she had felt a sudden chill fall like a shadow on her – but she thought no more of it, as it was a cold January evening. She had carried on towards the outskirts of the village – then had fallen unconscious a few yards from her own door.

A neighbour had picked her up and taken her inside, but there was nothing to be done for her. She didn't recover consciousness and although there was no sign of illness or fever, she was definitely dying. Her family had gathered around her motionless form and their wailing drifted up to Ursula through the stillness. Namkia was brief and unequivocal: 'A spirit struck her.' The wailing changed suddenly to a shriek, a death cry – and the old lady had gone.

With all the upheavals of Christmas and the ensuing festivals, as she settled down for the evening, she resolved to spend future Hgangis in civilisation. Like most New Year resolutions however, it was never kept.

At Hgangi Ursula had seen the strength of belief among the Zemi in the spirit world, and people pointed out to Ursula mysterious lights far away in the jungle – spirit-fires. Sometimes in the night the alarm was raised when staff claimed they heard cries and eerie whistling. Ursula was inclined to see the spirit-fires as being brushwood burning, and though she had heard the alleged eerie cries on two occasions and had no idea what animal could be making them, she remained robustly sceptical.

It was late in January 1941 that Ursula had no choice but to accept that the camp had acquired a poltergeist. The first manifestation was in Haichangnang's hut, at the far end of the servants' lines. At night he would see the door being shaken – sometimes so violently that it was flung wide open – and he heard pattering noises like a pig or dog running. Ursula was quick to suggest that he try drinking less zu, and gave the matter no more thought. However, the nocturnal door-slamming and running went on, and Haichangnang moved in next door with Hozekiemba, the new mali. The noises went on, and when Ursula returned a week later from a trip to Hangrum, a small deputation came to ask her to leave more men to keep an eye on the camp in her absence, as they had heard voices in her empty bungalow during the night.

Whatever it was, was working its way up the servants' lines, and soon everyone in camp had heard the noises in the night. With a childish, comic touch which caused Ursula to look further for a human culprit, the thing started blowing raspberries. If everyone hadn't been so scared, it would have been laughable, but the accompanying barrage of noise now reached the cookhouse. By the beginning of February, something disturbed the camp every night – there would be a crash like the falling of a whole stack of cooking pans, at which everyone would run to the cookhouse – where there was nothing to see.

If Ursula still nursed some doubts, these were dispelled in early February when the trouble reached her bungalow. She was reading by the fire in the living room one evening when she heard a pattering – like the sound of a large dog trotting down the veranda outside her window. Concerned in case Khamba had got free and might fall prey to a leopard, she rushed out with a flashlight. She could hear the noise just on the other side of the door as she flung it open – but found the veranda empty. She shone the torch all around the open ground, but there was no sign of anything. Calling over to the servants' lines she learned that Khamba had been safely chained up since before dusk – so it hadn't been him. This happened the next night too – and still nothing to see. By the third night she didn't bother checking outside – but she accepted that it was something.

The next episode, inside the bungalow, struck Ursula as little short of farce:

> It was the usual time in the evening, about an hour after dark, and I was just starting dinner. The camp table was pushed up to the partition wall between the two rooms and was just beside the connection doorway, and the hurricane lamp on it cast a ring of light round the table and myself for a yard or so through the doorway, into the bedroom beyond. I had a book propped against the sauce-bottle and was half-way through a plate of pumpkin soup, when off went a loud, explosive 'raspberry', as unmistakable and as concrete as a 'raspberry' can be, just beyond the doorway and within a yard of where I sat. I could tell the spot to a foot, and it was well within the ring of light. I put down the spoon and looked. There was the dog-bed, there was the doorway; there was the wall, there was the half-seen room beyond; and nothing whatever odd about any of them. Well, if a spirit wished to amuse itself by making rude noises in my bungalow, I could see no immediate way to prevent it, so I found my place in the book again and went on with my soup.

Not being accorded the attention it wanted, the poltergeist – or whatever it was – resorted to more alarming and physical manifestations. Again, this happened as Ursula ate her solitary supper. The shutters across her two small windows were held shut by a strong bar across the frame on the inside. The bar was held to the matting shutter by string, and the matting's natural springiness kept it in place. Hearing a faint noise,

Ursula turned to look at the shutters, and watched as the bar was slipped out cornerwise through the window-space as if someone behind her was pulling it. Then the whole shutter clattered to the floor. Owning to being startled, she called for the men to help look for what might have caused it, but of course, they found nothing. By way of sharing the phenomena, Ursula got Namkia to sleep in the bungalow thereafter.

The next evening visitation came at around six o'clock, when Ursula generally took her bath. She was standing in the bathtub and baling water over herself when the door creaked suddenly and then began to shake and rattle as if someone were trying to open it. More outraged at the intrusion on her privacy than frightened, she grabbed a towel, wrapped it round herself and rushed to fling open the door. The bedroom beyond was empty. Ursula started to think through the possibilities – and eliminate them. Any earthquake which could have shaken such a heavy door would have shaken the whole bungalow – and there had been no earthquake. She had heard no footsteps, human or animal, on the crackly bamboo matting. Although Ursula was innately level-headed, she did not discount the possibility of supernatural phenomena, and subsequent events only served to substantiate her grudging conclusion that some spirit force was at work.

After an uneventful evening Ursula had settled in her camp bed and Namkia was stretched out under his blanket against the far wall, 'like a big dog'. In the quiet, both were suddenly aware of a rasping, scuffling noise coming from the small storeroom at the back of the bungalow. Ursula's first assumption was that rats were raiding again, so she asked Namkia to take a look. In response he pulled his blanket tightly round himself and refused, saying that it was a spook. He insisted that he wasn't frightened to go and look – but there was no point in leaving a warm bed to pursue a spook which wasn't going to steal the stores. Ursula argued that he couldn't tell if it was a spook unless he looked – he remained convinced that it was no rat, and while this altercation took place the noise continued. Ursula likened it to a brick on a piece of paper being dragged over a concrete floor. Exasperated, she got up, grabbed the flashlight and went to see for herself. Namkia, shamed by his employer's courage, donned his blanket and followed.

Peering by torchlight into the small room, no more than ten feet square, they scanned the shelves, but found nothing which could be making the noise. Indeed, it continued around them, apparently no more than a couple of feet away, but in no distinct location. At least there were no rats, so they returned to their beds – but an hour later the rasping grew to such a volume that it woke Ursula up. Prepared for a long search, Ursula put on a warm coat and started a systematic trawl through the basha. She opened jappas and boxes – scanned the rafters, stamped on the floor and prodded with a stick in the regular rat-runs at the base of the walls. The noise just kept on, so half an hour later, when Ursula had found nothing, she left it scraping away and went back to bed.

The final visitation that Ursula experienced occurred when the rest of the staff had gone to a party in the village, leaving Namkia on bodyguard duty. They sat in the bungalow, talking by the fire until after eleven o'clock, when they both heard the sound of murmuring voices from the cookhouse some twenty feet away. Namkia crossed to the cookhouse, saying he wanted a word with the cook, and Ursula stayed put. Previously the staff must have presumed that she was asleep, so were whispering, but she expected to hear Namkia talking now – but while the murmuring stopped, there were no other voices. Namkia came back to say that all the servants' quarters were in darkness and everywhere, along with the cookhouse, was barred shut from the outside as the staff had left them. Needing to say no more, they turned in for the night.

The phenomena fizzled out by the end of March, and although Ursula looked for a physical explanation, no person or thing could be found responsible. The incidence most likely to be accounted for by human activity was that of the voices from the cookhouse, but when Namkia left the bungalow his range of vision covered the cookhouse, the lines and the open area between them and the scrub all round. No one could have got out and made it to cover in the couple of seconds available – especially if they paused to fasten the doors behind them. The same time-limitation would apply to anyone standing outside the lines and not indoors. The open area was steep and rough and it would have been impossible for anyone to run across it unheard or unseen. If an intruder had headed off in the other direction, Namkia would not have seen him – but Ursula would. She was prepared to accept that this disturbance, too, was some sort of supernatural phenomenon – but the Nagas were adamant. The spur, they said, was haunted ground, which had been used before the camp was built as a burial-ground for suicides and other unpropitious deaths. Villagers claimed to have seen the eerie lights moving on the site of the camp before it was built, and they had to conclude that in building Ursula's little settlement they had disturbed the resident spirits. For her part, Ursula kept an open mind.

16

News from Home

Running dispensaries was one of the best ways to earn the locals' confidence, and although at first people consulted her only as a last resort, they began to realise that they could save a lot of misery by seeing Ursula promptly. For injuries and malaria, they trusted her to administer modern medicine – but for other ailments, however, they preferred to place their confidence in their own traditional magico-religious ceremonies.

Ursula had to deal with all manner of injuries and infections but late in March she discovered the nastiest injury that could befall anyone working outside the village – a bear-claw case. It was in Boroneo, six miles away, and Namkia suggested delaying their trip until an advance party could build a rudimentary camp for them. However, Ursula was keen to get to the case as soon as possible. Slashes from filthy bear claws were not just deep, but easily infected, so she insisted that they set out at once – they could start early and make it there and back in a day. They slipped, lurched and fell through the hot, marshy grass and by the time they reached Boroneo they were two hours behind schedule and the day was steaming hot.

A group of headmen were waiting for them and one explained that since they had called for her, the village had sent out a hunting party to kill the bear – and now there were four more injuries to treat, including the senior headman. The day's work had expanded alarmingly, and as they walked into the village, Ursula learned how the first injury had come about. A boy and two bucks had gone out into the scrub jungle to get a porcupine, but they had met an old, black she-bear with one cub. As they struggled to get away through the undergrowth, she had caught the boy, pulled him down and attacked him until he had the common sense to feign death. The bear shambled away and the bucks were able to bring him back to the village.

The junior headman took Namkia off to give him lunch, so Ursula went to the old camp to eat hers:

> I sat down on a bamboo bench and opened my case. But there were no sandwiches, no chocolate, nothing – only a small banana and two minute curry puffs. In the rush of the start, the cook had packed the titbits and left the lunch behind. There is a special fiend – a malign spirit – who organises these things. I saw his handiwork so clearly in the day's course that I was quite certain there would be more to come.

They went to find the first casualty: 'The boy was a mess, poor brat, two huge gashes in his head (skull showing), cheek torn into hunks, eye all God-knows where, bitten through the hand and in the hip.' It was hard to know where to start – and even in the long misery of swabbing and sponging the swollen lumps of flesh, there was no sign of the boy's eye. Ursula knew that he would have to go to hospital, and this was the eventuality every Naga dreaded. It would be hard to make him go, but it would be his only hope of survival.

The senior headman had got off lightly, but the man who had come to his rescue had lost a third of his scalp:

> He sat and talked and joked and offered me zu while I washed and picked splinters from a wide, white area of bare skull. The third elder had a bad bite, which I was afraid would lame him, but his nephew was no more than inconvenienced by his injuries. Washing, probing, dressing, Namkia and I moved from house to house all the long, hot afternoon. It was five o'clock when we shook off the last, importunate offers of beer. We set our faces to the slope and turned for home – Namkia at least well fuelled against the journey.

On their route home, Naga hospitality required that refreshment be offered at all times, convenient or not, and at each village food and zu were pressed on the Laisong contingent. Tearing themselves away from the last village, part of the escort with spears and torches went out ahead of them and another similar party brought up the rear. Namkia, village diplomat and responsible medical assistant was, by this stage, thoroughly drunk, and was making slow progress, tacking gently from side to side and talking nonsense at the top of his voice.

At last they rejoined the bridle road, but Ursula was exhausted. They reached the ford at Jenam and waded in torchlit single file through the shallow black water, whose ripples reflected the light of the torches in shimmering orange. On the far bank a patch of grass under a tree offered a resting place and Ursula flopped down for five minutes to re-gather her strength, but Namkia was impatient. He asked Ursula for her flashlight and permission to go on ahead – and being too tired to argue, she let him leave.

The rest of the group set off again five minutes later. Ursula headed up the column, with Ramgakpa behind, followed by Ramzimba, the caretaker's son, then Hozekiemba. Behind him came the train of torches and spears. Ursula had just rounded a bend close to the river when there was a violent crash in the bamboo to the side of the path. The whole line stopped and turned towards the noise.

> The spears came up with a swift, concerted swing, a poising of twenty points, and, at that instant, I saw a white cloth in the thicket – a glimpse, a glimmer, where that idiot Namkia was playing tiger, for what looked like the last time, on an armed and expectant band. A spear at that range would go clean through him – it was split seconds – I screamed, 'Namkia! You fool!' I saw the spear-points drop a startled fraction, and then Namkia came scrambling out of the scrub, drunk as a tinker, roaring with laughter, full of his joke. The next thing I knew, he and Ramgakpa were hauling me out of the bushes and, for the first time in my life, I'd fainted.
>
> They pulled me to my feet – Namkia not too gently, for Hozekiemba was cursing him and he was venting his temper on me – and I jerked myself clear, and set off

> walking again, crying with shock and exhaustion and marching, to hide it, as fast as I could. We crossed the lower ford, below Laisong, and crawled, I nearly all in, up the hill to the village. Namkia was grumbling away aloud, rather sobered, but still resentful that his splendid joke hadn't come off. The air was steamy still, it was past eleven, and we sweated, dripped and trickled in the fuggy heat. On the stroke of twelve we came in and saw the lights bob in camp as the cook and what men were left turned out; and five minutes later I was in the house and sitting, in one pallid, wet heap, on a fireside stool, too exhausted even to stagger across to the bed. The cook came in and asked if he should serve dinner. I couldn't even answer. Down in the lines I could hear Namkia's voice, rising in angry defiance as the others got him alone and attacked him solo and chorus. Somehow I went to bed, but I don't know how.

The weekly dak bringing letters, newspapers and periodicals was Ursula's only link with the outside world, the sending of telegrams or wires being expensive and reserved for only the most urgent news. Even though the deliveries and collections happened regularly, Ursula often spent weeks without word from home. Undoubtedly the war was largely to blame for letters not getting through, and when they did, they arrived in bundles like long-awaited buses.

Among the home parcels that did make it through was a photo of Doris with Graham – 'Weasel' – and Ursula fixed it on the wall of the bungalow. The household gathered to admire the family, and easily accepted that Graham was Ursula's brother – a very handsome sahib whose photo they had seen before, and who, they intimated, must have much success with the memsahibs. When shown Doris, however, they were incredulous:

> I think they pictured my dear mamma as a venerable and silver-haired memsahib, and when I indicated as my mother what appeared to be Graham's fiancée, they thought it was a funny joke. Ha ha!

By mid-March Alexa was ensconced in Delhi, and Ursula sent her such news as she had gleaned from England. It painted a gloomy picture of how everyone's lives were touched:

> News from home comes in spasms. Mother's flat and 82 have had a few windows bust, but Daisy's (55 Lexham) has had all the windows blown in. Uncle Jim's (Pembroke Gardens) was utterly flattened, and with it all the family portraits and treasures! Mother was thinking Graham might get engaged, as he has had a 'nesting' feeling for some time. His friend Tommy Field-Fisher is a prisoner of war in Germany and Tommy's rather frightful blonde girl made a dead set at Graham on the principle that a boy in the hand is worth half a dozen in Germany – but owing to a skilled interception by Mother, Graham took to his former flame, Judy, rather a nice thing.

A letter from Doris arrived before the end of March, asking Ursula what she thought should be done with the contents of Humpus' London flat. Ursula replied with an unfounded optimism regarding the hoped-for end of the war:

> Re furniture, I think it would be a pity to sell the good family pieces, even if they are big, unless one can get some sort of a price for them. With all this furniture being bust by bombs it is sure to be scarce and expensive when anyone gets to wanting any again. However, the inferior stuff can certainly go. I should think the bookcases, my big desk, the piano, the dining-room table and the big yellow wardrobe are all worth keeping. I know the latter is huge, but it is the only one which holds evening dresses – it has a vast capacity, and the drawers move so nice and smoothly! My dressing table is cheapers (quite a lot of the small stuff IS cheap) and the drawers jam so frequently, I sweat off all my make-up trying to work them, and it holds about one stocking and a lipstick. The bookcases are enormous too, but what else can one put books in? Anyhow, you and Aunt Esmé have a nice long think about all the things that one would want and couldn't possibly afford to buy again, even as second-hand fumed oak, and then go to it.

Doris soon sent news that Graham was getting engaged – to the universally approved Judy. Ursula returned hearty congratulations,

> I hope the Weasel nests nicely. Give it my love, congratulations, etc. My staff is having a feast today in honour of the engagement. I don't know what to do about a wedding present, but I have some lovely onions I could send.

One of Ursula's old Roedean friends, Rosemary, was to marry a Mr Malkin in Canada, Graham was off the eligible list – and Ursula remained determinedly and unapologetically on the shelf. Stalwart, devoted Pat had kept his offer of marriage open, loath to send for the girl from home if there was any chance that Ursula might change her mind. Although his approach to matrimony sounded calculating, Ursula didn't think the worse of him for it – but she could see that they would not be happy together. He was looking for a partner who would settle down with him, and whom he would love devotedly, while Ursula wanted someone with whom she could share her passion for travel and exploration. She wrote to Doris,

> I have turned down poor Pat again after his last offer. I feel rather sad about him, but honestly, I think we should be in a tangle inside two years and we should be worse off than before. I feel very sorry for him, but you can't very well marry for that reason only! All things considered, I am afraid it is no good, and it seems better to say so now than prove it afterwards.

The Bower sixth sense manifested itself again in April. Doris had mentioned in a letter shortly after Humpus' death that she still felt her presence, and in April, Ursula wrote,

> It's funny you saying Humps feels still 'about', and wondering whether she had popped over to see me – which is exactly what she did do. I nearly told you in several letters and then didn't, as I thought you might think I was batty. She always said she would. It was most peculiar and most real, because it was when there were others in the room, and I knew what she said and where she was in the

> room, and everything. It looks rather wet written down, but it was extraordinarily vivid. She had a jolly good peep at us all. This wasn't only one occasion, but several. I had the 'feel' again one day last week.

She finished the letter,

> Your Christmas cheque arrived – and very welcome! With it I purchased the mithan (pronounced 'mitten'); rum – Winkles for delectation and warming of, bottles 1; and hams, half-boned, cooked, tinned – Winkles for the use of, 1. So, with a belch and a hiccup and a loud ho-ho, we now conclude.

It must have been strange, while immersed in Naga life, to have to consider such distant concerns as furniture, the state of the very remote war in Europe, her magazine subscriptions, her camera and car, Aggie. Luckily, they were of a different world for which Ursula nursed no great longing, indeed, had it not been for her family, she might not even have spared a thought for what was going on in the rest of the world.

17

Cats – Big and Small

Animals, domestic and otherwise, played a large part in camp life. Having first acquired Khamba – by now a huge, bounding Naga hound – Ursula unwittingly gave a home to two females, Lassu and Nagi, who were effectively his wives. Veterinary care being non-existent in Laisong, there was nothing to prevent waves of pups who

> rolled and staggered and growled and yelled, chewed the furniture and slept on the bed, until they were given away and peace returned; but they were pets as babies, with their fat, white pudgy paws.

The camp also acquired a cat. Ursula explained to Doris:

> The dak-wallah announced he had brought us a cat. I was sitting all peaceful when I heard faint squeaks, and investigating, found a mingey, skinny little ginger kitten, done up in a hen-basket and very cold and miserable. I took it in and talked to it, and it purred. Then the staff arrived and inspected the feline, which was still squalling faintly. We opened a tin of doubtful salmon, and when it got the smell it nearly went mad with excitement. By this time everyone had come in to see, and you'd have laughed solemnly while the massive and highly picturesque Namkia fed it tinned salmon in a piece of newspaper.

It took up residence in the cookhouse, and the cook reported to Ursula that the new addition had the right idea about rats, but being still very small and wobbly, it tended to arrive at the rat-hole long after the rat had vanished. As Ursula observed to Doris, the Naga word for cat is 'miaow-na' – brilliantly simple!

Sometimes the cat (named Monsieur Coty, because of its colour's resemblance to face powder) would score a hit, but if one rat was killed, there were legions waiting to replace it. Although unwelcome vermin, the rats and mice posed no physical threat, preferring to hide in the thatch or under flooring rather than try to attack – but it was the local leopard which caused the most upheaval. It had made its lair somewhere among the rocks of the deep cleft in the gorge behind the camp and regularly raided the livestock. On one occasion it caught and mauled Lassu, but she escaped and lived to tell the tale. However, there was suddenly a marked increase in attacks, and it was presumed that, perhaps injured, it was holed up in the scrub on the camp spur.

The first encounter was with Monsieur Coty – who responded so hysterically that he hurtled through the lines and up the cookhouse drain, and with a flying leap gained the cook's bed, where he joined the chef under the bedclothes. The first human sighting came two nights later. In the quiet of dusk, the peace of the camp was shredded by four screams, getting nearer and nearer. Ursula rushed outside and moments later the staff arrived en masse, torches and spears at the ready, with old Hozekiemba, who was gasping and stuttering as they helped him along.

He had gone into the jungle to answer the call of nature and heard a rustling noise coming towards him through the undergrowth. He dismissed it as a pig out after hours, and so watched amazed as the bushes parted and out stepped a fully-grown leopard, just fifteen feet away from him. Hozekiemba had been expecting to see a pig, and the leopard was hoping for a stray goat – so both froze for a moment. The first to move was the old man, and he ran shrieking towards the camp. The leopard, disappointed, slunk back into cover.

The following evening the cook spotted a large dog slinking along on its belly towards the henhouse. He flung a well-aimed pebble and was taken aback when the leopard, for such it was, drew itself up to its full size and walked away. Two nights later, Ursula and Ramgakpa were sitting by the fire in the bungalow, when they heard crunching on the gravel outside and a low, throaty grumble of a leopard muttering to itself. The assumption was that the beast was probably injured, and in its hunger it was resorting to risky public hunting and even, perhaps, breaking in. There wasn't a gun in the place and the rest of the staff were in the village – the worst-case scenario didn't bear thinking about.

Namkia dismissed it as hysterical nonsense and saw no reason for extra security. Ursula went down alone towards the H of P, and as the path turned, she saw something by the light of the half moon – a dark, grey and shadowy shape, hunched to the side of the path ten yards ahead of her. With only the light of a hurricane lamp, she realised that the shadow was looking at her with large, green, luminous eyes.

It certainly looked like a leopard – however, if she fled and it gave chase she wouldn't stand a chance… and if it turned out to be a village goat, she would never live it down. She decided to hold her ground, and raising the lamp for a better view, she watched as the green eyes vanished. The shadow rose up and with a low-slung slinking action, moved to the edge of the bushes. It turned, stood up to its full height and fixed her with a long, green stare before vanishing like a ghost into the undergrowth. Ursula told Namkia about the green eyes and suddenly concerned, he asked 'One eye or two?' 'Two,' she replied. 'If it was one eye, it was a demon. If it was two, then it was a leopard. Either way, you're safer in the house!' So saying, he grabbed her by the shoulder, rushed her before him up the path and pushed her indoors, barring everything shut behind them. He slept with his spear beside him that night – and perhaps disappointed at the camp menu, the leopard wasn't seen again in the area.

As Ursula travelled around the Barail communities she became aware of an inexorable decline among the Asalu villages. Impoi, Namkia's home, was one of these, so he was in a good position to explain the reason for the problem.

Their economic failure was largely due to the agricultural practices imposed on the Zemi by the terrain, and insensitive administration. The Barail Zemi had always lived by farming – only complete failure of the crops could impel them to turn from their agricultural habits to trade or outside work. Every event of the Zemi's year was dictated by the turn of the seasons and the harvest, from preparation, planting, tending and harvesting to the religious ceremonies and holidays.

Their main staple was rice, grown in dry fields, with some land given over to millet, maize and vegetables. The most obvious problems were the paucity of cultivable land, and the danger of exhausting the soil itself. To deal with this, the Zemi, and indeed most of the Assam hill tribes, practised a system known as jhumming. Every year a different block of jungle was felled, burned and cleared, and this area could be farmed for two or three seasons. After this it would be left to lie fallow, and as soon as cultivation ceased, the jungle would start growing back. The longer this fallow period could be extended, the more fertile the land would be next time around. The more land a village controlled, the longer the land could lie fallow between spells of cultivation.

It was the shortage of jhumming land that threatened the Zemi in North Cachar. Suitable land was scarce, so for jhumming to work, a village would need to control an enormous area. The jhum-land available for any village was too small to maintain itself indefinitely, so the Zemi in the Barail were forced to develop a system of cycle-migration. It would never have done to send just a small, vulnerable colony out to work a new parcel of land – the Zemi had spent too much of their history in a state of war. So, when one tract of ground became exhausted, they upped sticks and built a new village some distance away. The villagers would never abandon their ancestral graves and ancient sites, so when the land of the first site had recovered over the course of years, the community would return. Larger villages might have to move three, four, or even five times before their original site had become good for cultivation again – but they would always return.

This system worked until the British arrived and put the area under their administration. At the same time, Kuki tribesmen moved into the area in large numbers and settled in the Zemis' fallow land. The Zemis protested to the administration, but the officials had no idea about the cycle-migration system – instead the authorities concluded that the Zemis were laying claim to fantastically large tracts of land which they did not use. In the British view, they had abandoned their ancient sites, so the Zemis' attitude to Kukis settling in them was distinctly dog-in-the-manger. The British officer in charge overruled the Zemis' protests, disallowed their claims to the land and, much to the Zemis' fury, awarded their long-held land to the Kukis. Over time this must prove a recipe for disaster, as two tribes were now occupying land that could barely support one.

This misadministration set the Zemi against the British right from the start – without realising it, they had deprived them of the land that was their only asset. In an attempt to keep a balance between the two tribes, the authorities made rulings which seemed to the Zemis to be prejudiced against them, and they became increasingly angry. The British simply concluded that the Zemi were difficult and impossible to govern, and were ungrateful for the benefits they had brought them – not least protection from the menace of Angami raids.

It was not long before the consequences of overcrowding became evident. There were bitter disputes over boundaries and rights – neither tribe had enough land to afford a proper living, and the soil was soon exhausted and over-cultivated. Over years the forests receded, grasslands increased, and the intervals allowed for land to lie fallow grew shorter and shorter. Splinter groups left villages and went out in a vain search for land. In desperation, jhums were cut on impossibly steep slopes, so that even when crops did grow, they were washed downhill in the annual rains. As crops failed there was no longer any annual surplus, so the villages fell back on their grain reserves – but when these were gone, there was no buffer against starvation.

Unlike the Naga Hills, where the British administrators had studied the tribes and understood them, North Cachar was tacked on to the very different plains district of Silchar. The local officers were often only temporary, and none had the time or inclination to look for what lay at the root of the problem. Periods when an inspired administrator worked to improve the tribes' lot were looked on as Golden Ages – and Mills, of the Pangsha torching, was one such officer. As Deputy Commissioner for Silchar he visited the Barail and quickly understood the reasons for the economic collapse, and set about improving the situation.

No way could they find new areas to cultivate, so Mills looked for the Zemi to make a dependable living from the permanent fields – using a fraction of the area they had under the jhumming system. The neighbouring Angamis operated a system of wet-rice terracing which made good use of the land year after year, so the administration allocated funds and took on demonstrators to instruct the struggling farmers of North Cachar. From the start they were up against an ingrained belief among the Zemi that having water in the fields would cause death by dropsy, but such was the economic need that they agreed to try, and within a year several areas had been terraced.

The people hit hardest by over-cultivation were the Zemi villages at the end of a cycle – especially the Asalu tribe. They had been on their site – the least fertile of their three – for more than a hundred years, and now were having to make do with only one-sixth of their former territory. Around 1920, when their crops started to fail, they had nowhere to go.

Several families agreed to try terracing, but by this time Mills had gone back to the Naga Hills district as Deputy Commissioner in Kohima, and North Cachar was again suffering from administrative neglect. The wet-rice demonstrator, an Angami, skimped on building the water channels for Asalu and as soon as the rains began the channels broke and most of the Asalu farmers lost their crop. Desperate, they accepted work in the fields of neighbouring tribes for a pittance which would not feed their families – this meant they could not put by any stores for their family, and they would have to work for someone else again the next year.

Before the terracing system could be given a chance to work, a man in Thingje who had started wet-rice cultivation died of dropsy. At once his neighbours abandoned their irrigation. The new administrator tried to coax them back to work, but superstition was too strong. Impatient and angry, the officer fined some men who had let their terraces go and thereby effectively drove the last nail into the coffin of wet-rice cultivation. The Zemi were bitter, hungry and hard-done-by, and they retreated behind a wall of resentment and anger – Ursula now understood one reason for the anti-British feeling.

The Kukis, untroubled by superstition, persevered with their terraces and frequently took over land which the Zemi, fearing more government action against them, were relieved to let go. Soon the Kuki had their own wet-rice demonstrators, but for the Zemi, their first Angami demonstrator having been sacked, the post was vacant. It was Masang who took over the job and, rogue that he was, he turned it into a political sinecure. Masang had no aptitude for the job, and under his tutelage the destruction of the Zemis' soil went on.

Asalu was in extremis, and under pressure they split their community and moved on. Namkia and his contingent left to resettle Impoi where there remained a little cultivable land, but its unity divided, the Asalu community fell apart and resolved into small groups.

With more groups leaving, Asalu stayed in situ, decaying among its ancient graves. The splinter groups struggled and eventually had to go to work in Kuki and Kachari fields. The area was spiralling into decline, and only Impoi, with its small tract of fertile land, had any chance of self-sufficiency.

As Ursula and Namkia were out hunting pigeon in the Asalu grassland they found an area under cultivation. The rice was barely a foot high and thin on the ground – the other crops were ripe but terribly sparse. Namkia knew that a good wet-rice demonstrator might turn the tide of decay – but he knew too that no Kuki demonstrator would put himself out on a Zemi's behalf and Masang was no expert. It would be prohibitively expensive to get a good Angami to do the job, so it looked as if nothing could be done. It was with great sadness that Ursula and Namkia turned away from the tragic crop and headed home.

18

Masang

It was a long time since Ursula had seen – or even spared a thought for – Masang. He had gradually ceased to visit her when Namkia's hostility towards him became too much. If he visited the Laisong camp, Namkia stalked off and refused to interpret – and as he spoke no Hindustani, this was quite a bar to communication. From being a constant companion, Masang grew more distant and eventually he came no more.

When Masang's brother arrived at Laisong in November to ask Ursula to go to Kepelo to see him, she realised to her shame that she had as good as forgotten him. According to his brother, Masang was seriously ill and wanted to see her. His life had taken a down-turn since they had last met. He had been wet-rice demonstrator for the administration – but the SDO had eventually grown weary of his irregular behaviour and sacked him. Dikheo, his side-kick in the Gaidiliu affair, had been hunted down in his home by the authorities and a scuffle had broken out. He had been shot dead, so the last of Masang's old ties had gone. He was left without any distinction – now he was just an ordinary Zemi, who slipped inconspicuously back into village life. Now he was lying ill in Kepelo.

Namkia threw his hands in the air and said it was unthinkable that a she-sahib should trek off across country like a village woman, a dog at heel at the bidding of one such as Masang. Kepelo must show proper respect and prepare a camp and only then could she pay a visit. Masang's brother turned and left, apologising for troubling her – but Ursula remembered her old friend and mentor. Masang might have been a rascal, but he had been her right-hand man before Namkia. She was certainly not going to desert him, so early the next morning she was ready to leave. Namkia said he had no intention of going, so Ursula put together a day's luggage and a wallet of drugs and set out eastwards for Kepelo with Haichangnang for company.

At the edge of the village a reception committee was there to greet her – it reminded Ursula of the first time she had visited the district, when everyone had apparently gone stark raving mad, pawing her, forcing gifts on her, begging her blessing. Once again, the villagers seethed around her, calling out to her and touching her clothes, but Masang's brother ushered Ursula and Haichangnang to Masang's house, drew them inside and shut the door.

As her eyes grew accustomed to the pitch darkness inside she saw the rest of Masang's family gathered around a small fire. On the floor, on a mat to the side of the fire was Masang. He was a shadow of his old self. Instead of the tough, stocky ruffian, she saw a bag of bones, his skin covered with the soot and grime of two months' illness in the firelit room. All his muscle and strength had gone and now his skin was drawn tight and leathery over his frail frame. A bony hand like a claw came up and groped towards Ursula and she took it. 'My mother. Goddess. Save me. I am afraid to die.' Catching Haichangnang's eye across the hearth Ursula suddenly understood. To Masang she was, and always had been, the re-incarnation of Gaidiliu.

Comforted simply by her presence, Masang scarcely spoke as the day ticked past. He occasionally repeated his appeal to her, but mainly lay in the dark with his bony fingers on Ursula's knee or clutching her hand like a frightened child. A couple of times Ursula moved away, but his hand immediately stretched out after her and drew her back.

Ursula was glad that Haichangnang and not Namkia had come with her – she suspected that Namkia wouldn't have been able to resist gloating. Haichangnang simply sat watching them from across the fire, his face wrung with pity, speaking only to console and soothe. In this time of extreme emotion and fear, he showed a gentleness and humanity that Ursula had not seen before.

The long vigil gave Ursula time to think of the implications of what Masang had said. The pieces of the jigsaw fell into place. Masang, as Gaidiliu's most faithful prophet, had believed beyond all doubt that she, Ursula, was the new incarnation of his goddess, right from the first moment that he saw her. Apart from being female, Ursula could think of no similarity between herself and the renegade python-worshipping priestess/goddess who had caused such a furore back in 1931. Perhaps it was their very lack of similarity which had most convinced him – after all, Gaidiliu had promised to return in a form in which the British would never recognise her.

Unbeknown to Ursula, Masang had stood up at a mass meeting of villages in Laisong, just before her arrival, and announced that Gaidiliu had returned – that Ursula was the goddess they had been waiting for. The sane and steady among them – Namkia for one – would have none of this and reacted quite fiercely. This would account for his disinclination to work for her and his initial frostiness. Only over time had he learned that she had no pretensions to being a goddess, and they had become friends.

The main body of villagers had decided to sit tight and see what happened before committing themselves, but there were some, the very faithful and fanatical, who wanted desperately to believe that their goddess had returned, and so swallowed Masang's story, hook, line and sinker. This accounted for the adoring crowds, the gifts, the prayers and pleas for blessings. Now everything made sense. Headmen had fallen at her feet, calling her 'Mother' and 'She-spirit' – in the most fanatical villages they had been fulfilling their duties in leading the official worship of the reborn goddess.

This realisation shed light on another incident, when a four-man party from Bopungwemi had visited her in the camp shortly after all the madness had begun. Three of the men had engaged Ursula with a lot of chatter and gifts while the fourth had leant impassively against the veranda-post, watching her intently. This must have been Dikheo, Gaidiliu's other prophet. He had come at the risk of his life to see if Masang was right, and the goddess really had returned. By his behaviour Ursula realised that he was not convinced, so only Masang and his followers believed. The rest, who put their trust in Dikheo, thought better of their earlier impulsive devotion – and that was why the rush of adoring visitors had dropped off so suddenly.

With Masang representing the only believers, Namkia had seen him as the major threat – after all, the one person who should not know about this reincarnation business was at the heart of it, and only Masang was likely to tell her. Namkia had assiduously discouraged his visits and done all he could to keep him out of Laisong until he gave up altogether. What was so extraordinary was that everybody had known about the theory that Ursula was Gaidiliu – except Ursula herself.

When Masang had sent his brother to Ursula, Haichangnang admitted that he had asked not for her but for Gaidiliu. By coming at his request, Ursula had confirmed his beliefs and now he felt comfort in the presence of his goddess as he approached death. Ursula's new understanding of the situation and of the Zemi people as a whole came as a revelation:

> From that moment, I think, I became a Zemi. I understood them as I had never done before. Their faults, their follies, their sincerities, were all so clear. I would have said before that Masang's recognition of me, based, it would seem, on no good reason at all, was just a device to regain his former power. Given a goddess, he could be her prophet. But what to make of this? Masang was dying. He knew it and so did we; I could do nothing for him. He was afraid of death, but he was not asking me, myself, to save him. He was asking Gaidiliu, his queen, his goddess, in whom he so believed, in whom he trusted, whose hand he now, half-conscious, held and held; she for whose sake he had been beaten and jailed; she to whom, dying, he clung. I sat on and on there, quiet, the dry paw in mine.

With no arrangements for staying overnight, Ursula had to leave, but it was evening when she and Haichangnang pushed their way out through the awaiting crowd:

> For the first time consciously, but for the last time, I went down a village street as a divine being. They crowded and clung to me, as when I came. Now it was all simple and comprehensible.

Ursula realised that only Masang had been perpetuating the Gaidiliu myth – and when he died that would be an end to it all. Leaving the village Haichangnang caught her eye as the crowds finally dispersed and knew that she understood. They went slowly back to Laisong with an indefinable new rapport between them. It was a fortnight later that news reached Laisong that Masang had died.

Given time to reflect, Ursula admitted that perhaps there was some small physical resemblance between her and Gaidiliu, which had inspired Masang. There was not a lot of difference between their ages, and she, like Gaidiliu, was tall and quite strongly built. However, she vigorously objected to being linked with this renegade, and in particular to being dubbed the 'Naga Rani' by the British – as that was what they had called Gaidiliu. 'She was not a lady I would care to be named after'. Ursula couldn't deny that, when she had first seen Naga people, she had had an uncanny sense of déjà vu – but even with this new development, she never nursed even the slightest suspicion that she had any link with Gaidiliu other than in the minds of the Kacha Nagas. Although the worship dwindled after Masang's death, there remained a residue of allegiance. But as Mills had said, if they had to have a goddess, it might just as well be a government one.

19

War Comes to the Far East

Tucked away beyond the Barail range in Laisong, Ursula was blissfully separated from the outside world. There was an ageless calm – life was not easy but this very fragility made the Zemis' short lives rich and meaningful:

> I think the Zemi were a great deal happier than we. There one derived pleasure from small and transient things, from kindnesses, friendships, loyalties and the like, which because of their simpler, barer state were more deeply felt and of greater meaning. Then, too, there was always the sense of mortality and impermanence to quicken appreciation. Death was never very far from anyone in that malarial, doctorless country, and thinking back, I believe it was chiefly that which held one so firmly in the present and prevented too great building of hopes for the future. Certainly, to enjoy every simple pleasure as though it were for the last time sharpened the sense and gave life an extraordinarily rich texture.

All the same, global events were reaching out towards the timeless world of the Barail. Occasionally Ursula received copies of the *Illustrated London News* and the men were fascinated by the photos, which Ursula would give them to adorn the walls of the morungs.

Early in December Ursula took her annual holiday in Calcutta, again taking Namkia – but this time he insisted on Haichangnang going too. Ursula had good reason to want to take the pair of them to see the War Weapons Exhibition – it was inevitable that the British in the Far East would be drawn into the conflict, and she felt that it would do no harm at all for the pair of them to go back with reports of massive military potential. At the first opportunity, Ursula whisked them away to the exhibition, both men in full tribal dress.

The full panoply of Britain's martial might kept Namkia and Haichangnang occupied and oblivious to their surroundings – until they were a third of the way round. Then suddenly there were cameras and officials everywhere. They became the most photographed men in Calcutta – not just by visitors to the exhibition, but by the authorities who saw this as a marvellous PR opportunity. The pair submitted to a spell of flashbulbs and clicking – and in return were allowed the full run of the exhibition. A friendly sergeant-major ushered them away and when they wearied of sight-seeing in the heat of the day, he took them to the canteen and plied them with ice cream.

The three of them had a splendid time together, and Sergeant-Major Croucher approached Ursula at the end of the day. 'Whenever you want to park them, miss, you bring 'em along to me. I'll keep 'em happy.' So every day Ursula dropped Namkia and Haichangnang with their army escort and headed into the city. Each day they were photographed and filmed in and on every tank, gun, bomb and pavane in the place, and were allowed to work all the handles on the naval gun, winding themselves round in circles under Croucher's direction.

This time in Calcutta there was no Pat to escort Ursula. He had been in touch since her last refusal – and as promised, had written to the girl back home asking her to come and join him in his tea-planting life. It seems she had not even seen fit to answer and Ursula's heart was wrung by his loneliness. As she explained, again, to Doris by letter, she still had a very soft spot for Pat:

> I nearly did marry him, but didn't quite make it. It would have been marrying him in cold blood, so to speak, and with all the difficulties of bad climate, etc, etc, I just couldn't screw myself up to it. Some of the other planters' wives are pretty grim, and so are some of the other planters, most of them being 'verra Scots'. On the other hand, some are pleasantly so. Pat on a farm or something in Glen Ogilvie, between Kincaldrum and Glamis … Anyhow, I was in a very Balkan state of mind about it, and still am, in spasms.

The inevitability of war was already affecting Calcutta and the atmosphere was tense. It was almost no surprise when the first post to reach Laisong after their return brought news of Pearl Harbor – the Japanese air raid which brought the war to the Far East – and everyone in Laisong was as outraged as the rest of the Allied nations.

Changes were afoot in the administration too – on returning via Mahur, Ursula found that the SDO had been replaced, and the bungalow was now home to Mr and Mrs Perry. Knowing from experience that district officers could be less than kindly disposed to a maverick female, Ursula went to meet Perry with some trepidation. A very tall, slim man came to meet her and shook her hand with genuine warmth. To Ursula's enduring gratitude, it was the start of a lasting friendship. 'Many years later I can still say that there are few who have shown me as much kindness as Mr and Mrs Perry.' At least Ursula was assured that her position in Laisong would not be threatened from that quarter.

Even though the news of the fall of Singapore filtered through to Laisong, and the Japanese invasion of Burma brought the action closer, the threat still didn't touch Ursula and her camp. North Cachar was remote, and Laisong, shut off behind the Barail range was even more so – besides there were other more immediate things to occupy her. There were local worries such as the risk of jungle fires, how to provide milk for a motherless baby, treat the blacksmith's illness and re-thatch the bungalow.

Maybe it was the tension of looming war that elicited another visit from Humpus. Writing to Doris in October 1941, Ursula mentioned an occasion in mid-April when she was certain Humpus had visited her, and had been upset about something – which in retrospect Ursula felt must have been the bombing of Doris's flat. She owned that it had given her quite a start when Doris had written of the bombing and she subsequently linked the date with that of Humpus' visit. She went on to mention a further presence on 18 August. Again Humpus seemed distressed about something,

> Somebody was here last night. It might have been Daddy or both of them, for that matter. My big lamp has gone wrong and as I only have a hurricane lamp and night falls with a crashing at 6.30, I taught Namkia to play 'Beggar My Neighbour' – a simple game he enjoys greatly – and I was playing that and digesting my dinner when whoever it was came and stood just behind my chair and watched for some time. I thought at first it was Humps, but it didn't seem quite like her.

It was not until March that an opportunity arose to take a break and visit friends on the plains. Ursula found everybody in a state of high alert, with essential belongings packed and ready to evacuate at twenty-four hours' notice. The men were all awaiting their call-up and there was an urgent request for women to help with the stream of refugees who were coming towards India from Burma. All of a sudden, the war was on their doorstep.

Since the fall of Singapore in February 1942, the Japanese had been advancing northwards through Burma at alarming speed, and bridges were blown to slow their progress, leaving pockets of British troops cut off and vulnerable. In March, General Bill Slim was appointed commander of the 1st Burma Corps – effectively all the British, Indian and Burmese troops in Burma, but as events unfolded in April, he found himself in charge of a massive withdrawal over the Irrawaddy River at Mandalay. With the forced retreat of troops came the mass evacuation of civilians and the injured.

Ursula had no intention of leaving Assam, so she set about recruiting a team of Zemi volunteers and offered their services to the government on any refugee routes where they could be of use. Such was the Zemis' respect and loyalty for Ursula that she had no trouble drumming up support, and she worked with them to form an efficient unit for jungle work as they awaited orders.

The situation in Burma was desperate,

> The Japs were coming up Burma like a piston up a car cylinder, and quite a lot of the refugees had come out through the side exits through Manipur. But once the Japs got past those exits, there was only one way for the refugees to go, and that was right over the top, up the Hukong, over the most appalling mountains where no arrangements for food or anything else had been made.

Ursula heard reports that the route was littered with corpses and to try to prevent this carnage, the authorities were sending tribesmen and military units to try to catch the refugees as they crossed the Burma frontier into Assam. Ursula offered to go up with her squad of Nagas and take on escort duties. 'We knew jungle work. We were all strong. We could get on in the jungle, which a lot of women couldn't.'

When orders came they were a disappointment – women were no longer being sent to the refugee routes because of the appalling conditions. Ursula wanted to argue that she was not just any woman, but she realised that, to the administration, she was still an unknown quantity:

> The governor's wife didn't know about me, didn't know that I was perfectly competent with the men to look after myself in the jungle, and that we were a team. We all knew how to live in the jungle.

Ursula's letter offering the services of herself and her Naga squad eventually found its way on to Mills' desk and he wrote most sympathetically to her in mid-April:

> I am afraid I can hold out no hope of a job with Nagas, very able though I know you would be. A few Assamese have been put on the refugee route. I think this was right, but the men on the spot opposed it strongly on account of the awful crowd there is there, the sordid discomfort in which everyone lives. But you can be sure that if a job comes along, I'll let you know, for you are one of the few people who really understand the Naga mentality.

The sudden encroachment of outside events on their world caused a good deal of tension in the camp. Over time, Ursula and her household had become, in Naga terms, a kienga. The unity of the group had never come under this sort of test before and Ursula was unsure how their relationship would stand up. In all, she confessed, one couldn't expect too much.

Eventually a job was found for her – Namkia, Haichangnang, Ramgakpa and Dinekamba would accompany Ursula to Lumding railway junction to run a canteen – while the rest stayed in the camp looking after the house, dogs and livestock.

Ursula's imminent departure was common knowledge in Laisong, so it was with a sinking heart that she saw a deputation of headmen approaching the camp. What they had to say cast an entirely unforeseen light on her relationship with the village. The headmen were there to protest against the governor's orders to send Ursula to Lumding. The country was in a disturbed state and if invasion was indeed imminent, this was no time for a young woman to be out alone. The administration was failing in its duties – and if they were not willing to look after her, the Zemi would. They would take full responsibility, and the first stage of this would be to forbid her to leave the safety of the hills.

Ursula was extraordinarily moved by their care and their sense that she belonged with them, however, orders were orders and she had no choice in the matter, she explained. She must go. Faced by her determination to throw herself into the fray, the headmen swept out of the camp, giving strict instructions to her porters not to take any luggage anywhere, and headed for Perry's office in Haflong. Only by promising that he personally would see that Ursula returned to Laisong, no matter what, could he mollify the deputation. They relayed Perry's promise to Ursula – she and her small squad could go if they really must. Jappas packed and farewells said, Ursula, Namkia, Haichangnang, Ramgakpa and Dinekamba set off for Lumding.

Leaving the hills, Namkia was preoccupied and uncommunicative, and when they halted for their last night in the hills at Asalu, he hung anxiously around Ursula, evidently with something to say but unable to bring himself to speak. Ursula was writing by the light of a lamp when he finally steeled himself and walked resolutely into the hut. Quite overcome, he dropped to his knees before her where she sat and hugged her fiercely, his head in her lap, and began to cry.

This shocking collapse left Ursula momentarily speechless – but she asked what was the matter. No amount of shaking and questioning would stop his tears or prevail upon him to move, so Ursula extricated herself gently. As she stood, his head and arms collapsed on to her chair and he went on crying inconsolably. Remembering a bottle of rum in the stores, she rummaged about for it and poured him a stiff tot. Eventually he regained his control, picked himself up and perched on the edge of the table to pour his heart out:

> It was all right before I left Laisong. I didn't mind a bit and I wasn't afraid to go. But now my wife and mother have been at me, and I don't know what to do. Suppose Assam is invaded, and abandoned without a fight, as they say it's going to be? Suppose we can't come back? Suppose raiding breaks out again in the hills when the British go? Who'll look after my wife and children? I was in the village today, and heard what they're saying. They say this isn't our war, and we ought to leave it alone – we aren't Japs, we aren't British; we're Zemi. What's it to do with us? We've been together now, you and I and the others, for two years; we are like a family. How can I leave you? What about my children? Oh, my sister, my sister, I'm being pulled in two – which way shall I go?

Ursula could only answer with absolute honesty – she only hoped that her own uncertainty would be some comfort to him:

> I don't know what's going to happen, either. But my home's here in Laisong, and I'm coming back to it, whatever happens. After all, Lumding isn't far; we can walk home in four days. As for the rest, I don't think you Zemi will be able to stay as neutral as you think – certainly not if the Angamis and Kukis take sides; and I doubt if you'd find the Japs a fair exchange for the British. From what I hear they're rather more like the old Kachari kings you talk about, who made men lick knives, and flayed the soles off their feet and made them walk along thorny logs. Meantime, there are all these people coming through from Burma, in the devil of a state. I've been told to go down and help; and I'm going, with anyone I can find to go along with me. If you people won't come, it's my bad luck – I've had the orders, not you.

This seemed to resolve matters for Namkia. 'Asipui-ghao (dear elder sister) – don't be afraid. We're all in it together.' Wiping his eyes he shook her hand and went off to the lines.

20

The Burma Refugees

To call Lumding a junction was a misnomer. The cluster of railway buildings, yards and houses had been built in a clearing, at a point where it was intended that the Hills Section railway line would meet the one running up the Assam Valley. Lumding had already been built by the time the last part of the Hill Section was finished, and contrary to plans, it met the existing line about one and a half miles west of Lumding.

The threat of Japanese invasion had sent Lumding into confusion, so the yards were choked with wagons, there were unclaimed loads of building materials and bamboo, and consignments of goods in sidings had started overflowing on to the main line. If a mail train arrived, it would be held up at the signals outside Lumding, then there would be a frenzy of activity while trucks were shunted into temporary jams to let it pass.

In this chaos there was no provision for a canteen. Just one woman, Mrs Rankin, whose husband was a railway manager, pulled it all together and conjured up the basics that they needed. There was no shed, store, hut, cookshed, food or fuel – or space in which to run a canteen or in which workers could sleep. Somehow Mrs Rankin got tabletops and commandeered girders to put them on. Charcoal stoves were provided from the engine-sheds and a room found to accommodate the canteen apparatus, and by sheer persistence, Mrs Rankin got some makeshift buildings set up for the workers. There was a distinct shortage of food, proper catering equipment and helpers, and for the first two chaotic weeks it was only Mrs Rankin's local knowledge which enabled them to scrape together the wherewithal to operate at all.

Refugees were leaving Burma in their droves, and the trains rolled in packed to the roofs with exhausted, hot and hungry humanity. These trains were meant to pass through Lumding during the night, reaching Chaparmukh or Pandu in the morning, at which points they could be given a meal. Unfortunately the main urgency was to take troop trains up, so the refugee trains were shuttled off into sidings where they spent the night, arriving at Lumding at any time between five and eight in the morning, in desperate need of refreshment.

Ursula would receive a telegram at around two in the morning to say how many refugees to expect. An early start – three or four o'clock – was essential for preparations, so there was little time for sleep. Such rest as Ursula, Namkia, Haichangnang, Ramgakpa and Dinekamba could grab was taken in the main room in a traveller's bungalow, where Ursula had a camp bed and the rest slept on the floor around her – all under mosquito nets, as the area was heavily malarial.

Ursula's recollection of that time was of physical exhaustion – but they worked on, driven by the crying need of the demoralised, dispossessed, weary, and injured soldiers and refugees. The number they would have to cater for was usually around 200, some of which would be European and would want familiar food. Ursula recalled a typical day:

> We went down to the railway station, and the water for the tea had to be carried in four-gallon kerosene tins with a wooden bar across. You carried one in each hand. The five of us carried sixty gallons that way, and we stacked the cans. At first we just had open fireplaces on the platform with iron bars across to sit the tins on, but as we got a bit more organised, the railway built us a little shed with proper brick compartments. We went down to the railway coal-bunkers and came staggering back with loads and loads of coal. It was very sooty coal – I used to go down a blonde and come back a Carmen brunette – hair absolutely black with smoke and soot.
>
> We brewed up our tea, and then about five the train would pull in. We'd be swamped by these mobs and mobs of clamouring Indian refugees, and poor devils – it was very hot. They were packed into the trains. Half of them were sick with dysentery and cholera. If anybody died on the train they used to try to get the body out for proper burial or cremation.

The packed carriages often sat in sidings for hours at a time, and while the overall refugee journey was supposed to be around eight hours, a more accurate estimate of the journey time was twenty-four hours. If there were any dead in the carriages, the refugees had no choice but to throw the bodies out on to the line.

The five o'clock trains would be in for several hours, so Ursula organised patrols down the carriages to find out if anyone was concealing a body, and if so to try and get it removed. The service Ursula and her Nagas provided far exceeded the normal remit of 'volunteer work', and as weeks wore on, the cases coming out of Burma got worse:

> There was another Indian Congress canteen down the far end of the platform, and the organisers were very political and not frightfully friendly. They were a bit standoffish, but the men who actually worked on the canteen soon got very friendly with us and helped us a lot. When the train full of wounded from the front came through about eleven, the Indian Congress workers used to abandon their spare time and come and help us, because the wounded couldn't get to the canteen – or very few of them could. There were a lot of dysentery cases and wounded who couldn't walk, and it meant that we and our tins had to do about two hundred people in the full length of the train in twenty minutes – it was only meant to stand for twenty minutes. Four gallons of tea, one can in each hand, at the double up and down the best part of twelve carriages in temperatures of ninety and a hundred is no fun. It usually meant we could only do the first half of the train, and the chaps up the top were clamouring for second cups before we got down to the bottom.

Although stretched to the limit, Ursula always appreciated others doing their share and showing consideration for others:

> Only one chap – a brigadier – had the nous to hold up that train until every single one of his men had been fed. There was a refreshment room, where I'm afraid a lot of the other officers had gone, but he wouldn't go. He stood there with his foot on the step of the carriage, defying the stationmaster, the engine driver and everybody else to make him move – until every one of his men had had his tea. He was directing us, sending my men down to the bottom saying, 'Those chaps haven't had any yet – those chaps up there can have their second helpings. See those men are done.' He just picked a bun off a passing Naga's plate and stood there with his cup of tea, eating his bun and directing everything. He was the only one.

Her admiration was even greater for the wounded;

> They were marvellous. See[ing] me doubling down the platform with my cans, they were all leaning out of the windows saying, 'Take it easy miss, take it easy. All right, don't you worry – take it easy.' Then they used to pull out with everybody hanging out of the windows and waving and shouting, 'See you on the road to Mandalay. See you on the way back, miss.' Quite often there were badly injured men who had smelly wounds, whose clothes were in a mess, and they saw there were ladies on the canteen. I had one or two rather genteel helpers who weren't much use. They were much too ladylike to do a job of work, but they would pour tea in the canteen if I carried the jerry cans – and the wounded didn't like to shock the ladies, so they wouldn't go up. So again I had to do a patrol down the train, look in every carriage to see if there was anybody who wasn't getting anything. I found one chap who'd obviously been next to a friend who who'd been hit, because there was blood all over his uniform. I said, 'Look here, go up and get some tea. Can you walk?' 'Oh yes, I can walk, but there's ladies there, and I didn't like to go.' I said, 'All right, here you are,' and passed him in his tea and bun. He was very grateful. I went to another chap who had to be taken off with a great bit of shell splinter pinned in his neck, which had gone completely septic. He collapsed and we had to get him off and get a doctor. There was another one who had his leg in plaster right up to his thigh, and he was trying to get out of the carriage with the help of his mates. I said, 'Here, here – don't you bother to go up to the canteen. You stay where you are – we'll get you something.' 'Oh no miss, it's all right. I like walking in India.' And off he went, dot and carry, dot and carry, arm round a friend's shoulder, to the canteen. They were really marvellous. I think only once I had one rather gloomy one – that must have been one out of I don't know how many men – two hundred a day for six weeks.

Around midday the trains carrying the wounded left and Lumding sweltered in the heat. The station was temporarily empty and Ursula and team washed up, then went back to the hut for lunch. Indoors the heat was stifling – too hot to sleep – so everyone took turns to bathe, then at three o'clock there was the third shift. The heat was at its stuffiest when they went out to meet the up-mail and the odd straggling train loaded with trucks, ambulances or mules en route to the front. By seven or eight in the evening they had seen off the last trains and Ursula retired to the hut to deal with accounts and correspondence as a wobbly fan clacked overhead, scarcely stirring the heavy air. At about half past nine Ursula turned off the light and fell into bed in the midst of the already sleeping Nagas, to grab a nap before the telegram came through at two o' clock to start the next day's routine.

They worked eighteen hours a day, seven days a week – refugees in the morning, wounded troops in the evening and time between arrivals spent carrying coal, tidying up, and preparing food for the next day. Then, after two weeks, their workload dropped to a mere sixteen hours a day – but this couldn't last.

When they first arrived, Lady Reid, the wife of the governor, had organised a rota whereby the ladies of the Shillong hill station were firmly coerced into volunteering to do their stint. After a few weeks she was unable to stay on, so she left Ursula with her list – and suddenly all the ladies who had promised to do a relief duty sent word to say they couldn't come. 'All the hitherto-docile volunteers turned nasty and wouldn't do anything remotely uncomfortable.'

> Couldn't get a relief anywhere. Anybody who could have come was already doing a job. No, they were going to stay up in the hill stations, thank you. I'm afraid my fellow Britons, the ladies, came very badly out of it – very badly indeed. I was going to meet one of them who was coming down to take over, and I received a telegram from her mother to say that it was quite impossible for her to come. She was far too young to come down and work in the plains on her own. Considering she was a good many years older than I was, I took a dim view of that.

It was especially galling that no-one understood how hard they were working. Writing to Alexa she explained bitterly,

> It was decidedly an experience and I would not have missed it, but it was frightfully hard work. Nobody would believe it, which annoyed me so, for we had six or seven hours behind us and were going down for our second shift when the railway people were going to their offices, so they all said they couldn't think why we complained, as we didn't start work till 10 am! The first morning my relief was there we were just finishing breakfast when we heard there was a train in, which we'd been asked to meet, so fled to the station and did tea for 350 at short notice. Returning for a few seconds' rest before the second shift at 10 am, we were found finishing a bun each by one of our lady helpers. My relief later caught her in the shed telling the other lady volunteers what liars we were about our long hours, as we had been just having breakfast at 9.30 and must of course have slept till then. <u>Dear</u> creature!

Ursula and her Nagas kept up the relentless routine for six weeks and eventually she was relieved by 'an extremely gallant grandmother'. As soon as Ursula heard that she was going to come, she wired her to wait. The wounded were coming through in such numbers that Ursula felt that, exhausted though she was, she had to carry on herself. The new volunteer never got Ursula's wire and arrived without any support staff or any of the equipment that Ursula had told the Shillong authorities that helpers must bring. On arrival the new recruit began to understand the situation, and quickly wired for two friends to join her. Ursula stayed on for a day or two to keep things going while they settled in, then left her with the Anglo-Indian ladies of the station. This brave volunteer had to be stretchered home after little more than a week.

As Ursula put it, 'How she lasted that long, I don't know. It laid me out – and it also laid out four hefty Nagas. It was very, very tough going.' On her return to Laisong, Ursula received a letter from Mrs Perry, who had taken over as WVS organiser, to say that she had tried frantically to get helpers sent from their HQ – but in vain. As a very irritable Ursula explained to her mother in a letter, 'Mrs Perry then heard that there were 161 WVS members sitting pretty on their A-holes at HQ.'

She went on to enumerate more problems for the Lumding operation:

> It was pretty grim at first, mobs of Indian coolies ploughing through, with no regard for sanitation or anything else, shitting the landscape black all round the water supplies – and then cholera broke out. The Burma side was smelly hell, but the Indian side was quite well organised, although all the Congress have been howling to high heaven about 'racial discrimination', which means that European food was given to the Europeans when obtainable, though a lot of them had only dhall and rice for a month. Cholera having broken out on the short route, the Europeans were sent that way because they didn't mind being injected and were cleaner in their habits, and the low-class Indians were sent round the long, cholera-free route. More howls from the Congress. The refugees, with dysentery and heaven-knows what other diseases on them, would use the train latrines wholesale, when it was in the station – great fun for all concerned. Just imagine 800 of them, concentrated along 200 yards of line – or if you prefer it, don't.

She concluded: 'If the lovely ladies are not going to play up with the real work, it looks as if the plain-but-usefuls, including self, will have to stand by, as witness my experiences at Lumding! Will cable if I move.'

Namkia, Haichangnang, Ramgakpa and Dinekamba could well have argued, as had Namkia's wife, that it was not their war – so why should they run themselves into the ground for the British whose administration had let them down so badly? But they were there because they had faith in Ursula, and would never have let her go alone – and while their reason for going was personal, so was their response to the job in hand. Ursula expected nothing of them that she would not do herself, and recognised their loyalty and dedication:

> The Nagas were a tower of strength. What really moved them were the wounded – the British wounded. Once they saw the wounded train come out – a train full of them – and saw what their wounds were and how they were suffering and how courageous they were – the Nagas just looked at each other and they went into that job like furies.

Namkia put their sense of duty and honest humanity into words. He said that they were not going to stint themselves – they had seen the men who were putting their bodies as a shield between the Nagas and the enemy, and they knew where their loyalty lay – it was a debt to be discharged. She was amazed by their stamina, 'If they'd worked hard before, they absolutely doubled their efforts. They really were good.'

In the middle of May 1942, Ursula and her Naga team crawled wearily back over the Tolpui Pass towards home. They fell into the Haflong train and slept on the narrow wooden benches – and back at last in Laisong Ursula collapsed in the comfort of her bungalow and slept, on and on for a week.

When she finally returned to the land of the living, Ursula found that the Burma Army was falling back, with fighting reaching the Manipur border. Imphal was under bombardment and women and children were being evacuated as invasion was only a matter of time. As she admitted, even if Assam had been surrendered and the invasion had happened during the previous week, she couldn't have raised the strength to stagger even as far as Mahur.

Only the timely intervention of nature prevented the Japanese invasion. The annual rains broke and a constant screen of water divided Laisong on its mountain perch from the rest of the world. The Japanese could not rely on a spell of clear days in which to advance until autumn, so the immediate danger was lifted. It was another crisis entirely which now threatened Laisong.

The rains began and continued unabated for three weeks and then, on the first clear day, three men walked into Laisong. They were from Asalu – men Ursula knew – but they were all but unrecognisable. They were human skeletons, starving and weak. Horrified, Ursula called Namkia and he admitted that Asalu was in the grip of a terrible famine. Having lost faith in the British administration, and fearing reprisals about their abandonment of the wet-rice project, they had kept the situation secret from the government.

The wet-rice growing was not the only problem. During a previous time of hunger, twenty-one years before, a clerk in Haflong had arrived with bulging grain sacks and in a dramatic gesture, cut them open and invited the starving villagers to help themselves. He had omitted to mention that the grain was not a gift, but a long-term loan, which would have to be paid back. Years later, the people struggled to grow enough for themselves, let alone have surplus with which to pay off the debt, so a running IOU was handed down from the 'borrowers' to their next of kin. In an attempt to pay off the debt, the Asalu headmen organised a levy throughout the village. Although this was undoubtedly the best solution, the fact that the situation had arisen at all was seen by the Zemi as a deliberate trick to subjugate them. They swore never to be so fooled again, or be tricked into accepting help so mean. In future they would preserve their dignity and never allow their distress to be exploited for usury.

Once again, the Zemi were facing starvation. The previous August, a plague of grasshoppers had eaten the flowering rice and Impoi and Asalu had lost most of their crop. The authorities at Haflong had no record of this – so now the two villages had no grain reserves and no support. An epidemic of measles had laid out the working men who brought in only meagre day-to-day earnings on which the whole village depended – and now there was no food and no money.

The Impoi and Asalu headmen followed the first three. They too were skeletal shadows of the men Ursula knew. Their pride and determination regarding the government were unshaken, but Ursula was different. They hoped that she alone would be able to see them through their crisis with a private loan.

Ursula and Namkia sat down with the headmen and tried to sort out the problem. The clerk's crass mistake over two decades before had set a precedent and the headmen would not believe that, although loans were the norm in ordinary times, in the threat of famine, they would be given free relief. They were certain that if they told the administration of their plight, it would be no time before the government sent someone down to offer terms to squeeze every rupee and anna out of them and cash in on their misery.

It was heartbreaking to Ursula to see the terrible consequences of one man's ignorance. The ramifications had reached out across the decades and the only thing to do now was give them a loan from her own sparse funds – but Ursula felt the government owed the Zemi a responsibility of care and was not prepared to let the matter rest.

The next day's dak carried a letter from Ursula to SDO Perry in the hope that he would take positive action. She recorded in *Naga Path* the sudden unfolding of events:

> The crust of Zemi secrecy so rarely cracked that when it did, what emerged was startling. One moment all was peace and silence in the Barail, and the next a shocked Perry, still new to the district, was faced with a full-grown famine sprung out of the ground. There wasn't a thing on the books – not a hint from his predecessor – he couldn't believe it. He sent a man out hot-foot to confirm or deny. His report was enough. Things happened. As soon as the stuff could be sacked and put on porters, twenty loads of Government free relief rice were on their way up the road, while Perry himself, with the ample balance, was hurrying up behind. Like the clerk before us, he and I opened the bulging sacks and called on the people to take – and they looked at us long and dumbly, and turned away.

It was only through much cajoling that the most urgent cases could be persuaded to take a little rice. Ursula was wrung with pity as her old friend Miroteung arrived. She had last seen him playing with his plump, golden-haired baby on his porch – now he came from the baby's burial, and he himself was almost too weak to stand. He leant weakly against the doorpost for support and merely shook his head – he was too exhausted from the walk to her camp to speak, but he would not accept the rice.

Eventually he agreed to take just ten pounds when Ursula promised that if there turned out to be any catch in it, or any interest to pay, she would make it all up herself. She believed that Perry had supplied the grain with the intention that it should be free – but she had to be prepared to stand any retrospective charges. 'I said I would pay every penny personally. How I'd have done it, I don't know, but I promised and I would have done.'

Perry recognised the special trust which Ursula had established, and arranged to meet her in Laisong a week after the first relief deliveries. By this time the immediate tragedy had been averted – but it had been a close thing. What Perry and Ursula wanted to do now was find a long-term solution and prevent stupid misunderstandings from jeopardising the Zemis' very existence ever again.

In a very short time Perry had become almost as well accepted by the Zemi as Ursula herself. However, the overall mistrust of the government was far too deep-rooted for two individuals, no matter how sympathetic, to cure. It would be easy for Perry, already well-liked, to re-establish good communications and to maintain the

Zemis' trust during his time in office, but all that could be destroyed under another administration. There seemed no immediate way to secure a lasting trust.

By the end of May rumours had reached Mills in Imphal of the famine in Asalu and Impoi, so he wrote to Ursula for more information. He started by reassuring her of the situation among the Zemi in his area:

> I don't think the Zemi here anticipate that the administration will be withdrawn. It could only happen in the incredible event of the Japs being able to spread themselves all over the hills, and if they did that they would give the Angamis too many troubles at Lome to leave them time to turn on the Zemi. I didn't know till you told me that any Imphal fugitives had come through Tamenglong. The Bishempur Road was the favourite one. I'm very disturbed to hear of the shortage of rice. Is it due to a bad harvest last year, or have fugitives taken it, or what has happened? Will you let me know what it is due to, and how serious and widespread, for it has never been reported?

Confident in the support of Mills and Perry, Ursula prepared to sit out the rains then see if her services were needed anywhere else. As the monsoon continued, Ursula and her household were nervy and snappy, and squabbled among themselves. In the heat and the rain, malarial conditions prevailed even high in the hills, and despite all precautions Ursula went down with a bad bout which laid her low for a week. Although Namkia was as exhausted from Lumding as Ursula, he took over nursing as soon as she fell ill:

> No woman could have been more gentle, no nurse more devoted than Namkia was to me then, I was very ill for a time and quite helpless. For a day and a night he never left my room; every time I roused, he was sitting by me; at night he lay beside the bed and woke at my least move. There are no words for his tenderness, his delicacy and his care. This was a new Namkia.

The rains proved to be the windiest and most violent for many years and south-westerly gales rattled the rain like bullets on the walls and swept away the soil from the garden. Sheer force drove the rain into the bungalow and nothing dried properly – even the comfort of a fire eluded them as the damp wood smoked sullenly without a flicker of a flame. Recalling the first hailstorm she had experienced, Ursula assumed that her bungalow would withstand the battering, so she was still sleeping like a child in the end room when the front and then the side matting were whisked off the roof and hurled away, and the thatch simply blew off in all directions across the spur.

The men did their best to effect repairs, and all was well until the next hailstorm. Ursula lay wrapped in blankets on her camp bed, Namkia a huddled form across the room in his usual corner, as rain drummed against the walls, streaming through cracks and chinks and the whole house creaked under the pressure. As occasional flashes of lightning lit up the room, Ursula saw Namkia looking anxiously at the roof, but she felt safely wrapped up against the weather and was half asleep when a crack overhead brought her to her senses. The whole house was going, and Ursula and Namkia bolted for the living room, where they stood, holding on to the sup-

1 A reluctant debutante, Ursula obliged her mother and grandmother by 'doing the London season'. In her debutante portrait she wears a wistful smile – she was never at home in big social gatherings and was vehemently not in the market for finding a husband. (Betts family archive)

2 A portrait taken after Ursula's return to London. As recipient of the Lawrence Medal and awarded the MBE, Ursula had to handle the requirements of sudden celebrity, sitting for publicity photos and attending formal functions. (Betts family archive)

3 By the time Ursula returned to England after her work with husband Tim with the natives of the remote Apa Tani Valley, she was a respected anthropologist, and while Tim convalesced in London, She became something of a celebrity at social gatherings with her mother, who would probably have urged her to sit for this formal portrait. (Betts family archive)

4 Ursula's smile suggests that this portrait may have been taken on one of her forays to Calcutta to by clothes and have a perm. After leaving Nagaland and the Apa Tani Valley in 1948, never to return, she wrote, 'We had been torn up by the roots. The wound ached unceasingly,' and she knew she would never feel truly happy away from her Naga home. (Betts family archive)

5 Ursula with daughters Catriona, right, and Alison, in much treasured Naga costumes. Although prevented by Indian border restrictions from showing them the land she loved, Ursula brought the girls up immersed in the culture of her adopted Naga people. (Betts family archive)

6 This professional portrait accompanied a newspaper article detailing the improbable jungle activities of the lone English rose, living alone among former head-taking tribesmen. While the press, particularly in America, exaggerated the savagery of Ursula's Naga scouts, the reality was still remarkable, and her position of trust in Slim's Army was unique. (Betts family archive)

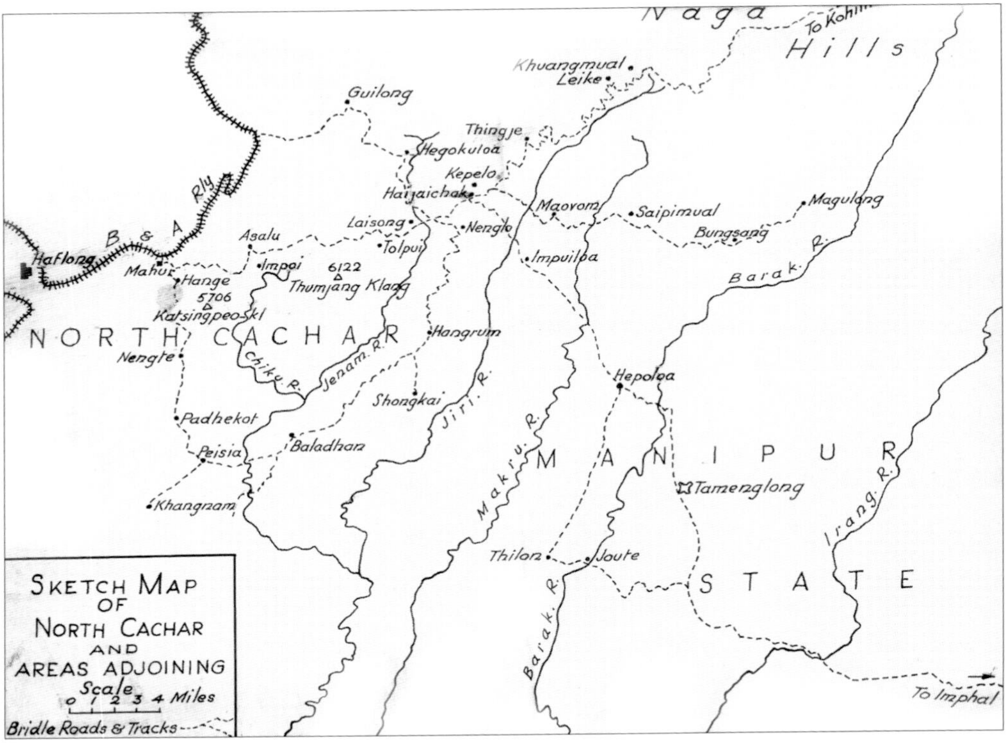

7 Although Nagaland is small in area, travel was a slow process on rough bridle paths and up steep and tortuous ravines. The journey from Ursula's base at Laisong to the Haflong railhead to assist with incoming refugees represented a major excursion for Urusla and her volunteers. (Betts family archive)

Reached the village about 2.15, had tiffin. The Nagas still hanging about the bungalow, scarlet blankets all among the trees. Fine looking men, but given to wearing old European (8) clothes underneath, which rather spoils the effect when they throw their robes back. Many of them had their hair cut Naga fashion, with a tail down the back and the sides shaven, and one had cock's feathers in the tail. Managed to photograph a good many, but the light was poor. {\B.51988=51992\} Hauled out cock's-feather & a young buck with an enchanting grin & took them close up. {\B.51995=51996\} Also took the headman. {\B.51999=52004\}

In the evening a party came round & offered to dance for us. We told them to come at 8.30, which they did, pretty well ginned up - or rather zu'd. They stood in (9) a line & sang several songs in a kind of chorus, one man giving the words, like a psalm in an old Scots Kirk, one man singing it solo and the rest joining in the chorus in harmony. There was a very deep, chesty bass and two or three parts on top of that. It was really very effective, especially when they go warmed up to it. Then they did a song & dance and skipped about the light of the verandah lamp, old Red Slippers, the 2nd headman, well to the fore. Then they did a sort of Nuts-in-May dance, formed in two lines. It was supposed to be two villages bargaining over a (10) bride, and ended, amid shrieks of glee, with the hauling of one little man over the other side. At least, it ought to have ended there, but they went on with another verse, possibly about what happened afterwards. I don't know, as it wasn't translated for us, Pongse and the Ukhrul lumbu being both moderately zu'd. Last of all they did a war- dance. My young buck let out the best screech of the lot, but he was too zu'd or too shy, or both, to nip in and do a solo. The headman's brother or cousin leapt about with an imaginary spear, and then dashed off & came back with a hedge-stake (11) with which he did the most marvellous war-dance. It was really thrilling, and he acted marvellously. Old Red-slippers grabbed another stake & joined in and they bounded about and crouched and stabbed and challenged for all the world as if it was the real thing. The headman got between them at the very beginning and leapt about with arms outstretched while they tried to break past him. Of course it was all pretend but Col. T. said that when they are actually dancing with spears the young bucks get so worked up they would certainly go for one another so the headman gets in and keeps them well apart, however much they try to get by. They went on till they were both exhausted, and nobody would take their places. I hopes the young buck would, but he was too shy. He led one song, very well, but adequately lubricated.

To-day, after Mrs T. & I had gone ahead out of Kungthak, Lt. Col. T. was following on when he heard the two medicine & tiffin japha-coolies bursting into full song. (They were two of the 13 from Mao, and both young lads, about 17 or 18). He asked Pongse to translate (13) and was told they were saying they were jolly glad to have the medicine & tiffin jobs, because they got all the zu to finish after it had been presented to the Colonel by the reception committees. They had had 5 bottles of zu between them on one hour and had a gorgeous lift on.

Nov. 13th

Left Tuinem about 8.30, slightly ahead of the coolies & escorted by headmen & chorus, who appeared to have slept at the bungalow instead of in the village. We sang a good bit of the way. Hope the Nagas (14) enjoyed it. It sounded pretty bloody to me. Feet hellish sore & badly blistered, but well greased & plastered up. Escort left us after a couple of miles. Photographed them right & left, and so parted. {\B.52005=B.52006\}

Kept meeting parties, some going to work in the fields. One man shouted across the valley, a sort of high yell which carried the dickens of a way. I suppose it was about us. The Nagas were a fascinating sight on the hill-paths, men & boys & women, with all their blankets & bead necklaces. Several sick by the road, but Colonel T. sent them all down to the bridge at the bottom (15) where he took out the medicine box & held court with Pongse. {\B.52008\} Tried to

8 Ursula immersed herself immediately in every detail of life on a dispensary tour, quickly absorbing the vocabulary and revelling in the idiosyncratic behaviour of the Naga people. This diary entry, typed later from a hand-written book, encapsulates her total absorption into her first Naga experience. (Betts family archive)

9 Ursula's love of ancient sites and wild places often drew her to drive 'Aggie' to Scotland and take the ferry to Skye, to go hill-walking in the shadow of the Barlam Range. Here she overcame her tendency to vertigo, which would have rendered her Naga treks impossible. (Betts family archive)

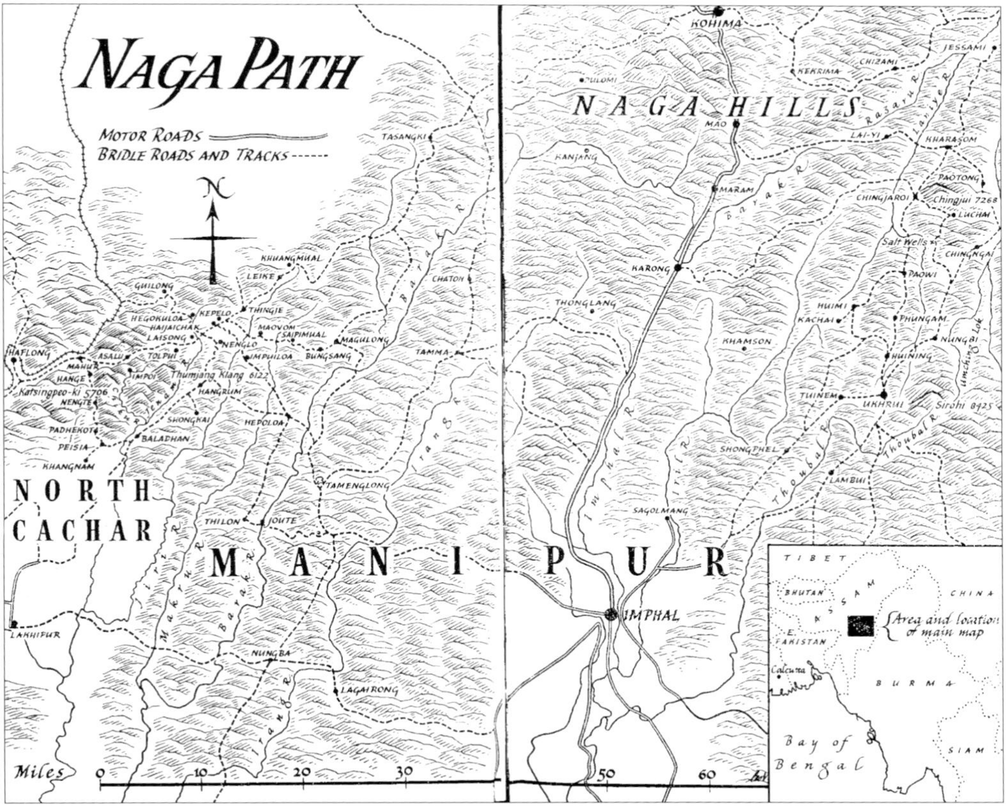

10 A roughly drawn map of Nagaland shows the remoteness of the main groups of villages from the capital, Kohima, and the steep ridges between which a few bridle paths and tracks – and even fewer motor roads – wove to form the only transport system. (Ursula Betts collection/*The Naga Path*)

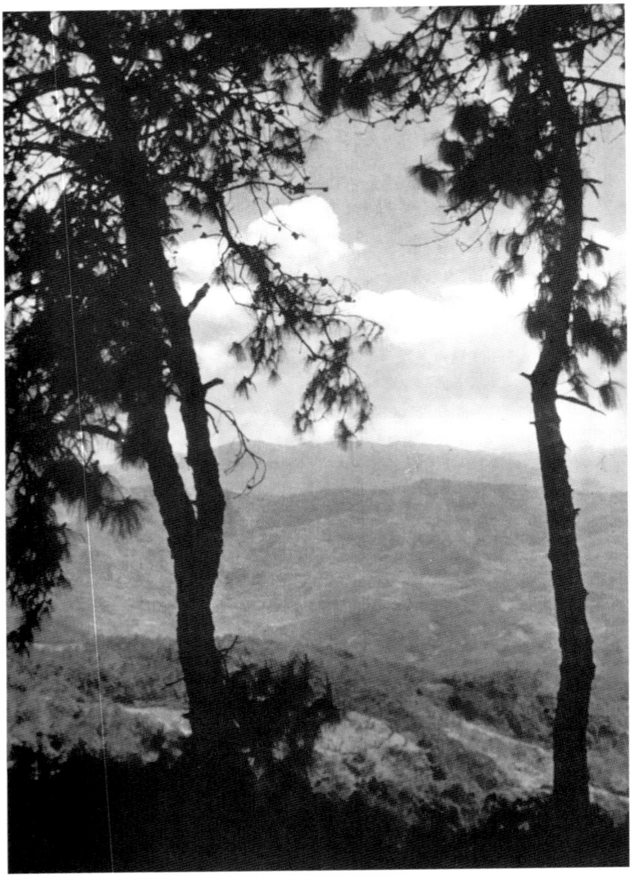

11 The road to Manipur. The rugged scenery drew Ursula in, and after her first tour she recorded, 'There is no describing the fascination of the hills. Neither heat, sweat, dirt nor discomfort could break their hold.' Although few of the European community expected Ursula to stand up to life on the road, she returned more determined than ever to go back as soon as she could. (Ursula Betts collection)

12 The Kabui Naga village of Kambiron, the last stop on Ursula's second tour in the hills. Only later would Ursula learn of its part in the uprising of 1929, when the British called in and the figurehead priestess, Gaidiliu, was finally imprisoned – promising to return to her followers in 'another form' – a prediction with strange ramifications for Ursula. (Ursula Betts collection)

13 The eerie landscape of morning mist in Tangkul Naga country. This was the area where Ursula made her initial dispensary tour, and the locals left a profound impression with their distinctive cockscomb hair, bead and bone collars and crimson and black togas. When she returned she was aware, 'Life had changed'. (Ursula Betts collection)

14 Ursula's first experience of the Zemi Nagas was in Laisong – a village of some eighty houses – where a feast and dance were arranged to welcome her. Touring dancers, Naga musicians, red-cloaked headmen and a sacrificial bull set the scene for an entrancing celebration which lasted far into the night. (Ursula Betts collection)

15 A Zemi Naga morung, or men's clubhouse. These village halls were normally the sole province of the elders and Naga bucks, with adjoining dormitories for the young girls but, granted extraordinary status, Ursula was given permission to sit in and observe local rituals in the morung itself. (Ursula Betts collection)

16 Masang, cutting Namkia's hair. Ursula observed that the two men fell into two wildy differing camps. Masang and other Kabuis welcomed her with 'a hospitality which was frightening', while Namkia and the Zemis initially regarded her with dislike and suspicion. This tribal difference remained an enigma, only solved when Masang was on his deathbed. (Ursula Betts collection)

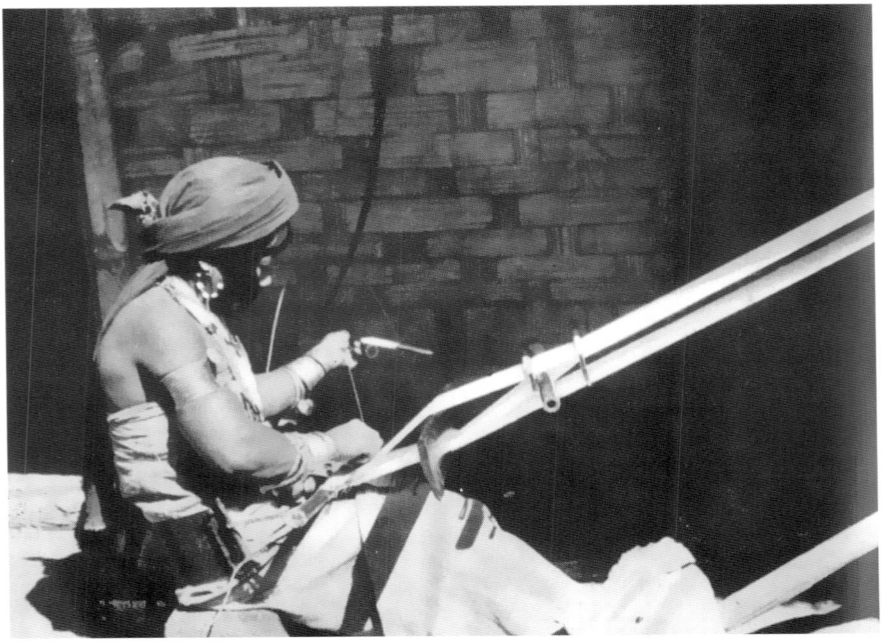

17 A Kabul Naga girl weaving. With the exception of von Fürer-Haimendorf, no proper pictorial anthropological studies had been made of the Naga people and their culture. Although untrained, Ursula had an unexpected talent with a camera and a way of putting people at ease – which combined to create a unique and lasting archive – now housed at the Oxford Pitt Rivers Musem. (Ursula Betts collection)

18 A mother and child in Chingaroi in Tangkhul country. With neo-Tibetan features, the Nagas always maintained their tribal and national independence from India, even before the British administration. India gained independence and claimed Nagaland as an Indian state, triggering years of conflict. (Ursula Betts collection)

19 A Naga girl in Chingaroi. The stepped village, high on a hill, had been a Tangkhul settlement, but was wiped out by raiding Kuki Nagas, and since this time the empty site had been gradually colonised by emigrants from outside the area, creating a mixed-tribe community with its own dialect. (Ursula Betts collection)

20 The Zemi Naga long jump at the hazoa – the sacred jumping stone, close to which the Zemis traditionally buried heads taken in battle. In Ursula's time the stone was the centre for hotly-contested sporting events, including the long jump from the stone, which she filmed in colour – a unique record. (Ursula Betts collection)

21 Naga dance. Local festivals and celebrations were an opportunity to abandon daily hunting and routine, and events could last for days with travelling dancing troops adding to the traditional village dances. (Ursula Betts collection)

22 Luikai with Ursula's first Naga hound, Khamba. Poverty stricken and in debt, Luikai arrived at Ursula's camp seeking work and, despite his grimy condition – and the fact that he had 'the itch' – she took him on, and he proved a grateful retainer. (Ursula Betts collection)

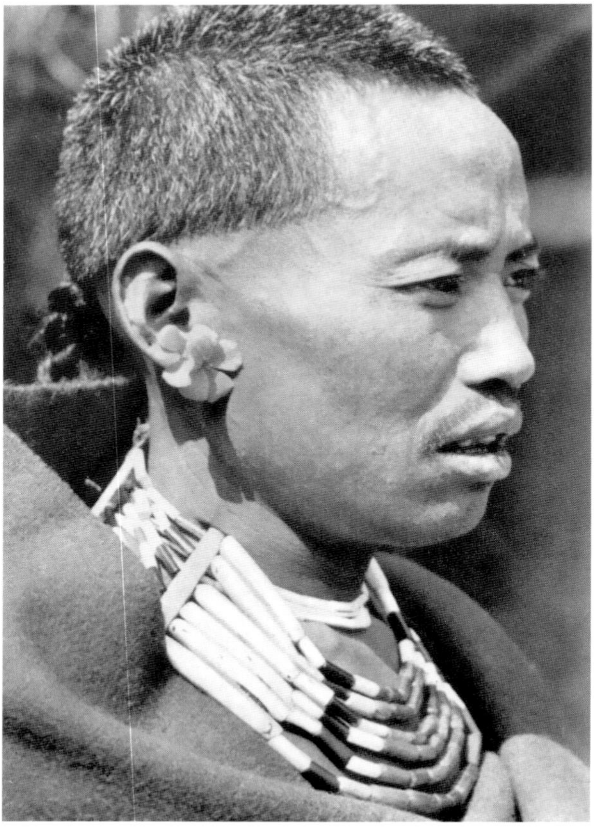

23 Nagas in Jessami, a village with a reputation among Ursula's staff for jadu – black magic – where she got her first experience of the power of superstition. The Nagas believed in magic and the existence of evil spirits, ever ready to punish the unwary or take revenge for ceremonies improperly performed, and Ursula witnessed numerous incidences of mysterious death and what appeared to be curses. (Ursula Betts collection)

24 The headman of Jessami. The villages on Ursula's dispensary tour were grateful and anxious to give her a warm reception, so it was a source of acute embarrassment and shame to the headman and elders to find that someone had left a black magic spell at the village gateway. (Ursula Betts collection)

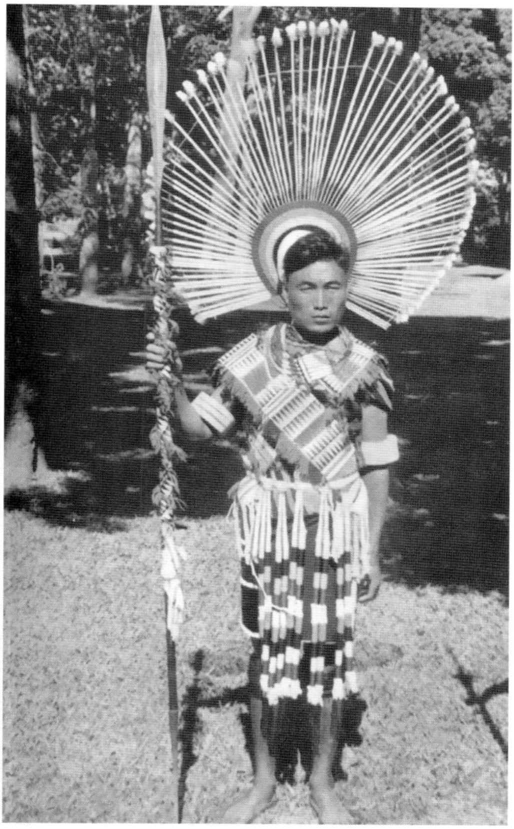

25 An Angami Naga in full dress. Historically, the Angami of the Naga Hills south of Kohima were an aggressive and warlike tribe, who harassed and raided neighbouring tribes, exacting tribute. The shortage of good agricultural land meant that territory was often hotly contested, and there was much inter-tribal fighting before the British administration. (Ursula Betts collection)

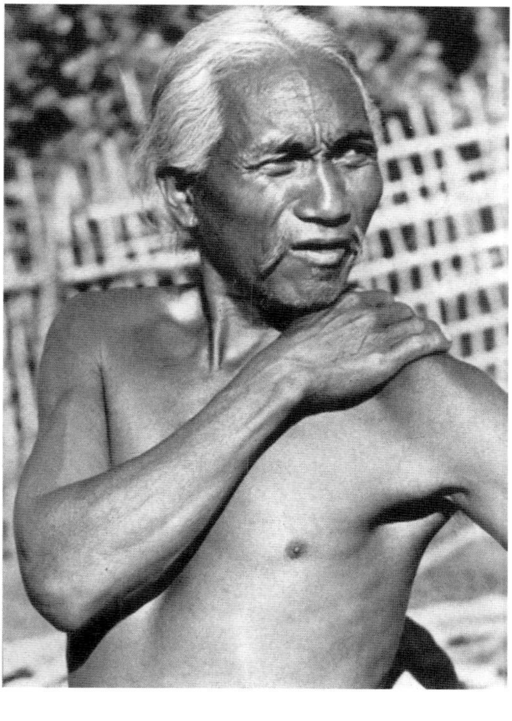

26 An old Kuki Naga gentleman in south-west Manipur. Ursula needed to gain the trust of her photographic subjects – her camera initially posed a potential threat of jadu, especially among the older tribesmen. However, over time the people accepted her, and she was able to create an extraordinary photographic record of the Naga tribes. (Ursula Betts collection)

27 A Tangkhul Naga headman in Tuinem, wearing traditional woven cloths for which the village was particularly well known. Ursula took advantage of a dispensary tour to gain the villagers' confidence so they would allow her to film their traditional crafts. (Ursula Betts collection)

28 Masang of Kepelo who, eight years before Ursula's arrival, had been one of the few staunch supporters of the imprisoned priestess, Gaidiliu. Since that time he had been waiting for the prophesied embodiment of Gaidiliu's divine self to arrive, and he nursed a silent conviction that this was Ursula. (Ursula Betts collection)

29 A Naga drummer in Laisong. Remote from 'civilisation' and using only home-made tools, the Nagas created a variety of musical instruments to perform their traditional songs and accompany their dances. (Ursula Betts collection)

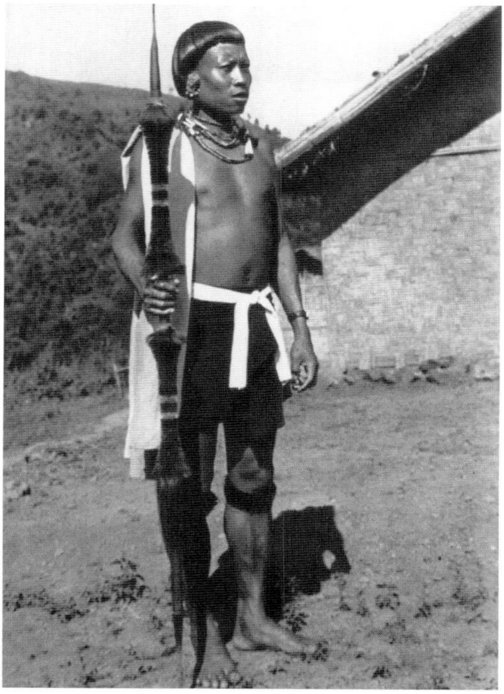

30 Namkiabuing of Impoi. Although initially a very reluctant addition to Ursula's staff, this outwardly warlike man became Ursula's most trusted adviser and friend, and he took great pride in introducing Ursula to his home village, south of her Laisong camp. (Ursula Betts collection)

31 A Zemi Naga buck in full dress. For special occasions the young men adorned themselves in their best woven cloths and kilts, green beetle earrings, elaborate necklaces and dazzling coloured feathers, with their legs whitened with pipe-clay. (Ursula Betts collection)

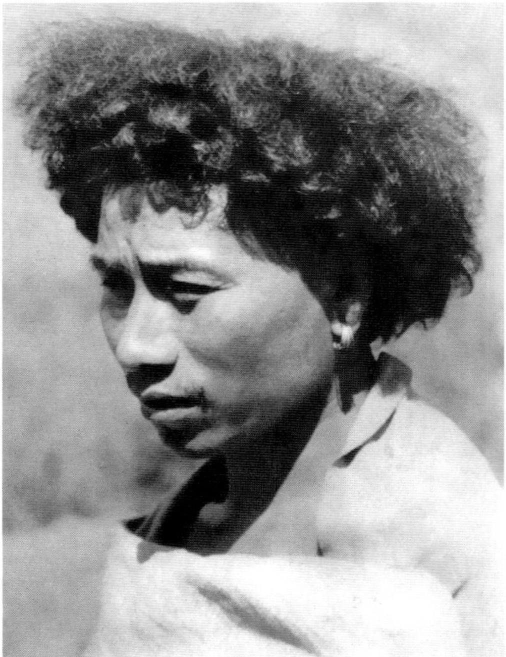

32 Paodekumba, V-Force scout. When the Japanese threatened to invade their homeland, the Nagas had two choices – to take their chances and sit it out, or take positive action against them, so risking violent retribution if they failed. Trusting Ursula to lead them, her Zemi friends made final arrangements in their home villages and returned to Laisong to defend their territory and pride. (Ursula Betts collection)

ports and waiting for the crashing to stop. When it did, it was replaced with the sound of rain drumming on the floor. Gingerly they crept back into the bedroom – the rafters had been splintered and the bindings holding them together had been stripped away, along with all of the thatch, so the room was open to the sky.

Eventually something had to break the tension of the imminent invasion. It was known that the Japanese were waiting for the right moment to strike and rumour and counter-rumour spread throughout the area. In a nutshell, 'The Zemi were afraid. Talk magnified our defeats; Jap prowess was exalted. Invasion in the autumn seemed certain, and what to do when it came was a problem for all of us.'

Ursula asked Namkia how he and the rest of the Zemi felt their situation was. Overall, he explained, they felt that it was not their war, and they would just like to be left to their own devices in the hills where they had always lived and forget about the whole thing. With this understanding, Ursula received a message in July – over in Manipur, the Kabui, Zemi and Lyeng had held a meeting to discuss what to do if the administration were to withdraw. They wanted to know if Ursula would stay on and be their leader.

21

'V' Force

The invitation to lead the Nagas was a bolt from the blue – but it was an immense vote of confidence. Ursula sent back a non-committal reply about the leadership – but reassuring them that even if invasion came, she fully intended to stay put.

Namkia, Haichangnang, Ramgakpa and Dinekamba had seen for themselves the state of the soldiers coming up through Lumding and understood how bitterly they were fighting to keep the Japanese out of Assam and their homeland. Others still saw the war as something that should not affect them, but Ursula felt Namkia should point out to them how it might soon become impossible to ignore. If the Japanese were coming through, they'd come whether the Nagas sided with the British or not. The whole area would be fought over, and they would be part of it. Ursula strongly recommended that they think very hard before cutting themselves off, but it was probably Namkia's conviction, having seen what he had at Lumding, that tipped the balance. When Ursula started to raise and co-ordinate intelligence scouts in the area, the Nagas opted to join her.

In early August a message came from Haflong that a Colonel Rawdon Wright was on his way to see her. On the day of his arrival Ursula was watching from the bungalow veranda, and around noon she spotted a party approaching – an unmistakably European figure in shirtsleeves and an escort of Nagas. Ursula sent Dinekamba with an invitation for the colonel to join her for lunch, but when he returned an hour later he was alone. Scribbled in the margin of her note was an apologetic line, 'So sorry, but I've got a gammy leg. I'd better go straight on down to the resthouse.' Ursula and Namkia set out to meet the colonel and found the party still way back from the village – and given the state of the colonel's leg, this was no surprise. He was not a young man and his leg was held completely rigid by a strong bandage. She and Namkia escorted the limping colonel to the resthouse and when he rallied a little after his long walk, they lunched on the veranda.

Rawdon Wright had heard a lot about Ursula and it turned out that they had met before. As she wrote to Doris,

> Who should turn up but Rawdon Wright, Eric's old friend from The White Hart! He didn't connect me with your little daughter until I had persisted in recalling it to his mind for some time, and then it all came over him in a rush, so to speak. He had heard of me from Mills and didn't connect me with my White Hart self at all.

Old enough to have fought in the Great War, and nursing a gammy leg, Wright had had a tough job finding any service that would have him when war broke out. Eventually he got a ground job in the RAF, but then the fighting approached Assam. This had been his old stamping ground when he was in the Assam Rifles between the wars, so he pulled all possible strings to get posted there again. He managed to secure a desk job – not what he had wanted, but at least he was in the right area. When Singapore fell, he wangled his way out of the RAF and into the Army and had flown out heavily disguised as a civilian – now, despite his wounded leg, he was ready to go back into active service.

He was fed up with being treated as an old crock, so he set out to walk the full fifty miles through the hills to meet Ursula. If she was impressed with his determination, the impression he made on the Nagas was even greater, and they agreed that they had never seen anyone, Naga or otherwise, with such guts.

Wright explained that he was undertaking reconnaissance for a guerrilla organisation known as 'V' Force, tasked with recruiting the hill tribes to work as army scouts. This had become a matter of urgency as the Japanese were ranged along the length of the Burma border, ready to invade. In India, the Congress Party had been fomenting internal trouble which promised to give Britain more problems – indeed there was a possibility that the Congress Party was planning an uprising against the British government to coincide with a mass Japanese invasion. Certainly the Japanese would be watching events in India, and if the Congress Party created enough havoc, they would take advantage of the situation and invade.

'V' Force was charged with watching the border areas, including North Cachar and the area of Manipur just in front of it. There were several tracks crossing this territory, converging at Haijaichak and then moving on to the railway. No doubt there would already be Japanese spies and agents undercover on the Indian side of the border who would want to cross back to make their reports, and the area would be crucial in the event of an invasion. Wright wanted to raise a volunteer group of scouts to patrol the area – a 'Watch and Ward' operation. Knowing Ursula's unique relationship with the Nagas, he wanted to know if she thought it would work – and if she did, would she take on the job of recruiting?

Spreading out a map, they assessed the routes the Japanese could use. There was the road from Kohima, and Naga paths from Maovom and Impuiloa, which met at Haijaichak at the eastern end of the pass. The remaining route, from Hangrum, emerged at the west end of the pass near the Laisong resthouse, and Laisong village would have this one covered. Only one other way through the territory existed, from Hangrum up the stream-beds via Tolpui, but it was a difficult route and anyone tackling it would need local knowledge or guides. In any event, Hangrum was in a position to watch over that route. All the strategic villages that would be involved in a scheme to patrol these routes were Zemi settlements – there were Kuki villages, but with the exception of Khuangmual near the Naga Hills border, they were small, widely scattered and built a good distance from any of the routes.

Wright was aware of the sensitive relationship the Zemi had with the British – from his days in the Assam Rifles he knew all about the Gaidiliu affair and its legacy. Did Ursula believe that they could rely on the Zemi to support them?

Ursula explained that there was a sound element, typified by the likes of Namkia, who had a lot of influence. Wright could probably rely on support from Asalu and Impoi – on the other hand, by far the larger group in the area would likely say they didn't want to get mixed up in anything and just wanted to be left alone. With regard to Gaidiliu's followers – none of the ring-leaders were left, but she couldn't predict how any remaining faithful might respond. Unfortunately the only way she could accurately describe the majority of the Zemi was 'pretty sticky'.

All the same, Wright said he would like to go to Hangrum and perhaps beyond to see how people were disposed. Ursula immediately offered to accompany him, at least as far as Hangrum – they knew and trusted her, and would respond more warmly if she were there than if he visited them as a stranger alone.

The following day, Ursula, Wright, Namkia and the porters set out – and it soon became apparent how badly his wounded leg hindered him. On the flat they were making only about one and a half miles an hour, but on steep ascents he was almost incapacitated. Wright had to rest on the shoulder of one of the men, and where there was not room for two abreast, he dropped on to his hands and knees and crawled. Despite the pain and the laboriousness of his progress, he uttered no word of complaint.

The village was in a flat spin about their visit – as Ursula knew, absolutely anything would scare Hangrum. Leaving Wright limping gamely behind her, she went ahead with Namkia to meet the welcome committee. Before Ursula could greet them, Namkia could contain himself no longer and broke in:

> That Colonel Sahib – he's not a man, he's a tiger! He's got a wounded leg. He got it in the German war. His bearer told me. He goes up the hills on all fours, like a bear. He comes down the hills like this, on a man's arm. And not one word, not one! The courage! Anyone else would be weeping aloud by now. I tell you, he's not a man, he is a tiger!

They all turned and watched his tortuous progress down the zigzag path, and he arrived amid an awed silence.

Wright limped through the village in silence – but it was not the usual hostility reserved by Hangrum for strangers. It was one of speechless admiration. In the evening Wright sat with Ursula on the veranda and they stared out towards the Manipur hills as the sun set. Always moved by their magnificence, Ursula waxed lyrical and with a knowing nod he observed, 'I think you're in love with the hills.' 'You're right', she replied. Kindred spirits, they sat with their drinks as the light faded.

The headman and elders arrived by torchlight later that evening – they had had a discussion and they wanted Wright to have a litter. They offered to make one specially and arrange for the best porters to carry it, free of cost as a gift. Namkia translated for him and Wright shook his head. 'Please tell them, I'm a soldier. I'm not going to be carried about the country like a woman.'

The next day, Rawdon Wright set out on foot up the long, narrow scramble over Hemeolowa and Ursula stood with the elders as the white speck of his shirt moved slowly and painfully away, leaning on the shoulder of the interpreter. At the turn of the road he paused, looked back and waved – then was gone from sight.

By the time Wright got back to Haflong he was weak and exhausted and Perry was shocked at his appearance. He had impressed everyone he met with his courage, and therefore been his own best advertisement with regard to setting up a Watch and Ward operation. He made his report that it should be done, then left 'V' Force to set up a Porter Corps.

It was at this time that he became ill, the massive effort of the reconnaissance trip having been too much for him. At the end of November his leg had to be amputated and after struggling to survive for three weeks, he finally died in December. It was left to the remaining officers of 'V' Force to pick up his legacy and accomplish what he had started.

Fortunately, the Japanese held back from attacking over the border throughout August and September, as no progress seemed to be being made with the Watch and Ward plan. Then, in October, Ursula received a visit from another 'V' Force colonel. On Rawdon Wright's recommendation, Critchley had come to discuss recruitment with her.

After a long meeting, Ursula returned to camp with a clutch of papers, a credit of a 1,000 rupees in the Haflong Treasury and the go-ahead to recruit among the Zemi and Kukis to set up a Watch and Ward operation. Ursula knew that the Zemi particularly had good reason to distrust the government, but she also knew that they had faith in her and that with some help from the administration, she felt she could persuade them to support her. She also had another ace up her sleeve; 'I knew every single bad hat in the district, because they'd all been in to worship me. It was extremely useful.'

A few days later, Ursula met Perry to discuss the scheme. They agreed that, while this was the golden opportunity they had been waiting for to heal the rift between the Zemi and the government, if they failed to keep their word in any detail, they would not just lose the Zemis' support, but set relations between them and the British back decades.

Ursula decided to start recruiting in Hangrum – in the wake of the Gaidiliu fiasco, it was the most suspicious and aloof of the local Zemi villages. If recruiting went badly there, things could only get better. Ursula had one un-pressed volunteer – Paodekumba offered his services as a scout as soon as he heard of the plan, and for a fortnight, he had the honour of being the one and only recruit.

When Ursula and Namkia went to Hangrum, things didn't look promising. The immediate reaction was one of distrust, and the headmen wanted to put the matter to a village meeting. The village gathered in the open space in front of the headman's house – there were some forty or fifty, mainly householders, clustered around a bench where Ursula and Namkia sat facing them, with the headman beside them to chair the debate.

The whole scene struck her as absurdly staged. Behind the little gathering the village street stretched away towards the distant hills, whose contours showed crisply against the clear autumn sky. Towering over them like some extravagant operatic backcloth, the curved grey front gable of the lower morung was silhouetted against the sky.

The headman explained the purpose of the meeting, then Namkia took centre stage. Once he'd stated his case the objections and accusations came thick and fast. The mistrust of the British government was deeply entrenched, and the first reaction was that it would turn out to be a trick – they'd be sent away and would never come back. Namkia assured them that there was no hidden agenda – it was a genuine recruitment drive for a scouting force.

All the anticipated arguments were raised – 'Why should we fight for the Sahibs? We didn't fight for the Kacharis, we didn't fight for the Manipuris – why should we fight for the British?' Namkia's response was well prepared. 'Why shouldn't we? Did the Kacharis or the Manipuris stop the Angamis raiding? Haven't the Sahibs done that? Haven't they given us roads and salt-markets? Haven't they given us protection and peace? Don't we owe them something for that?'

Someone with a long memory recalled the porters they had sent with the British in the Lushai War. Hardly any had returned – they suspected the same thing would happen again. Namkia could not deny that most of the porters had died of cholera – but he pointed out that that was fifty years ago. It wouldn't happen again – there were medicines, injections. He reassured them over and over again that they would not be sent away – they would be serving in their own country, in territory that they knew well. No-one would expect them to work for nothing – they would be properly paid and armed with guns. The Japanese were threatening to invade *their* country – it was important to protect it from being overrun.

A ding-dong battle developed with shouts of 'Lies! Lies!' and denials – 'No, it's true. Truth! Truth!' Ursula was so frustrated when they wouldn't believe Namkia that she joined in. 'If you Zemi won't do it, then the Kukis will! Or else there'll be troops here to do the job for you – how would you like that? I'm offering you guns – where are your own guns? When did you last have guns?'

'So be it', they replied – 'bring in your troops. Let them get on with it'. She urged them to remember the last time troops were brought in, and they had played fast and loose with the female population. If they made this Watch and Ward scheme a success, they could keep their guns. The main fear seemed to be that of being taken away from their own territory – but Ursula stressed that what was important was how well they knew their own area. Still, nothing would convince them that they were not about to be tricked into leaving, then never be allowed back home, and eventually the meeting broke up. No resolution had been passed – one or two people had spoken privately to Namkia, but the village as a whole were against it.

Recruiting in Asalu and Impoi was much more successful. After the famine they had no resources and were unable to set by any stores of grain or foodstuffs for themselves because they were working in the Kacharis' fields to scrape a living. If Ursula and Perry both supported the scheme, they would support it. After all, both she and Perry had kept their word and helped them in the famine – and they should do something in return.

Ursula and Namkia toured all the Zemi villages and Kuki settlements – and all were willing to co-operate. Only Hangrum, Shongkai and Baladhan were holding out, so Perry promised to talk to them, and accompanied Ursula and Namkia back to the recalcitrant villages.

Hangrum was accustomed to dominating the area – it was a large village and other smaller settlements had always followed their lead. Now their authority was challenged, and this was a dangerous precedent. Namkia was a well-respected man from a founding family, and even small and vulnerable villages were prepared to stand out against the mighty Hangrum to support him.

In the open gathering, the Hangrum diehards shouted abuse at the recruits from the village who had joined Namkia – and the recruits said to hell with their dictatorship. Perry reassured the elders and villagers that there was no trick – they would be paid and armed; would operate locally – and that was a promise. The tide suddenly turned in Perry's favour, and Hangrum's two 'vassal' villages came round. Shongkei and Baladhan had turned up with a number of would-be recruits in their pockets, so to speak, waiting to see how things went before producing them – and now the headmen left the meeting, summoned in their recruits and shoved them at Perry.

Perry gave Hangrum a week's grace, and when Ursula and Namkia returned, a committee of headmen rushed to greet them. As Ursula observed dryly, it was the sort of effusiveness which generally meant that something had gone wrong. However, Hangrum had raised recruits – the headmen reassured them of this as they plied them with zu. They would bring the recruits to meet them that evening.

Hangrum, being a large village, had a good number of big, strapping young men of just the constitution Ursula wanted for scouting and running. Some had even come forward secretly and promised their services as long as the village council agreed. At four o'clock the headmen arrived and sheepishly ushered in the recruits. They had certainly enlisted their full quota – but it was clear that they had scraped together only the halt and the lame whose absence – or even death – would be no loss to the village. Of the ten, only three had two good eyes, all were over forty, most of them had no teeth and one was a cripple.

The headman was not surprised at Ursula's reaction – it had been a gesture of the purest optimism on his part. The recruits were quite happy when she sent the whole lot packing and told the headman that they would have to come up with men who at least had the full quota of limbs and all their faculties.

The next day the headman was back with a fresh offering:

> One or two of the old ones were, it is true, still there, but the more noticeably damaged had been replaced. There was, too, a new tone apparent in this consignment. They were more or less volunteers and they had not the resignation of the other crew.

Even so, they appeared very apprehensive and it seemed they wanted some guarantee of protection. Namkia stood aloof while the headman stammered and dithered as he tried to explain what he wanted. Namkia evidently disapproved strongly of whatever it was, and told him as much. Now he reluctantly came to his rescue and explained to Ursula that they wanted her to swear formally, on her life, that they would not be sent away from their own territory.

It was, Namkia said, an insult. Sahibs didn't take oaths – their word was enough. If a man lies, then he is no Sahib. He was disgusted – the very idea. Ursula, however, was quite happy to give her word, and if that was what it took, there was no need to take offence. He grudgingly announced her agreement, then stalked away to watch from a distance.

As soon as they understood that Ursula had agreed, one recruit came forward with an egg and offered it to her – and Namkia had to snap out of his sulk in order to tell her what to do. She must repeat the words of the oath, calling on the earth and sky to witness the truth of what she promised, and offering up her life as a forfeit if she lied. The egg would then be thrown down and smashed.

For the Zemi, such an oath was a very solemn undertaking, because the death of anyone who broke it was absolutely inevitable. To take an oath in court would be such a token of truth that those who did so would immediately win the case – no further argument. Ursula stepped into the open air, since the oath had to be taken where the earth and sky could witness it. She took the egg, repeated the oath he quoted to her and then, since she was a novice in the egg-throwing stakes, handed it back to him to break. 'He did me proud. He took two strides and dashed it on the ground. It hit a knob of rock and burst like a hand-grenade. Shell, yolk, shot into space like bullets.' The crowd trooped off to where the egg had landed and the spattered remains seemed to have spread themselves over a most impressive radius. The egg had been so totally dispersed that what she said was undoubtedly true. Namkia harrumphed scornfully as they went to pack to return to Laisong.

22

Watch and Ward

Throughout November Ursula prepared for the Watch and Ward scheme, and trained the recruits to work as a team, inculcating the necessary discipline for undercover work. The original intention had been to extend the field of operation along the Barak from the village of Henima downwards, but pending invasion, it was restricted to a triangle extending south from Khuangmual along the Jiri River to where it joined the Jenam, with its peak at the railway at Mahur.

The object was to pick up Japanese spies or agents, moving in either direction, who might try to go via the hills on their way to or from the small, unfrequented Hill Section halts. It was a key area in which three main cross-country tracks converged.

Ursula stationed a small group of five scouts in every village that covered an entrance or exit to 'the triangle', and with them were a pair of runners. She had reached an agreement with the village morungs to have runners stationed with them all along the main routes, so that each messenger would only have to cover a short distance to get information or orders through in the fastest possible time. The scouts were to patrol the area and bring to HQ any strangers passing through who were not hill men or government servants or otherwise properly identified. If they saw any aircraft crash they were to report them, but apart from that they should keep Ursula informed at her HQ in Laisong of anything at all going on in the region.

The scheme went into action in early December. After just a week the scouts were reporting back that people weren't taking them seriously. Perhaps if they had more sense of self-importance they might have been able to carry off their role without any recognised sign of office, but the Zemi had been everybody's whipping boy for so long, being downtrodden had become a habit. They wanted some official indication of their status – most particularly a red cloth, which was *the* universally accepted indication of authority in the hill territories.

Ursula immediately sent an SOS message to 'V' Force HQ at Barrackpore – she had given her word that she would support them, and if they wanted red cloths, they should have them. Two weeks later an officer strolled into the quartermaster's office and made a casual remark. 'Lovely grey blankets for North Cachar – wouldn't mind one myself.' The quartermaster, who already had a whole sheaf of urgent requests from Ursula on his desk, looked up wearily. 'Grey? Did you say grey?' 'Most certainly – look.' The blankets were indeed grey.

The importance of supplying blankets as promised had been well drummed into the staff at 'V' Force, for reasons of showing commitment and keeping promises as much as for providing a badge of authority. A captain jumped into a jeep and drove to

Calcutta where he went round all the military hospitals and managed to commandeer or nefariously 'liberate' nineteen scarlet British Military Hospital blankets. These were soon distributed so that there was one for each group of village scouts and a few for the Laisong staff. Literally 'dressed in a little brief authority', the operation was up and running – and at last the Zemi were beginning to feel that they had some clout. It was a year later that Ursula discovered what had happened to the original consignment of blankets – they had been sent in error to Kohima where the 'V' Force base had made them into drapes for the mess.

The next administrative hiccup was with the cash-flow. At the start of recruiting, Ursula had 1,000 rupees with the Haflong Treasury, but this office was open only very occasionally, and drafts of money due in did not seem to be getting through. Still able to send uncensored letters, she wrote to Doris in January to say that she got no money from Westminster Bank during November or December, and the Army 'a) forgot to pay me when they said they would, b) sent the draft too late to catch the next Treasury day,' so funds became very short. By as early as the start of November, the 1,000 rupees had been all but used up and Ursula found herself with just thirty rupees to last her six weeks.

The demands of organising Watch and Ward operations meant that Ursula had to keep touring the region, and she was constantly aware of the pressure on her as a woman to prove herself capable. Even without sufficient funds to keep body and soul together, she kept working on iron rations. Doris would have been delighted at the slimming effect of this regime – Ursula lost thirty-five pounds in weight. As she wrote to Doris, 'I got quite slim!' From her usual thirteen to thirteen and a half stone, she was suddenly a very svelte ten stone eight.

She wouldn't have dreamed of complaining to 'V' Force about the lack of funds – she felt her job was very precarious: 'As a woman, I was a freak in the job, and I was always afraid that they'd find an excuse to fire me. They said that sooner or later they'd send a British officer to take over.' Fortunately, when she went to join the Mills family for Christmas in Shillong, Mills quickly guessed by her appearance what was wrong, and wrote at once to 'V' Force HQ.

In the New Year Ursula was surprised by a much-needed pay rise and HQ granted her an allowance of rations – which helped enormously, as supplies were growing scarce and prices were soaring in response. She now received a captain's pay and had a regular Army imprest account for expenses and paying the men. It spoke volumes for Naga honesty that there was not a lock in the whole camp – Ursula would get 10,000 rupees at a time to deal with pay and supplies, and leave it all in a sack in her living room. If she left the camp, the money was protected by one elderly scout with an equally elderly muzzle-loader – and they never lost a single anna.

By the time she received a visit from Colonel Scott, Assistant Quartermaster General, 'V' Force in early January, the situation was improving, and he set his seal of approval on the way Ursula was working. From then on he made sure that she wanted for nothing. As he observed, 'Tough for a woman. Always wrong twice – once for being wrong, and once for being a woman.'

The scouts' self-esteem had grown with the provision of red cloths, but when the promised guns arrived with Colonel Binny, a wave of confidence spread through the watch. Binny, who as commander of 'V' Force Assam Zone was Ursula's immediate

CO, arrived to inspect operations. Satisfied with what he saw, he left the consignment of guns with no misgivings. The Zemi were never an especially warlike group, and had never had many firearms – and those that they had had were confiscated by the government during the 'troubles'. When she arrived, the only gun Ursula knew of among the Zemi belonged to Namkia's father.

The guns may only have been antiquated muzzle-loaders, and as Ursula would have been the first to admit, the Naga scouts probably couldn't hit a barn door from six feet using them, but they were tangible proof that Ursula meant to fulfil her promises. This gave them confidence – as did the fact that they now had something with which to defend themselves and enforce their orders. Given the antiquity of the guns, it was just as well that Critchley doubted that it would ever come to face-to-face fighting – and Ursula agreed. 'I myself felt that it was most unlikely that they would ever, in Critchley's phrase, "stand behind a tree and poop off at Japs".'

But a gun was a gun, and since civil guns, used to keep animals out of the crops, had had no powder-rations for two years, the scouts who had been issued with powder and shot 'for practice', were much sought-after in any village where game was plundering the crops. On their leave they were welcomed with open arms and had an excellent opportunity for target practice. Ursula's 'decorative and unlikely army' were improving their guerrilla skills and their confidence was high.

Small details still had to be worked out. The scouts could not read English, so there had to be a system of passes devised whereby authorised people, on lawful business, could go through the area without being hauled in at gunpoint. A simple rubber stamp was designed, which only Ursula or Perry possessed, and this worked well until Binny sent a British signaller up from Imphal with a convoy of stores and rations. He didn't pass through Haflong, so Perry never authorised his passage. Instead he arrived directly in Mahur, and unaware that he needed a pass, he immediately aroused suspicion. Ursula was away at the time, and was not available to intercede, so a bizarre convoy arrived in Laisong. The signaller had marched his party through the screen of scouts who were alerted when he offered no permit, but unable to communicate effectively, and quite definitely barred by protocol from arresting a Sahib, they could only follow him closely. The Asalu and Impoi scouts padded into Laisong in the wake of the unsuspecting signaller who, in Ursula's absence, was greeted by Paodekumba. He was in bellicose mood and was all for arresting him, but didn't want to make a mistake, so he instructed Ramgakpa to serve the Sahib tea while he conferred with the rest of the staff.

They concluded that he had to be a Japanese spy. Although they had never come across any Japanese, they knew they were dark-haired, and the only Europeans they had seen were fair or brown-haired. There was no room in their acquaintance for dark-haired Europeans such as this unfortunate Welshman, so Paodekumba sent to the village for reinforcements and he scuttled around for some rope. As the unsuspecting signaller ate his supper, Paodekumba briefed his posse and was all set to take serious restraining action when a runner turned up from Ursula. She was two days away in Mahur, but would be back very soon. Ruefully Paodekumba dismissed the men and prepared to mount a two-day guard on the suspect.

It was a very bewildered signaller who greeted Ursula on her return. He'd delivered the supplies – but the Nagas would not let him leave. He'd spent a couple of days enjoying Ramgakpa's hospitality, but he wasn't at all happy about Khamba, and Ursula felt the signaller wasn't really happy about the Nagas, either.

Paodekumba was profoundly disappointed when Ursula explained who the visitor was – but even he had to admit that not even the most brazen of Japanese spies was likely to commandeer a convoy of British supplies and march them into 'V' Force camp in Laisong. When the Japs did turn up, they would be a good deal harder to extricate from cover.

For security reasons, Ursula could give her mother absolutely no idea what her 'wild and woolly Winkle' was up to – but in the early part of the year she was reassured of her safety with a letter:

> We are having a shortage of cigarettes such as England had a while ago. All the English brands are off the market, and replaced by cigarettes with the old, familiar names, but made in India; and composed, as someone said, of 10% Virginia tobacco and the rest camel dung. If one can't smoke these, the only refuge is cheroots or a hookah!

In May, the best she could explain about how she spent her time was to say that 'my job, by the way, is much the same as Eric's in 1940, allowing for local variations.' At least Doris learned that she was still alive.

A trip to Calcutta in August with Namkia was an eye-opener for Ursula. It was no holiday – Ursula needed to have a wisdom tooth out. While there, she indulged in two new dresses and had some existing garments altered and re-dyed – but new clothes were scarce and prohibitively expensive. The shock of the visit was the extent of the Bengal famine:

> Starving people were about all the streets, having wandered in in search of food, and corpses were being picked up daily. The waifs were chiefly on the outskirts, away from the business and shopping centres, but there were some even there. Owing to petrol rationing, etc, the dustbins weren't being emptied often enough and mounds of garbage overflowed across the pavement even in the smart residential streets, and there was usually a beggar or a human skeleton of sorts hunting for scraps in the pretty whiffy refuse while cats and crows competed with him. Once one got away from the central part there were haunting sights, near-dead people lying on the pavements too weak to move, and children – especially babies – with every bone showing.

Back in Haflong, Ursula found that the governor, Sir Robert Reid, was visiting, and following her meeting with him, an item appeared in a Calcutta paper:

> The Former Governor of Assam, Sir Robert Reid, today described how head-hunters were aiding the Allies by forming themselves into guerrilla bands on the frontier hills of Assam.
>
> 'A most valuable guerrilla corps has been built up, and in forming this irregular army, the civil authorities of Assam took pride in the fact that they went ahead with the idea themselves.

> These guerrillas are a match for anyone in the world in the art of moving through and fighting in jungle. For the Nagas – one of these hill tribes – head-hunting is the breath of life though they find it irksome under peace-time administration to have this pleasure interfered with. Under present conditions, I have no doubt that the taking of Japanese heads would give them infinite pleasure.'
>
> Sir Robert said that these hill tribes were looking to Britain for protection and should have it. In the meantime, there should be an interim period of 'political tutelage', until they were fit to play their part in Indian politics.

As the year progressed, Ursula's 'comic-opera force', knocked into shape and kept in discipline by Head Scout Namkia, went from strength to strength. No British officer arrived to replace her, so still a civilian, Ursula carried on in charge. In 'V' Force Assam, perhaps it had sunk in that no-one could better inspire the loyalty and dedication of the Zemi … besides, if pressed, they would have had to admit that she was doing an extraordinary job. Especially for a woman.

In December Ursula was delighted to receive Doris's Christmas parcel and cards from the family. In her thank-you letter she mentioned hearing 'some sinister bangs and thumps in the distance this morning; don't know if it was a raid or someone attending to a recce plane, as there were aeroplane engine noises as well.'

Things had been relatively quiet throughout 1943, but as the Japanese drew nearer in '44, there were moments of serious excitement. On one occasion a Japanese aircraft flew low and looked as if it was going to shoot up the camp – it came so close that as it made a pass over Ursula's HQ, it came within rifle shot. As Ursula observed ruefully, 'If I'd had a machine gun, we'd have got him.'

Ursula's camp, on its very visible spur, was a tremendous lookout point with a clear view for miles around – but this also meant they were very vulnerable. Having only ancient muzzle-loaders with which to defend themselves, there was little hope of bringing down any enemy aircraft.

With a new airfield built for the RAF on the plain at Kumbhirgram to the south of Khangnam village, planes were quite a common sight. Sometimes they cut through the Barail passes, or swooped so low that they lifted the thatch on the Impoi morung and tore above the Laisong camp. On occasions the aircraft got lost and Ursula would receive a message via the Haflong police asking her to put out search parties, but due to lack of detail and accurate information, a lot of time and manpower were wasted. It was decided to position a dedicated observation post and base for search parties at Khangnam, overlooking the airfield on the plain.

It was for this reason that Ursula trekked south, to visit Khangnam for the first time. It was far from any other village, tucked away in deep woods, and uniquely it had kept its stone defences. It was a village long accustomed to battening down its hatches to repel intruders, and the passage of time gave the villagers no reason to de-escalate their defences.

Ursula's camp was on a ridge beyond the village, and it offered good views south into the heart of the plain towards the airfield and north towards the Barail. The path into the village from camp led between the dusty rocks of a ridge, then down into the broad main street where some fifty houses clustered round the two morungs. Ursula and Namkia had reached the outcrop on their way to the village – it was nine o'clock and the quiet of the morning was broken by an insistent and piercing hum, which grew louder until two big formations of bombers came into view. They were flying so high that the fighter planes accompanying them were only visible when the sun glinted off their wings as they headed towards the plains.

Ursula was just about to comment 'they must be ours', when puffs like distant exploding mushrooms appeared below them – and these in increasing numbers. Then there was the boom of heavy artillery fire, and the dull crump of falling bombs reached them from the direction of Kumbhirgram airfield. The airfield was just out of sight of the village, so everyone ran to the nearest viewpoint.

The plain below was engulfed in red dust, but they could hear the hum of receding bombers and the occasional loud report from within the dust cloud – either anti-aircraft fire or the sound of exploding ammunition. As the cloud of dust settled there was one large building on fire, but it was too distant to make out details. Namkia came rushing over to Ursula, 'The guns hit one! We saw something falling, but we couldn't see where it went because of the sun!' He couldn't be sure if it was in the Watch and Ward area – but he suspected it was more towards Manipur.

There was nothing that could be done from such a distance, but the raid had brought the war very close to home for the villagers of Khangnam. With the need for such an observation post firmly underlined, Ursula made all the necessary arrangements and returned to Laisong.

23

The Japanese Arrive

By March 1944 Ursula had been managing the Watch and Ward operation for eighteen months. On the whole, administration and operations had developed so that things ran on rails. The guns – still the old muzzle-loaders – had been man enough for what the scouts needed to do, and the men had become proficient with them. There had been a bad outbreak of smallpox in the Khangnam area to the south, where Ursula had set up her aircraft observation post – and it came at the worst possible time when the area was cut off by the annual rains. A vaccinator had visited the village, but had not been thorough enough, and twenty per-cent of the population had been wiped out. Following this tragedy, many villagers were still incapacitated and unable to bring in the harvest, but because of good communications and the ready exchange of information that Ursula had set up, 'V' Force relief arrived in the nick of time to prevent the additional scourges of hunger and starvation.

In fact, the Barail area had never had such a high level of government assistance. Ursula was determined to deliver on her promise, and once 'V' Force HQ appreciated the effectiveness of her operation, they were happy to support her. They had mepacrine, red blankets, powder and shot – all that had been promised – and more. They even had the full-time service of a medical officer, and Ursula was satisfied that she had earned all the support and trust that she had demanded when they were recruiting.

In January, Ursula had given Doris a hint of her occupation, signing a letter, 'your "Jolly-near-a-subaltern" Winkle' Her mother could only guess at what her daughter was up to on the other side of the world. In fact, she was, in all but title, a military commander, and she was leading from the front.

With her hereditary affinities, Ursula chose a Scottish example to illustrate her theory on leadership:

> I think it was Dundee who said that no-one could lead a Highland Army who had not shaken every man in it by the hand, and much the same is true of the Assam Hillman, to whom any leader is first among equals and nothing more. His attachment is not to the unit, but is entirely personal, and you cannot count on any man unless that attachment exists.

All the same, 150 miles behind the frontline, it seemed unlikely that 'V' Force's scouts would have to deal with anything much more than a handful of undercover Japanese operators in their territory. It looked as if Ursula's dedication and absolute insistence on fulfilling every promise to her Zemi recruits, to the letter, would at best turn out to have been a brilliant Naga-relations coup. Even as such, it was of incalculable value to the government, but in March, the situation changed.

On the 28th, Ursula tuned into the amenities radio for the midday news and was stunned to hear that the Japanese had attacked along the Manipur front and were driving forward. Other details were not forthcoming. Perry had written to her days before to warn her to keep her eyes peeled for infiltrators, but had been unable to commit to paper any better detail.

Shortly after midday Namkia joined her in her bungalow. She could tell by his look, as surely as if the dogs had started barking, that she could expect strangers. 'Who is it?' 'Two Sepoy-Sahibs.'

Two British sergeants were waiting for her on the veranda and they were quick to deliver their news. 'It's like this. Fifty Japs crossed the Imphal road at Kangpokpi about a week ago, and they ought to be here by now. We wondered if you'd heard anything of them. We've been sent from Silchar to see.'

Ursula was stunned at the implications of fifty Japanese at large, but she later recalled hearing herself adopt a bright tone and asking the sergeants into the bungalow for tea while they talked it over.

The existing frontline was along the railway – it was no longer 150 miles in front of them. It was 20 miles behind them. So Ursula and her Nagas were now the only thing between the railway and the advancing Japanese.

Maintaining a veneer of calm, the sergeants asked Ursula what forces she had at her disposal – and she replied that she had 150 native scouts, one service rifle, one single-barrelled shotgun and seventy muzzle-loaders. They agreed that Ursula would put every available man along the line of the Jiri River, with a brief to report back immediately on any Japanese approach. The sergeants assured her that they would report to HQ and do their best to have support sent up from Silchar.

The 150-mile buffer area between them and the frontline was now unsafe – gone. Hers was the most remote area of all in respect of Japanese infiltration, and now all that distance had been swamped and, as she put it, 'rolled up'. There were pockets of resistance at Imphal and Kohima – the former being under siege – but the rest of the region was open country which was quickly filling up with Japanese.

Ursula called up her scouts and, with studied calm, gave them their orders for the watch along the Jiri. Paodekumba was marvellously unmoved and set off at once. She then gave Namkia most of the news, expressing her expectation that support troops would be with them in no time. Then they briefed runners to go back, away from the Jiri, to call up the best men from the villages to the rear.

By the next day, Ursula was satisfied that the frontier was adequately covered – but her men still didn't have the full picture. It didn't take a military genius to realise that her own camp, up against a steep-sided hill with a single entrance channel would make a deadly trap. She would have dearly liked to decamp into the jungle to sleep at night, but that would set off a real panic. She couldn't afford to do that, so she cultivated an air of nonchalance and slept as usual in her bungalow.

In an area where communications had previously been extraordinarily slow, messages were now passing at remarkable speed, and Ursula soon received a note from Perry summoning her to a conference in Mahur on 1 April.

She found the small town's station in an anxious flurry of activity, all available troops being mustered and deployed against the immediate threat of the Japanese arriving. Indoors the atmosphere was tense, as Ursula, Perry and a number of officers gathered around a table in a small, lamplit room. The bald facts were that the Japanese were on their way, but no-one could say where they would arrive first. It was crucial that they find out immediately, as there were not enough troops available to cover the whole of the line. There was no wireless communication set up, so they had to rely on the railway telephone. This being open for anyone to listen in, they adopted a code including the term 'one elephant' to signify 'ten Japs', which would have been quite serviceable until someone arrived at the Silchar border with a genuine herd of forty elephants, thereby causing untold panic and confusion. As far as they knew, it was still a group of fifty Japanese that was at large in the area.

The immediate plan was to send out a patrol of company strength the following day in search of those fifty elusive Japanese. This was a job for 'V' Force, and Ursula decided to contact overall HQ, which had joined general Army HQ in Comilla. Her cable read, 'GOING FORWARD TO LOOK FOR THE ENEMY. KINDLY SEND RIFLES AND AMMUNITION SOONEST'.

Shortly after sending this, she received a signal, evidently sent before her cable arrived at HQ, the gist of which was 'get out, and get out quick!' Colonel Scott at HQ could respond in one of two ways – he could support her and get the rifles sent up, or order her out of the area. On reflection, she concluded that the latter was the more likely, however, she would carry on as if this were not on the cards. The one thing that she knew beyond any doubt was that if she buckled and ran away, the Nagas would not stand firm. There was no question of deserting them, and she needed to get back to her base as soon as possible.

The following day, Ursula and Namkia headed back towards Laisong with the patrol of the Chamar Regiment. The men, sepoys recently mustered from the plains, were below top fitness and couldn't keep up with her and Namkia on the steep ascents, so they only got as far as Asalu by nightfall. Even after a night's rest, the men were soon flagging, and three of them were so exhausted that they couldn't carry their kit. The company commander, Willy, picked up one pack, Namkia and Ramgakpa another apiece – and then a fourth man went down. Willy had been chivvying them along, covering double the distance as he marched up and down the column, and when he reached the latest casualty, he gave him a shake and explained that there wasn't far to go. The man just groaned, so Willy reached for his kit bag. 'All right. The Miss-Sahib'll carry your kit. Up you get – come along.' The man grabbed back his kit and marched on to Laisong unaided.

The patrol proper went out the following day, first to Thingje, and then to Hangrum, through burning heat and on hard, dry paths. All the way, the scouts foraged through the thick woods and vegetation for any signs of the Japanese having passed that way – but there was nothing. In the meantime, as Ursula neared her Laisong camp, one of her scouts, Zhekuingba, came out to meet her. 'There's a 'V' Force Sahib here.'

Ursula's first thought was that this was probably the officer sent to take over from her, and that she was about to be ordered out, but she resolved to put on a brave face. She turned the corner of the veranda and saw a tall, fair-haired captain sitting by her table. On seeing her, he jumped to his feet and introduced himself. 'Hello. I'm Albright. Scotty sent me along.'

As she shook his hand, something on the floor in the corner of the room caught her eye. There, all stacked up, were cases of rifles, tommy-guns, ammunition, grenades and, oh joy, extra rations. 'V' Force was backing her up. Apparently, when her cable crossed with the wire telling her to get out, Colonel Scott had responded immediately:

> My OC clapped his bush hat on his head, looked at my signal which was quite unintentionally pure Nelson, and rushed round to see Slim. He slapped the telegram on the desk and said, 'From Miss Bower, Sir!' Slim looked at it and said, 'We must support her.'

And support he did, not only by giving her the material assistance she needed, but by giving proof that he had confidence in her.

Unfortunately the good news stopped there. Albright gave her a summary of what had happened in other areas. 'V' Ops 2 and 3 – the Imphal and Kohima groups respectively – had broken up and were now scattered all over the map. A good many of their Kuki scouts were from groups involved in the 1918 rebellion and had no wish to fight for the British, so they had played a double game. When the Japanese had appeared, they dropped all pretence of support for the British and openly joined the enemy. Disastrously, they had led them to every 'V' Force camp and supply cache in the region, and now the majority of the officers were missing. Some had managed to escape and had made it to HQ in Comilla – only time would tell how successful the rest had been in avoiding capture in what was now Japanese-held territory. Murray from 'V' Ops 3 had made a fighting retreat from Shangshak, Ruther from the same group had managed to get into Kohima town itself, while another officer, Betts, was still missing. There was a desperate manpower crisis as HQ staff had been deployed throughout the area to fill in the gaps, so Scott was left with only a skeleton support and the clerks at HQ.

While small numbers of Japanese might recce the area under the cover of the forests, large troop numbers would need to use recognised roads, so it was Ursula's scouts' task to hang on in the area for as long as possible and keep watch over these main arteries for any enemy movement. On first sighting, they should send word to Haflong and then decamp to safety.

However, even though the scouts were armed only for their own protection, such was the enthusiasm with which they threw themselves into the task once they had better arms, that a method of patrolling was regularised across all the Watch and Ward areas, with potential for taking aggressive action. One scout would go fifty yards ahead of either the next scout or the main body of the patrol with an officer. There would then be another fifty-yard gap and a second officer. The patrol would progress cautiously through whatever terrain they had to tackle, the rationale being that the fifty-yard gap would allow the first scout time to make a silent, invisible retreat if he spotted any enemy en route, and inform the rest of the patrol so that they could set an ambush. The Japanese were well trained to set up their light machine-guns and get them into action quickly, so the idea was to launch a lightning ambush, and if they couldn't take out all the enemy, they should get out as fast as possible down the road before the Japanese got into action. If the patrol had to disperse into the cover of the jungle, they would reassemble at an appointed rendezvous. If the Japanese kept on coming, the patrol would ambush them again, and again if necessary.

The speed with which the Japanese had overrun the Imphal and Kohima areas had left the British no time to set up a screen between the Barak and Jiri rivers, so Ursula's area was left vulnerable to attack. She had recruited her men as scouts, not as a fighting force, and with no proper military defence in front of them, they would be easy meat for a strong advancing Japanese contingent – even with their new guns. Their triangular patrol area now lay before them as a void with no field telephone or wireless transmitter, and where there were no contacts or outposts from which to receive information. Their frontline was now along the Haijaichak pass, and from there they would have no more than an hour's warning of any advance.

The immediate need was to set up a chain of communications to pass on the alarm if the enemy was sighted heading up from the Imphal Plain. Ursula organised a string of beacons and a back-up of runners, stretching from the frontline to Laisong and on to Haflong. If a beacon was lit, it meant that they had contacted the enemy. Although there were some false alarms caused by spring grass-fires, the system served well enough in the absence of wireless communications.

On a longer term basis, there were patrols to run every day, and Ursula's Naga scouts liaised with the regular troops to guide them in the jungle. Life in the camp took on a very different aspect from the days of anthropology and dispensaries. Ursula likened it to living like gazelles when lions were about. Everything was arranged so that they could decamp into the woods at a moment's notice, and everyone kept their guns about them, even on forays to the kitchen garden. The twelve new rifles were distributed among Ursula's top scouts, there were a few tommy-guns, and Ursula carried a Sten gun:

> I had a Sten – a tommy-gun was too heavy, with the .45 ammo. I didn't like a Sten – they go off when you look at them – but the .38 clips were much lighter to carry. I could take two full clips instead of staggering along under two tommy-gun clips, which held much fewer rounds. So I had my Sten and at various times I had a .38 automatic sidearm – and my kukri. And at one point I had a .32 automatic pistol.

All this weaponry held no fear for Ursula:

> My father started me on a .22, and while he was still in the Navy, he gave both my brother and myself training using the standard Army rifle – the .303 – so I was quite used to both of them. And I could use a shotgun and automatic pistol too.

Her father could never have envisaged how handy these home-taught skills would prove to be.

Everyone watched for the beacons during the day – although if they came, the Japanese were most likely to come under cover of darkness. With this in mind, the Chamars, Ursula and the scouts (effectively now her personal bodyguard) left the camp at night to sleep in hollowed-out shelters in the area of dense low scrub to the north.

While marauding Japanese might spare unarmed villagers, there would be no mercy for armed scouts, so just one man was left as a sentry in the camp with instructions to fire a single shot if the Japs arrived.

Over the next three weeks, the Nagas hollowed out a veritable honeycomb of tunnels and chambers in the scrub, and they alternated from one group of shelters to another every night so that no outsider could ever know where they were. Provision was made for holing up en route out if they had to escape, and caches of tinned food were buried along all potential exit roads.

For Ursula, the worst element of this nocturnal exodus was the sense of treachery she felt, creeping back into the camp each morning, having effectively left all there to their fate overnight. There was always the chance that the Japanese could have arrived and overrun it:

> The old friendly camp was a potential enemy; all those green tunnels of roads, where I had walked and where the dogs had run, known to the last twig – tunnels where we now went in single file, scouts out, expecting ambushes, looking ahead for danger.

One thing was certain, if the Japanese arrived, while the Nagas might be able to blend into the background, there was no hope at all of Ursula being able to conceal herself in the village – she was much too tall and light-skinned. While her hair was normally quite dark, it had become very sun-bleached, so everything about her marked her as a European. If she had to make a run for it, it would have been madness to try in broad daylight. At a stretch, and under cover of darkness, she might have passed for a Kuki – but it would have been a very long shot.

Adamant about staying put, Ursula needed a contingency plan – so she and Namkia came to an arrangement. Looking back, Ursula was the first to admit that it was terribly melodramatic, but the tale had reached them of an officer in Burma who had given himself up and who had been slowly and mercilessly tortured to death. She had no intention of letting this happen to her. If the Japanese threatened to capture her, she would shoot herself and Namkia could take in her head if the pressure on the villagers to give her up grew unendurable. As she reflected after the war, 'Fortunately it never came to that anyway – for which I was devoutly thankful.'

With the Chamars in position, Ursula would have quite understood if the Watch and Ward recruits felt that they had done enough and could leave the defence of the area to the trained soldiers. With the Japanese expected any day, it would have made sense to save their skins and try to survive to look after their families. Ursula's heart sank when her twelve rifle-bearing bodyguards reported to her and asked for twenty-four hours' leave:

> I thought, 'Here it comes – they've reached the limit, and I don't blame them. We never recruited them for this, they're not trained for it, they're not armed for it, and I cannot hold them. We've got this very small chance of getting out of it alive, and I simply cannot ask them to go with me on a suicide mission.' So I said, 'All right – you go,' never thinking I would see them again. Much to my surprise, every single man was back within the stipulated twenty-four hours, and it wasn't until

about ten days later, when the excitement was over and we had time to breathe and reinforcements had arrived, I noticed that Namkia was not wearing his beautiful gold and yellow deo-moni bead necklaces, which were such a valuable feature of his costume. I asked him what had happened to them, and he then explained that all of them had gone home, arranged for the guardianship of their wives and families in the event of their death, which they expected to take place within three days, had made their wills, handed over their heirlooms and property to their families for their heirs. They were all comparatively young men, they had young families, quite young children and everything to lose – and they never thought they would survive. I didn't think I was going to either, so we were all square on that, but they had returned to meet the end with us, and they now wore only their beads for burial. I'm afraid I rather goggled at Namkia. This had taken me so much by surprise, and he said, 'What did you expect? How could we have we abandoned you – left you, a woman, alone to face it, while we fled to safety? How could we have lived afterwards, to hear our children called after by others in the village street, "Child of a coward!" It was far better to remain and die with you.' I felt about six inches high.

24

Meeting Slim

The parlous situation without updated information or proper communications continued into May. Kohima was under siege and the Imphal Plain was crawling with Japanese – this much they knew – but otherwise, Ursula and her scouts, in their camp perched on a very visible spur at Laisong, were in the dark.

While there was still the prospect of the Japanese arriving at any time, another diversion took their concentration away from the main event. As the only force available, they were tasked with rounding up some forty or fifty men of the Bengali and Madrassi Pioneers who had managed to get out of Imphal, and who had deserted as their officers marched them out through the Tamenglong subdivision. This took around two weeks, and as a 'spur-of-the-moment' exercise, proved very unsatisfactory. One of the reasons for desertion might well have been the desperate shortage of food, but once they'd rounded them up, Ursula and her scouts had nothing with which to feed them either. All the men were left to camp out, bedraggled and hungry, in the market sheds.

Further distractions stretched the capacity of the scouts in the wake of the Pioneer problem. The Japanese, although surprisingly not advancing into the Barail from the plains, were overrunning the Imphal road running west, taking over major camps en route. In the panic preceding the Japanese arrival, the camp personnel started leaving in their droves. Some went out in good order, while others took to the road in dribs and drabs, straggling towards the hills, hungry and exhausted. The men were mainly drivers, mechanics, artisans, water-carriers and auxiliaries from all over India – not regular troops – and they were not trained or disciplined for sustained marching. They were joined by small groups of Naga refugees from the mission stations, mainly pastors and teachers, some families of Gurkha graziers and a few ragged prisoners who had managed to escape from Japanese captivity. This human tide had to be rounded up and given food and medical attention as necessary, questioned, then escorted to the rear. It was the armed stragglers who proved the most serious problem, as in the Manipur area, between the Barak and Jiri rivers, they were running out of control. The local Naga people tried to help them, but the armed fugitives were roughing them up and looting their property. With no way of defending themselves against firearms, the Naga villagers had been forced to take to the woods, abandoning the villages where observation posts and runners had been stationed. In only a matter of days, the whole intelligence network was falling apart.

Ursula had been joined by an under-strength platoon of Mohendra Dals – Nepalese State Troops – so she was still hopelessly under-powered to handle any major insurgency in her area. The arrival of Albright with a platoon of Gurkhas to swell the ranks came as a gift from the gods.

Albright foresaw all manner of problems with a civilian woman being given command of a platoon – let alone one of proud, highly trained Gurhkas from the Assam Rifles. He couldn't predict how they would respond to being given orders by a woman. The officer had his orders, however, and he was to leave the platoon with her:

> Leave it he did, and it wasn't for us to look a gift-platoon in the mouth, especially just then. They hadn't been with us more than a few days when the main surge from the eastward came. I could do nothing with the stragglers without rank-badges, so we split Albright's. He wore captain's pips on the left shoulder, I on the right. It was most effective.

Ursula and her new 'bodyguard' had been practising ambushes on a road in the Jenam valley one day when a massive thunderstorm drove them to take shelter in the rest-house. They were sheltering on the veranda when Albright spotted two very wet Nagas running towards them. One was a senior figure, as he wore a red cloth – and by their haircuts Ursula marked them down as being from the Thingje group. Once in the shelter of the veranda, one of them talked very angrily about something to Namkia as he wrung out his soaking cloth. They had come from Impuiloa, and they had just been subjected to a looting spree by some of the refugees from the Imphal road. Four or five of them had swept in wielding guns, and looted the headman's house and other nearby villagers' homes. The looters were now heading towards Haijaichak and would probably be there by now. The two of them had taken a short cut out of Impuiloa to get ahead of them – now they needed help to capture the thieves.

Ursula, the Mohendra Dals, Namkia, the scouts, Albright and six Gurkhas set off for Haijaichak, some four miles away. As they neared the village, two Nagas rushed out to meet them – it was Hailamsuong, a scout from the village, and his lieutenant, Gailuba.

Based at Haijaichak, Hailamsuong had created an efficient team. Now, however, the visitations by looters were threatening the lines of communication on which they depended for advance warning. Menaced by gun-toting robbers, men were forced to leave their observation posts, and they had just suffered such a raid.

The looters had arrived from Impuiloa, driven the look-out from his post and then swept into the village, looting and forcing the inhabitants from their homes. Alarmingly, their numbers seemed to have swelled en route to around thirty, but the Haijaichak men couldn't wait to get at them. With some armed support they could restore the villagers' property and teach them a lesson.

Everything was quiet as they approached the village, and as they paused at the foot of a path leading up to the village, some local scouts joined them. Looking up, Ursula and Albright held their breath as an armed man hove into view and seemed to gaze right down on them. No-one moved and miraculously they seemed to have gone un-noticed, as the man turned and disappeared. If he had seen them, he must have taken them for another bunch of refugees.

Pushing Ursula behind a large standing stone, Albright issued his orders. She was to stay put with her scouts, and he and the Mohendra Dals and Gurkhas would go ahead.

His parting shot was, 'If we get in a jam – well, use your head and join in.' Ursula saw that this was no time to argue, so watched as Albright took five sepoys into the village. The Gurhkas were just visible, bayonets fixed, checking the abandoned houses. While some of the local troops had only recently been brought together from the plains, the Gurhkas were career soldiers, hardened by gruelling and intensive training, and they had no qualms about taking on six times their number in close combat.

Hailamsuong stood at Ursula's shoulder, agitated. 'Will there be shooting, my mother? My wife and child are hidden in my house.' Ursula was firm and, even if half expecting to have to go in support, reassured him immediately. 'The Captain Sahib is very clever. He will take them without shooting if he can.' They waited in silence as minutes ticked past and there was no shooting – in fact, no sound of anything.

Suddenly Albright appeared, smiling. They had been conducting a methodical house-to-house search when a villager had beckoned them over and whispered that the looters were all in the morung. Albright had tiptoed up and peered through the window – the men had left all their guns in a stack against the wall and were enjoying a meal of looted food. It was all embarrassingly simple – the offenders were no hardened gangsters and had set no lookout, so Albright and the Gurkhas had simply walked in, rounded them up at gunpoint and taken them prisoner.

The exercise had been a resounding success – the local people rushed back to their homes and any looted goods were restored. The prisoners were a rag-tag lot, especially when deprived of their arms – and they trudged off under armed escort, the Naga porters carrying their weapons in baskets behind them. The immediate problem solved, Ursula and Albright arranged to set up a Bren-gun post for Hailamsuong, to prevent any recurrence of the trouble.

Another incident which underlined Ursula and Albright's authority was when the Staff Captain shot a looter who tried to break away from his escort after he had been arrested. As she explained to Doris by letter,

> The SC was a bit shook up, so I had to collect the bits and bury them. I thought I was never going to manage it, but when it came to the point, I was so wild about having had the villages looted that I didn't care a hoot, and I got the whole thing done. It was a godsend, because the word went round that we meant business, and the looting was under control from then on. The Gurkhas thought we were the goods.

The arrival of the Gurkhas gave everyone a lot more confidence, and with regular training, Ursula was honing her Laisong recruits into a disciplined fighting force. What they didn't know about surviving in the jungle and the hill regions wasn't worth knowing, and with plenty of practice in team tactics and use of their new weapons, it might just be that, Japs or no Japs, they would get through.

The Japanese had been besieging Kohima since 6 April, and the garrison came under relentless fire until the troops were driven into a small area on the aptly named Garrison Hill. By the middle of the month the situation was desperate. There was heavy fighting around District Commissioner Pawsey's bungaslow, garden and tennis court, and the Japanese held the road west of Kohima Ridge closed against any supplies getting in. While food and ammunition were short everywhere in the besieged area, the garrison was fast coming to the end of their drinking water. Eventually, as

May drew to a close, the wounded had been evacuated, and the British 6th Infantry Brigade moved in as the fighting continued for Garrison Hill. Monsoon conditions turned the area into a quagmire, making fighting on the hills of Kohima Ridge almost impossible. However, the British Army brought in mountain howitzers, 25-pounder field guns and 5.5-inch medium guns, and by sheer force of arms began to drive the Japanese back. The tables turned and by the end of May, Japanese supply lines had been cut and it was they who were feeling the pinch.

With the relief of Kohima, the Japanese were driven from one of the roads leading to Ursula's area, and this released a half-section of the 3rd Assam Rifles who, triumphant but exhausted, joined her at Laisong, along with Lieutenant Bill Tibbetts of 'V' Force. They dug themselves shelters, took off their boots, put down their bed-rolls and slept for forty-eight hours. They re-emerged, washed, cleaned their kit until it sparkled – and were ready to take on the Japanese again.

Ursula soon got to know them – they were highly trained and disciplined fighters with morale soaring from their success in Kohima. Lance-Naik Supbahadur Rana and Rifleman Riki Ram (known as Mickey Mouse due to his skinny appearance) were Gurkhas, while the other four were Nagas – three Lhotas and one Ao. Their arrival injected new spirit into the growing Laisong force – these were men who had the measure of the Japs and were up and ready to go kill some more. This rubbed off on Ursula's men, 'We had rather the same idea ourselves, but unfortunately there were no Japs.'

Ursula handed over operations to Bill Tibbetts and worked in close liaison, as she dealt with 'Ack and Quack' – administration and quartermaster – along with the co-ordination of intelligence. With Ursula's help, Tibbetts quickly gained the trust of the Zemi people – to such an extent that Ursula began to feel that if Slim should ever insist that she be taken out for safety's sake, the Nagas would very probably stay and follow Tibbetts. However, leaving was not an option.

From time to time Ursula would go to 'V' Force HQ in Comilla – the staff there obligingly used to summon her down at intervals on the pretext of collecting supplies, but they all knew that it was largely an excuse for her to carry on to Calcutta and get much needed new clothes and, a rare vanity, a perm. On one such occasion, her commanding officer came rushing to her hut, shouting as he ran, 'Miss Bower, get your best clothes on – Slim wants you!' Ursula's cool head and unflappable composure went to pieces as she prepared to meet the commander of the Fourteenth Army:

> I hurriedly changed into the best dress I could find anywhere, was hastily inspected by my CO to see that my stocking seams were straight and my petticoat wasn't showing, was bundled into a jeep and driven down to HQ. There I was taken over by a very smart brigadier. HQ building was an enormous long block, and the veranda seemed to go on for ever. We walked up this and all along the right side, brass hats all round, until we got to a point where there were full colonels pushing tea trolleys – then we got to the last office. The brigadier swung sharp right, knocked on the door, saluted very smartly and said, 'Miss Bower, Sir.' I was so scared I missed my cue, my knees were knocking, and it was a good five or six seconds before I could get under way. I shut my eyes, marched straight forward, which I judged was about right, and then turned left and opened my eyes. There behind the desk, looking astounded as I

was, was Bill Slim. He leapt up, held out his hand, shook mine warmly and said, 'Oh thank God. I thought you would be a lady missionary with creaking stays.' After that we got on like a house on fire.

With General Slim's support and Colonel Scott organising equipment and supplies, communications suddenly got better. An entire W/T set-up for a net of four stations was sent up to Ursula. The equipment came with instructions that the network was to be called Bower Force, in support of Miss Bower of 'V' Force. The senior officer who received it thought it a splendid joke and laughed as he read it. 'Ha ha – very funny. Who made this up?' The officer who had delivered it was quite straight-faced. 'Excuse me, sir, but it's not a joke.' All this wireless kit had been scraped together at a time of crisis to support what Ursula termed, 'a sideshow such as ours', but this confirmed the importance of her role. Endorsed by General Slim, Bower Force became an operational network.

The plan was to position a wireless post at each of four strategic villages – Silchar, Tamenglong, Nungba and Laisong, each manned by a signaller and a junior who would protect him as he worked. The signaller sent to work directly with Ursula was a man called Ison, who had a marvellous understanding of the cumbersome and often capricious piece of kit that was his wireless set.

With Bower Force's field of operations expanding, she was pleased to receive reinforcements in the shape of a company of Mahrattas under the command of one Captain Archer, who took the place of the Mohendra Dals. The aim was to have as many scouts as possible trained to be proficient with a rifle, and Namkia, who for some time had been using a Bren gun, was learning all about tommy-guns from Archer's Havildar-Instructor. It was during one such instruction session between the bungalow and the garden, that a Japanese fighter plane came screeching down over them, and everyone dived instinctively for cover. No-one had been hurt, but the incident convinced Archer that he needed to find a site concealed from the air for his camp. At last they found a spot on the east face of the hill where there was good cover from the tall bamboos and thick jungle. One drawback, even before the camp was built, was the fact that, from the abundance of pug-marks, Ursula could see that it was in the middle of a regular game run, but Archer was convinced that animals would avoid the area once they got the whiff of humans.

The camp went ahead and the Mahrattas moved in, with field-telephone links set up between that camp, Haijaichak and Laisong. It was of no satisfaction to Ursula to be proved right regarding the likelihood of large animals using Archer's new camp as a thoroughfare, but she was amused by one particular incident. One night Archer's quartermaster noticed that the camp's three goats were in a state of agitation and, looking beyond them, saw a large leopard crouching, just a few yards from him, ready to pounce. In a rash burst of courage, he ran over, untied the goats and with two under one arm and one under the other, staggered down to the quarter-guard's lock-up shed, then got the guard out. Needless to say, the leopard had gone, but they searched around until they came to a crossing of paths, one of which led to Archer's hut. While they were discussing what to do, the leopard walked out of Archer's hut and out on to the path, fixed them with a contemptuous green stare and vanished into the jungle.

Archer had been in bed, under his mosquito net and enjoying a last cigarette before turning in, when in the dim light a large creature had pushed through the door curtain and settled on the floor beside his bed. He couldn't see it once it lay down – it was too far under the edge of his camp bed so, assuming it was 'one of Miss Bower's dogs' he thought no more of it. It then dawned on him that Ursula's dogs had been sent on to Silchar – so perhaps it was a village dog. Craning carefully to see through his mosquito net, he realised that the shape next to him was too large to be any sort of dog. He was then gripped by a series of impulses which he was sure would make the thing turn on him. He felt fluff in his throat and needed to cough, his cigarette had burned down to his fingers and he needed to put it out – and he fought an irresistible urge to turn over. His bed seemed to creak even as he breathed – eventually he could hold back a cough no longer and he spluttered as he tried to suppress it. The leopard, for such it was, rose with great dignity until it was sitting, looking at him like a huge dog. It fixed him with a look of contempt and stalked out.

Undeterred by leopards, the Mahrattas built their machine-gun post on Ursula's spur, which had a commanding view over three river valleys. Now they had a good chance, with skilful marksmanship, of bringing down any low-flying Japanese aircraft. It wasn't long before the opportunity arose to try it out, as the lookouts spotted an aircraft diving down towards them from out of the sun. Tibbetts squinted into the brightness and, a former ack-ack man, he knew the silhouette of every plane at a glance. In the nick of time he recognised its outline and stopped the gunner – it was a communications plane from Imphal and probably full of generals. Slim might not have felt so kindly disposed towards Bower Force if their machine-gunners were responsible for a lot of dead generals in the vegetable garden – still, it was a foolhardy thing to dive out of the sun over a position which the pilot must have known housed an armed post.

As the dissemination of intelligence improved throughout the area, it became apparent that the Japanese had not tried to infiltrate through Ursula's original area of command, but instead diverted the troops south from Manipur to the plains. Now the situation was changing, and as Bower Force's command area grew in size, new information suggested that the best hope of locating the Japanese would be to move forward.

35

Searching for the Japanese

After the relief of Kohima in late April, the forces from Imphal and 2nd Division from Dimapur were going through Kohima and forcing the Japanese together at the north of the Imphal Plain, so there was a good chance that some of them might try to break back through Ursula's expanding area of operation. Tamenglong was the most forward of the wireless posts, and Ursula asked for permission to set up a screen of observation right forward into Manipur towards the plain itself, to keep an eye on Japanese moves. Albright had started the plan, but was recalled to HQ, however, once Tibbetts took over from him, all arrangements were in place and in the middle of May permission came to advance to Tamenglong.

The move was no small undertaking, and Ursula and Tibbetts set out with six Assam Rifles, fifteen scouts, Ison the signaller and 100 Zemi porters. A Mahratta patrol had cleared the route ahead of them as they moved out towards Kangpokpi, and shortly after them, Archer would bring in his company to take on any Japanese that the scouting parties found for them. Across the swollen Barak River, they carried on towards Tamenglong, where Ursula found the camp she had inhabited in 1938 completely overgrown and lost amongst the grass and creepers. The summerhouse lay in ruins, and Ursula remembered the time, so long ago, when she and the SDO had sat there, looking out at Hemeolowa mountain towards Hangrum. Duncan had explained to her about the disastrous Hangrum attack, and Ursula had wondered at the time if she would ever have the chance to go there. A lot of water had passed under the bridge – she had little thought when she first visited the fort with Mrs Duncan, that she would be commanding the area against Japanese invasion.

Shortly before their arrival the village had been strafed in error by the RAF. Consequently, although there had fortunately been no serious casualties, the tin roofs of the bungalow and other camp buildings had been perforated like pepper-pots and leaked like huge shower-heads. Two minor casualties were sustained – there was a bullet-hole through the Gurkha NCO's only pair of trousers, and the SDO's cat had its shoulder slightly winged. A message had been sent to ask the RAF not to do it again, but there remained a risk until further confirmation – and the hut roofs were now in need of urgent repair to be habitable during the rains.

Something seemed to be holding up Archer and his men, so Ursula sat tight in the resthouse and used the time to get a full update from the SDO. He had been soldiering on single-handed since the start of the invasion without any support or orders from the Army and with the minimum of resources. He had set up his own intelligence screen, covering an area extending three days' march away, through which he was able to get news by relay-runners within twenty-four hours.

The SDO was haunted too by the unknown fate of a man called Sharp. As an officer in the Indian Civil Service in Imphal, he knew the district well, so when invasion loomed, he was taken into the Army and sent to set up an intelligence screen in the gap between the Watch and Ward area and the Imphal–Kohima road. Sharp had never reached Tamenglong, and the SDO feared that the Japanese forward party had turned back towards the south and come out at Haochong between Imphal and Tamenglong. Sharp had probably arrived at the Haochong resthouse just after the Japanese and it seemed inevitable that he had been captured there and killed. Strained by his long period working alone and exhausted, these incidents still caused him a great deal of distress.

A week passed and still no Archer, and as Bower Force watched the Laisong road for any sign of him, Ursula had a gut feeling that something had gone wrong with communications with Imphal – signals were sent, but there was still no answer as to why the fighting force hadn't arrived:

> We sat and chafed in the small rest-house. The holes in the roofs leaked; the pine-branches scuffed on the tin; and out between the trees we could see the hills where the Japs were. To add to their woes, mild dysentery broke out, attacking all of us except Ison. Bill Tibbetts, for some reason, had it badly and was almost incapacitated for the first few days of June.

Ursula's men extended their patrols in the hope of locating the Japanese. At least now intelligence was good, so that information was coming in from far out in Japanese-held territory about three days' brisk march away – some thirty miles. Ursula received reports every day of Japanese foraging parties, with tales of dumps left unguarded and mule convoys carrying supplies escorted by just a couple of men. Already some Kuki villages were assisting the enemy, and with maps laid out, Ursula and Tibbetts could trace the Japanese progress, just three or four days away, as they went to villages to get food. Some of these easy pickings were within close range, but orders were to wait for Archer's men, so they sat and waited.

Just once the chance to raid a Japanese forage dump seemed too good to miss – after a night march from Tamenglong, fit troops could launch a surprise dawn raid. Information was that the dump was full of looted rice, and since the Japanese had no idea that there were British forces within range, it was practically unguarded. Ursula envisaged a short, sharp raid, attacking with machine-guns and grenades at dawn – the whole dump could be up in flames in minutes and the enemy deprived of at least a month's food. Tibbets briefed the Mahrattas with the plan, guides were engaged, and since Archer and his men were not there to lead the attack, a young Punjabi lieutenant took command.

There was no question of Ursula accompanying them,

> I would not go on any long-distance raid – not unless there was absolutely no alternative. I just hadn't got the marching capacity, good though I was, of the men. I should have been a liability, so I stayed where I was and minded the house and prepared to send reinforcements or messages or do anything that was required.

The party got to within six miles of the dump – and the lieutenant simply lost his nerve and ordered everyone back. It was more than frustrating – the Mahrattas, some of whom had fought in the Western Desert, were experienced veterans and wanted to get into the action. This was such an easy raid and the men were furious at not carrying it out. The oldest of the NCOs was 'a delightful old gentleman Subedar' called Sarungki-Sahib – 'a dear old gentleman who couldn't have been a better soldier or a nicer person.'

Ursula was waiting when the raiding party returned:

> When they got back with nothing achieved, I saw what I never thought to see – Sarungki came into the office where Bill and I were sitting. He tore off his tin hat, threw it on the ground and burst into tears with shame – the sheer shame that had been brought on his regiment by this windy boy turning back when they were almost in sight of the objective. If only Tibbetts or Archer had been there, they'd have made it. The reason the chap gave was that they were running late and it was getting too light. But that wouldn't have stopped the Mahrattas – they'd have gone in. We had the most dreadful time comforting poor Sarungki. It was an absolute disgrace to a very fine regiment. I really felt for him.

It was all too frustrating – but worse was to come. Ursula received a signal to say that 200 Japanese and a field gun were approaching Tamenglong so they should all get out at once. From the diligent work of all the scouts, everyone in Tamenglong knew this to be untrue:

> I think it was pure funk on the part of the authorities on my behalf that made them send us back. Because there was no truth in the signal they sent us that a Jap force was advancing on us. It never was and it never did. They merely wanted to get me back and out of the danger zone, which annoyed us very much.

There had been too much waiting, bungling and, most of all, waste of all the good work put in by Albright and the SDO. Now Ison was left alone with his wireless – and Ursula felt that if it was not safe enough for her and Tibbetts, then it was unsafe for Ison too. Her only consolation was that she felt he had bonded well with the Nagas there and if he had had to move out in face of imminent Japanese invasion, they would have made sure he got away safely.

Bitterly, Ursula packed up her camp. As they marched out, Tibbett's dysentery came back with a vengeance, but he took his medicine, kept going and never complained. Despite his illness, they went on to Hepoloa the next day, where the Observer Corps, going in the opposite direction towards Tamenglong, were occupying their quarters. All orders seemed to have gone crazy, and the only thing they wanted was to get back to Laisong and restore communications directly with HQ. Back at 'home', Ursula learned that Archer had gone down with dysentery just before he was due to set out for Tamenglong and his colonel, old and about to retire, refused to send another company up, despite the fact that his British officers were up in arms in protest and, as Ursula suspected, knowing the Mahrattas' spirit, the troops as well.

It was a while after their reluctant withdrawal that Ursula got news of events in Tamenglong. The SDO had found himself alone again and entirely unsupported, and tragically shot himself.

Ursula knew that she had the trust and loyalty of her own Zemi Nagas, but it was not only in the Barail region that the Nagas fought for and supported the British, often beyond the call of duty. Ursula made a point of recording incidences of extraordinary bravery and self-sacrifice.

On one occasion two Naga tribesmen serving in the Assam Regiment escaped when their position was overrun, changed into native dress and went to the nearest Japanese HQ. They grovelled about how pleased they were to see the Japanese who would liberate them from the brutal British, and asked if they could have a job. They were taken on as water-carriers and sweepers – which enabled them to scout about the HQ for some ten days. The Japanese never suspected that the tribesmen were trained sepoys, and were not surprised, given the co-operation of the Kukis, at their claims of resenting the British. They found out how to open the 'secret' safe and then, one night opened it, swept all the papers into a bag and lit out towards Imphal. They passed their haul over to the first British soldiers they could find. Naturally, all the information was in Japanese, but after it had been translated, it landed on Slim's desk and he was amazed. In it was the Japanese battle plan for the advance on Kohima and Imphal. Interesting as it was, he assumed that the Japanese would realise that their whole battle plan was compromised, and therefore make alternative arrangements. Again, to his astonishment, the Japanese carried on with the original plan – they evidently thought that the two Naga thieves had taken the safe contents thinking it to be money. As soon as it became evident that the plan he had before him was indeed operational, Slim was able to deploy troops to forestall them – it was a crucial point in the battle, and possibly a major influence in turning the tide in Britain's favour.

Before Bower Force was extended throughout the Barail area, one man in another Watch and Ward patrol sacrificed his life for his colleagues. As Ursula had taught, the scouts patrolled

> with a Naga scout out fifty yards in front, then the first part of the patrol with an officer, then another fifty-yard gap before the second part of the patrol with an officer – which in this case was generally me.

On this particular patrol there was no visibility beyond three feet on either side of the path – a very intimidating situation – and the leading scout, the statutory fifty yards ahead of the patrol, turned a corner and came face to face with an advancing Japanese patrol. He knew that if he doubled back they would go after him, and he'd lead them straight into an unsuspecting patrol behind him. Instead, he raised his muzzle-loader and shot the nearest Japanese. Seeing no more back-up behind him, they took him to be a single passing Naga, and they opened up on him. His body was instantly riddled with automatic fire, but as he died, the sound of firing ahead alerted the patrol. They dived for cover and set an ambush, so when the Japanese continued along the path they were able to take them easily. The lead scout had had no second thoughts and had given his life for his friends.

Another man from the warlike Sema tribes found himself in a minority in his village when a vote was taken not to try to hold up the Japanese advance. This so offended his loyalties that he spoke out against the decision – it was dishonourable and even if they did not want to fulfil their duties as subjects of the King, he would. He had no firearm, but took up a spear, dao and shield, and went out single-handed against a Japanese patrol. He got within close enough quarters to kill five of them in hand-to-hand combat before he was shot – but he went down fighting, a proud servant of the King.

These stories of selflessness and sacrifice were just a few among the many which filtered back to Ursula and, if it was possible, strengthened the bond she felt with these honest, honourable people.

Absurdly, when the alarm signal was sent to Ursula in Tamenglong to move out, the Japanese were pretty much in retreat, moving back towards Burma and the River Chindwin, however, the Watch and Ward operation continued through the summer. There were still pockets of Japanese on the Imphal Plain, and there were agents, escapers and stragglers in Ursula's area, and they had to be collected and dealt with.

All the same, it was an anticlimax. Since the pressure was off, Ursula decided to take some overdue leave, and travelled down to Calcutta, leaving Tibbetts in charge at the camp. After so long sleeping in her clothes to be ready to move at the slightest alarm, it was a real effort to undress for bed. Putting on pyjamas left her feeling vulnerable – it was hard to accept that the city and the hotel were perfectly secure. On the second or third night, Ursula woke on the floor in the dark, groping about for her Sten gun. As leaves went, it was neither relaxing nor restful, and she was grateful to get back to Laisong and carry on with routine patrols and administration.

Ursula and Tibbetts continued touring the area, checking on the wireless stations and making sure that the villages had no food or health problems – and were not being harried by stray Japs. One of the villages they visited was the Kuki settlement of Jampi, in north-west Manipur. At the time of the Japanese invasion, Kukis all the way from the Burma border to Ursula's area had sided with the Japanese and some villages went further than others to support the invaders – and Jampi was one of them. When the Japanese were in the area, they had put up a bounty of 100 rupees to bring in Ursula's head, and after the Japanese were driven back to the east, there was a distinctly uncomfortable atmosphere when Ursula visited them, escorted by a guard of Assam Rifles. She personally felt no rancour, but the village had a bad conscience, and feared reprisals:

> There was no point in doing that – we had no authority to do so, either. And even if we had, we wouldn't have done so. After all, they hadn't attacked us. The headman refused to appear at all, and a very nervous young man arrived with a bottle of rice beer and a chicken. He sat there looking at us in terror. We were rather cool with him. I was sorely tempted to point out that I was in possession of my head and the Japanese weren't – could I please have the hundred rupees, which I felt were due to me. However, I felt it was no good rubbing salt into the wound, so we just went on in a rather chilly manner.

By November the war had moved back to Burma, and with no further need for patrols, the operation was wound up. The role the Nagas had played was fully recognised by General Slim:

> They guided our columns, collected information, ambushed enemy patrols, carried our supplies and brought in our wounded under the heaviest fire, and then, being the gentlemen they were, often refused payment. Many a British and Indian soldier owes his life to the naked, headhunting Naga, and no soldier of the Fourteenth Army who met them will ever think of them but with admiration and affection.

Perry, Scott and Albright returned to Laisong for the final meeting, the scouts came in from villages all around, and the camp and village were seething with visitors wanting to be part of the celebration. Magulong had sent a troupe of their very best dancers and Namkia managed to find a really massive pig with which to feed the hordes, mithan being unavailable due to inflation.

It was a cool bright day and the cloth on the camp table flapped in a brisk wind. On three sides of the table were gathered the scouts – the Zemi in their scarlet blankets, jet black hair shining in the autumn light; the Kukis in their white turbans, and here and there the jungle green of the Assam Rifles. The atmosphere was of a passing out ceremony – a final presentation. The scouts came to the table one by one and were given their 'prizes' – guns, ivory armlets, knives or cash – and their formal discharge papers. Eventually the crowd dispersed, and those who had been given their guns hurried away to take part in Albright's shooting competition with prizes of flasks of gunpowder. The day wore on, the pig was cooked, the Magulong troupe danced and the party went on through the night.

It was wonderful that the danger had passed and that the Allies were confident of victory in Burma – but it was a sad moment the next morning as the battered boxes of guns, including Ursula's Sten and Namkia's tommy-gun, were loaded up. The porters set out, along with the Assam Rifles, Albright, Perry and Scott, winding up the village street and reappearing at the point where, so long ago, Ursula had spotted the approach of Rawdon Wright.

With all the military paraphernalia gone, the camp was a civilian settlement once more – but so much had happened, it could never be the same again. Every scout, now back in their villages, had experienced something unique and life-changing. In the direst crisis, mutual trust had cemented the Nagas and the British together, and they had worked as a unit to repel the Japanese threat. The guns and orders might have gone, but something else had gone too, eroded, rejected and forgotten in the atmosphere of trust and a common objective. The wall of reserve between the Zemi and the British had gone – and Ursula had achieved her original goal.

The White Queen of the Nagas

Ursula was a civilian again – although strictly speaking, she had never had a military title or rank. She was, simply, the senior woman in all of 'V' Force, and the only woman in command of active troops. This alone had sparked off a lot of romanticised publicity in the Indian press, and someone, clearly unaware of Ursula's actual relationship to the Nagas and the unfortunate misunderstanding about her being Gaidiliu, dubbed her 'The White Queen of the Nagas'. To her embarrassment, her fame now extended beyond the sphere of 'V' Force to the rest of the English-reading public in Northern India.

One cutting, of unknown date and provenance, promulgated the Ursula myth:

Likeable Head-hunters

I have just been hearing more about 30-year-old Miss Ursula Graham Bower, who has spent two years among the Naga tribesmen on the India-Burma frontier playing her part in the war against Japan.

Miss Graham Bower in 1938 began medical work among the Naga headhunting tribes. She likes them – 'some of the pleasantest people I have met', she says – and they return the compliment.

She has a small Naga bodyguard, lives in a bamboo hut two days from the nearest white man and when the Japanese were in the immediate neighbourhood slept in the jungle to avoid capture.

Nelson Touch

At one moment she was ordered by the British Military authorities to withdraw. Her answer, in the best manner of the Intelligence officer, was to move forward and ask for 15 more rifles.

When the time comes for the next Lawrence Gold Medal to be given by the Royal Central Asian Society this remarkable young woman's achievement can hardly escape passing under the review of those who award it.

The Statesman of 2 December 1941 included a 'Photo of Naga tribesmen from Assam photographed at the War Weapons Exhibition in Calcutta'.

Two interesting visitors to the War Weapons Exhibition in Calcutta yesterday were two Naga tribesmen from Assam, named Namkiabuing and Haichangnang.

They are the servants of a European lady who is on a short visit to Calcutta, and the men have taken advantage of the occasion to inspect the display of war weapons in which they appear to be greatly interested.

Sturdily built and picturesquely clad in their national costume with a richly embroidered handspun cape draped round their shoulders, a string of Deomoni (or sacred beads of Assam) round their neck and red plumes hanging from their ears, the men went from section to section minutely examining the various exhibits with childlike curiosity. Their presence and activity attracted great interest among the visitors.

Namkiabuing, the elder of the two, has been to Calcutta before but his comrade is a newcomer. They both belong to a warlike tribe and are greatly interested in the war, and appeared to be fully aware of its latest developments. An example of their interest in the war is to be found in the fact that Namkiabuing has been investing half his pay every month in Defence Bonds since the war began.

Following their employer, the men went round the different sections but their chief interest lay in the big guns, particularly the anti-aircraft and naval guns, the mine-sweeping appliances and tanks. With the permission of the authorities concerned, they climbed on to a tank and showed the greatest interest in its mechanism. Similar was the case with one of the naval guns which they wheeled round, a British sergeant major instructing them in the operations. 'We would like to operate these against the Germans,' said the elder man, with a broad grin, to a representative of *The Statesman*, who watched their activities and added regretfully that they did not know how to fire these guns.

Some of the Nagas of the tribe to which these men belong have already joined an Assam regiment which the Assam Government are raising.

Back in England no-one had any idea about what had happened to Ursula. When the Japanese were in the area, not only was there no time to write, but dak runners could not be spared to take post to the nearest depot. In November, after Watch and Ward had been disbanded, she felt able to send more informative letters – not least because the press had been 'spilling the beans, so I suppose I can'.

She filled in background details about setting up the Watch and Ward operation, the promise of a relief officer – who never came – and the myth of the 'White Princess of the Nagas'. She explained how there had been a great deal of speculation about the 'lady-officer' who worked for this undercover 'V' Force operation, with rumours of her being guarded by six foot Naga warriors. She didn't bother to explain that none of the Zemi Nagas was much over five foot six, or to refute the legend that she herself was six foot tall and had a deep bass voice. Her actual appearance could have put the lie to all of these myths, but the war correspondents had got hold of the story and there was no controlling it:

> Although this job was really a military one, I and my *Volksturm* turned over very well till March this year, when the Jap advance came on like a tidal wave, and we suddenly found ourselves some 200 miles in advance of everyone else, responsible for locating the advancing enemy, and officially warned we could expect the enemy any minute. Poor old *Volksturm*, they had to grab their muzzle-loaders and rush out to patrol the frontier. They had the heck of a five days before troops came up.

Ursula put her responsibilities in a nutshell:

> From 6th of April, when Albright arrived with the arms, we were left with a handful of troops – twenty-two men – and the *Volksturm*, the larger body of troops being withdrawn. Three routes, all from enemy territory, converged in one pass, so we sat down on a hill commanding it, and had to do the best we could for about a week.

> For various reasons we had a very hectic time and some narrow squeaks, but the Japs failed to arrive, which was the main thing, though there was a little minor excitement with a fighter. We were a bit of a forlorn hope, as we were expecting 200 men and knew there were 2,000 on the road, but all we had to do was make sure the beacons got lit, and withdraw in good order. This wasn't quite as easy as it sounds, but DV, I think we should have managed it all right. Albright's job was to light the beacons, and mine to lead off the survivors. There were all sorts of refugees and pseudo-refugees and non-combatants, and enemy agents and Lord knows what coming through all this time, and we had to deal with them as well as defend the pass and keep track of the enemy – so we were pretty busy.

She concluded her summary of her role, saying that her 'zoo and the *Volksturm* have had handsome bonuses and presents from a grateful government'. However, far from declining with the level of danger, her renown seemed to be spreading. Having met Slim and got on so well, he had insisted that the Army paper give her a write-up with a photo – which she enclosed with her letter:

> If the papers really have said that I repelled Jap attacks, it is b____s, but Heaven knows, we expected to have to repel them. However, it's *not* quite the same thing. You might relieve the suspense and let me know what they *have* said.

In another letter to Doris, Ursula enclosed a cutting from the American magazine *Time*, 1 January 1945, China-India-Burma edition:

'Aré wa ittai nan dai?' ('What on earth is that?') cried a startled Japanese officer as a burst of elephant-gun fire whistled past his ears and a troop of half-naked Nagas leaped out of the bushes. He found out, but too late. He and his jungle patrol were wiped out. But last week other Japs who had survived the fight in northern Burma knew more about the Naga raiders and their leader.

The half-naked tribesmen from north-eastern India were directed by a white woman; pert, pretty Ursula Graham Bower, 30, an archaeology student who looks like a cinema actress.

In 1939 Miss Graham Bower went out from England to India 'to putter about with a few cameras and to do a bit of medical work, maybe write a book'. She disappeared into the Assam hills to study the Nagas. These lithe-limbed tribesmen live in fortified hilltop villages, lead a somewhat humdrum existence punctuated by occasional raids to cut off their neighbours' heads, which they carry about in wicker baskets.

Miss Graham Bower managed to keep her own head on, and presently won the friendship of the Naga chieftains. Now and then people in the outside world got letters from her, exulting over the pictures she was taking of the primitive dances and ceremonies. Some of the more pretentious Nagas wore a little apron in front, but most just wore bracelets. They cultivated little patches of cleared jungle for rice, and, like the South American Indians, used drugs to catch fish. They begged Miss Graham Bower to name their babies. She named most of them Victoria Elizabeth.

When the Japanese armies surged across the Burma border and threatened to spill into India, Miss Graham Bower declared war on Japan. She placed herself at the head of the mobilised Nagas. By her orders, guards were posted on main and secondary trails, a watch-and-warn [sic] system was established. Over these trails thousands of evacuees, deserters, escaped prisoners and baled-out airmen, fled from Burma to India, Miss Graham Bower also directed Naga ambushes of Japanese search-parties.

She is still leading her pleasantly active life among the head-hunters. In Leigh Hall, Cricklade, Wilts, Miss Graham Bower's mother commented on her daughter's fighting blood, added proudly, 'An extraordinary girl, she never would sit still.'

To which Ursula's response was, 'And did you, Mother darling? The things you say!!!'

There were other matters to catch up on, too. 'Did I tell you that poor old Khamba died in February? Poor hound, I loved him so.' Then there was the matter of what her cousin Keith was doing – was he safe? Less importantly, she wanted to address the dearth of reading matter to fill her leisure time. 'Could you arrange to pay a Times Book Club subscription for me out of my own funds at home? It comes one third cheaper than paying from here.' Adding only her bank address, as she had hopes of going to another job, she signed off with lots of love from 'your Guerrillarina Daughter, Winkle'.

'V' Force did have a new role in mind for the newly demobbed Ursula. Her description was 'they got me a job in a jungle training camp down near Badarpur, the foot of the hill section railway'. In fact the camp had been created with her in mind, and the idea was for her to set up a jungle academy with a group of selected Nagas to teach the RAF survival techniques. It was a six-month assignment, and apart from the creation of the original brief, she was in charge.

The camp itself was tucked away in deep jungle, and was accessible only by means of an almost dried-up stream-bed. To the amazement of the RAF trainees, there were regular visits by tigers and elephants, but apart from their being awed by their environment, they had no problems with receiving training from a woman. Tales of Ursula's Bower Force had spread and made her something of a legend among the forces operating into Burma. Each fortnightly batch of trainees found themselves full of admiration and respect as she more than lived up to her reputation.

The weather was hot and dry and where there was no jungle there were foothills covered in stubby trees and jungle grass. Higher up the hill, behind the camp were the bamboo forests, leading to proper mountain woodland – it was an ideal place to train without the threat of malaria.

Ursula was disappointed that very few of the men really took to the jungle and most remained frightened of it to the last, their biggest fear being the wildlife. Some arrived with romantic misconceptions, imagining it was all grapes and Dorothy Lamour – these men needed their ideas knocked into shape. Of all the RAF men who graduated from Ursula's jungle training, only four really took to it, and applied to stay on as instructors.

Ursula wanted the men to learn a smattering of the language so they could communicate if they came down and were met by Nagas – they had to trust that the Nagas were on their side and would help them. The focus was on survival and getting back to the nearest ground base, while avoiding enemy contact. She designed a curriculum to develop the men's instincts and give them the knowledge to distinguish edible foodstuffs from poisonous ones, harmless creatures from dangerous, and how to handle any situation.

One of her graduates, on whom the experience left an enduring impression, was Ebenezer (Eb) Butler. He had joined up as RAF aircrew at the age of eighteen and trained in America. He had returned to the UK a fully-fledged pilot – along with some 700 others – for whom there was no real need at the time. To begin with, these superfluous pilots were shuttled around England, but after the attrition of the Battle of Arnhem, the Glider Pilot Regiment had lost a lot of men, so the fledgling pilots were given a choice: stick around in the UK and hope to join a squadron, or join the Army Glider Pilot Regiment. Eb Butler took the latter option and was shipped out to Lalaghat in India. After the privations of wartime Britain, this was heaven on earth – but still there was no call to action. Their main work was to provide squadron transport, ferry in reinforcements and lift out the wounded. The latter was often quite harrowing and Eb confessed to feeling concerned that his being there might be keeping out a trained medical man who would be of much more use to the sick and injured.

While Eb was at Lalaghat an opportunity arose for a break. 'They said there's a body called 'The Naga Queen', and she wants to train you lads in how to survive in the jungle.' Eb's unit and a bunch of Americans volunteered, on the premise that a change was as good as a rest. It did cross Eb's mind that it could be the worst thing he'd ever let himself in for, 'It's all very well having jungle queens and stuff, but I don't fancy being stuck out in the jungle…' However, on arrival, prospects started looking up:

> We went to a little clearing, and she was there. Everything was spotless as she would have it – spick and span – a woman's touch. We thought, 'You'll have to mind your manners here', but she introduced us to the Nagas, and although we couldn't speak their language and they just had a smattering of English, they were smiling and graceful, so we just got along with them…

Ursula explained what she hoped they would learn over the next two weeks:

> She said, 'God forbid, but it may be, that you're stuck in the Naga Hills if your aircraft comes down, or if you run short of fuel. If you make contact with the Nagas, you're fine, but while you're waiting for the Nagas to find you, you have to learn to live off the land and cope with the terrain, because it's Lake District plus – jungle and peaks and ravines.'

Ursula accorded the same respect and courtesy to everyone alike. Eb recalled,

> What got me was her cultured accent – and she was always very feminine. Even in the jungle, her hair was swept back, and she had this clear skin. She was just so delightful. Nothing at all was any trouble – she was so laid back. She was so compassionate towards everything. She saw that the camp cat had being going around with its tail up, so she arranged to go off for a day, and announced she was going to Sylhet. 'For supplies?' we asked. 'No, no, the cat needs company.' And she took the afternoon off and took the cat into Sylhet. When the cat came back, her tail was down, and sure enough, she was much happier after that. That's the kind of person she was. We never got very close to her – we would eat an evening meal together,

> but then she'd be off, back with the Nagas in their little encampment, and we were with the rest of the RAF and the Americans.

Ursula kept to a standard syllabus:

> We used to take the men out into the jungle for various exercises – stalking and hunting techniques. With the aid of the Nagas there was a drill for teaching the men how to approach a doubtful village, how to approach a villager and try to make friends with him – and then to go and hide yourself somewhere when he went off to the village. The RAF were trained to hide themselves somewhere from which they could retreat without any difficulty or getting trapped. Then they would see whether the villagers who came back were friendly or were returning armed. The Nagas who represented the armed and hostile gang had a great deal of fun chasing the RAF lads. The Nagas could run much faster than the RAF could, especially uphill. One day the 'hostile gang' arrived, and one RAF chap started on the obvious exit – which was up quite a steep hill. He was going very well – quite a fit little man – and one of the Naga boys started after him. Well, if anybody can run uphill, it's a Naga. The chap thought he was doing well, then all of a sudden, a hand reached out and tapped him on the shoulder. I shall never forget his face. The Naga had overtaken him at something like twice his speed.

In a final trial, the men would be jeeped out and dropped in the jungle about twenty miles away, then be left with only a compass and some emergency rations of chocolate and glucose. Their challenge was to find their way back to the camp. They had been taught by an ex-Burma forestry officer that if you met a tiger, it was probably not hostile, but would prefer to be left alone. If you hear a deep growl in front of you in the undergrowth, turn round very quietly and creep away and he won't bother you. This instruction had met with derisive laughter until two men on their final trial walked in on a tiger. Too scared to do anything other than what they had been told, they tiptoed away and it worked like a charm. As Ursula knew, they hadn't believed it until then, 'but after that, the reputation of the instruction went up a lot.'

Some sixty years later, Ebenezer still has vivid memories of his training:

> She explained how there were paths and tracks, rivers and ridges – and the Nagas showed us how to build a little basha. We were saying, 'But it's only for one night,' but they insisted. 'Oh no, you must have protection, because there are snakes and even elephants – if you hear a thunderstorm and see no rain, it's because elephants are coming.' We asked what you would do if elephants charged down on you, and the Naga explained, 'You have a fire', and he cut off a chunk of bamboo and flung it in the fire. I got the fright of my life – it went off like a bomb. 'That will frighten any elephants.' It certainly frightened us!
>
> Over the course we had leaned to use bamboo for cooking and as little cups to scoop water, and the instructor said, 'You may be short of water, but it must be boiled. You use this bamboo cup.' I asked, 'What happens if the bamboo burns?' He said, 'By that time the water will be safe to drink.' We learned what to do if you're caught unarmed, or if you have to enter into hand-to-hand combat. The Nagas cut

> these bamboo slivers – spikes – and they push them into the ground around them. As Miss Bower said, 'They may be bamboo, but they'll go through the strongest boot the British Army has ever designed – it will impale your feet.' Then they did a dance – a sort of hypnotic thing, where your antagonist is wondering what you're going to do next. Every now and then, the dancing Naga slips back, and as he backs away, the enemy comes forward, not thinking, puts his foot on the spike and he's caught.

Ursula taught the men jungle lore in person: how to keep clean, how to check the water for snakes, and always to carry a sharp bamboo stick to deal with them, not to drink the water without boiling it, and never to pick off leeches because it would leave the head in the flesh and turn septic. The answer to leeches was to burn them off with a cigarette. Eb particularly appreciated these little details – stuff you didn't find in textbooks. It was clear to everyone that she knew her stuff.

Ursula would turn out every morning to greet them, immaculate in her army fatigues. Eb remembered her English rose charm. 'Good morning boys. Have you had a good breakfast?' 'Yes thank you, Ursula.' 'Today you're going to learn about defence. How to use the bamboo as a weapon.' She would then show them how to sharpen the end to make a spear or, given the right sort of fibre, make and string a bow. As before, she had a standard army-issue gun, and the Nagas had Lee Enfield .303s along with their daos, which they used for cutting and jungle clearing. It was clear from the start that she had enormous respect and affection for her Nagas, and she was very ready to explain that they were no savages. Certainly they were warriors, and they would fight to the last man with her. Eb recalled that no-one ever heard the British forces say anything but good of the Nagas – they were universally respected.

By the end of the fortnight, Eb and his colleagues were deemed ready for the final test:

> It was a big adventure. They took us way down and dropped us off in a lorry. We went off in different directions in four groups with the Naga guides, then they left us at a place where we would be near to water and where we could settle. As Ursula had pointed out, 'We've spoiled you, you know. When you come down in your aeroplane, you won't always land on a flat piece by a river.' We built our basha and slept the night, and as soon as dawn came, we were on our way back. We had compasses and maps, but the maps were no good because we couldn't follow the routes and, truth to tell, our group got lost. We felt we'd let the side down badly – and we said, 'She'll come for us – but what a show-up if she has to come and get us out of the jungle, after all the time she's put in with us.' We trudged along, arguing about the way to go. One said if we followed the river downstream we were bound to get somewhere – another thought that was the way we'd come. Eventually we decided we had to follow the stream down, and we were hacking through the jungle. Someone had the idea to go up on the ridge to find a path. Once we were up there we looked round for fires or any sign of habitation, but we couldn't see anything at all. At that time, I thought this was all part of it – I was fit and I could manage – but back at the camp there was an RAF regular, and apparently he was panic-stricken. He thought he'd lost four of his lads. He later said that Ursula gave

> him some advice, and he was pleased that she did. 'Look at it this way, if you rescue the boys before they're thoroughly lost, they're going to feel cheated. They're going to say that they could have got out. You want to make sure that they really do want to be rescued, and if you could catch them on the road coming into the camp, that would make everybody happy'. And that was what happened. She had judged it to a nicety. She confided, 'We're all very pleased to see you – but you've got some questions to answer to your officer… such as how come you got so lost, you clueless lot.'

To meet this extraordinary Englishwoman was an experience in itself, but to work and train with her was a privilege, which allowed a unique insight into her relationship with the Nagas. Eb looked back on the days in the jungle as an unforgettable time.

> We had the highest regard for her, and she was wonderful. After our course, when we left, she was sweetness itself. 'Now boys, keep safe, and don't forget the words I've told you.' And I remember them still: 'Umri saibrung da mutai kalao' which is Naga for 'We are friendly airmen, take me to your chief.' That was drummed into us all the time. I said, 'Chances are, if we do come down, it won't be Nagas – it'll be some other lot, who'll take our head off.' But it stuck with Eb, and all the rest who trained with her. Back at Lalaghat, the men couldn't wait to hear about the 'White Queen of the Nagas' and if she lived up to all the hearsay. The jungle course graduates couldn't speak highly enough of the extraordinary Miss Bower – and probably more than one of them came away just a bit infatuated.

37

The Proposal

In May 1945, Ursula found herself at a loose end for the first time in years. She had turned down a second term at the jungle school as she felt a further contract would curtail her freedom too much. Instead, she had written to Mills to see if he had any work for her. He'd put forward the idea of a period among the Daflas in the northern hills on the other side of the Brahmaputra Valley, and Ursula was excited about the opportunity – however, there was no point in moving before the end of the rains, so she settled down to write up her notes in Laisong. There was another incentive to get working, too – Barbara, her step-mother, had got her a commission to write an article, and Ursula was determined to deliver something she would be proud of, on time, and without the use of a typewriter, which had had to be sent for repair.

Far away in Europe, events had gathered momentum as the Allies surged through Germany. It was the end of the war in Europe as Germany signed an unconditional surrender on 7 May, and the following day, VE Day celebrations broke out all over Britain and Europe. Things took a little longer to percolate through to Ursula's neck of the woods, but by mid-May, just in time for Ursula's birthday, VE Day celebrations were held in Haflong. Ursula reported a riotous and exhausting time:

> There was quite a do – sports, both on land and in the water, football, hockey, native dancing and finally a torchlight Naga dance and gala at the Club. It made a break, but was rather wearing, as events followed so close after each other and it was hellish hot.

Ursula had never been one to seek the limelight, so although she relished the excitement of Bower Force, she was relieved to get away from the unwelcome fame her war efforts had earned her. She saved one particularly inane item from a California newspaper and sent it to Doris:

British Beauty Leads Burma Head-Hunters
Organises Fierce Tribesmen on Own Initiative;
Secret Bared of her Battles Against Foe
By James E. Brown
Staff Correspondent Int'l News Service

NEW DELHI, Dec 8th The dramatic story of a female 'Lawrence of Arabia' emerged from the wild jungles of Burma today – the story of a fabulously beautiful British woman who has been leading fierce head-hunting tribesmen of the Naga Hills against the Japanese.

She is thirty years old Ursula Graham Bower and – until it was finally revealed today – the thrilling record of her resourceful deeds on behalf of the Allies was one of the top secrets of the Southeast Asia command.

Thousands of miles from her native London, Miss Bower lives in a rough 'basha' on a solitary hilltop in the rugged Naga country, a hard two days' march from the nearest white habitation in the town of Haflong.

Solitary Life

On her own initiative, this young woman established an intricate network of observation posts throughout the North Cachar Hills which supplied the British Fourteenth Army in Burma with one of its most valuable sources of military intelligence.

For six years Ursula lived a solitary life among the Naga head-hunters, studying the natives and taking photographs of them while collecting material for a book.

In 1942 when the Japs invaded the Naga country, the tribesmen were very wary of British influence in view of Britain's traditional frowning on such activities as the collecting of skulls as souvenirs. But today, thanks to Ursula, the Nagas are completely in sympathy with the British.

Call for Rifles

And many fine Japanese 'trophies' now can be found adorning the bashas (huts) of native chieftains.

When the Japs at one time were reported within fifteen miles of her hill-top 'headquarters', Ursula was advised to leave. But she replied with a request for 30 or more British rifles, adding:

'I am going forward to find out what is happening.'

Marching towards the enemy with a group of her Naga followers, Ursula established a screen of observation posts. She set up a warning system of beacons and native runners so that the Fourteenth Army would know in advance the direction and time of the Japanese raids towards the vital Assam railway running into Northeast India.

Ursula's 'headquarters' became the focal point of much intensive military activity and a centre for the concentration of pack-mules, weapons, ammunition and food.

Arduous Marches

The British describe the London girl as 'a great organiser', able to withstand arduous marches through the jungles and mountains. Yet this remarkable young woman is not the Amazon type.

On the contrary, those who have seen her declare she has a completely feminine personality, that she is a great beauty of charming manner.

Wherever she goes she is accompanied by two armed Naga tribesmen – her faithful 'bodyguards.'

'I thought the one in *Time* took the uttermost biscuit, but this walks away with the whole ruddy cake shop!' But there was more to come from another American paper, a copy of which was sent to her by a Fouteenth Army man who had been posted to the States. She shared the lunacy with Doris:

> It is headed, 'The White Princess – a Royal Jap Headache' and contains more fiction to the half inch than Rider Haggard. At the top is a fancy illustration of a whamsy female in early 1920 costume (God knows why) sitting in a cane chair amid tropical leaves, with a set of the best silver tea-things and a bowl of grapes at her elbow. Her feet (in 1920 court shoes) are on a cushion on a log, and she is gazing, like a housewife who has been sent chops instead of cutlets, with faint disapproval at a resigned-looking human head presented to her gaze by a female

Dyak (!), who appears to be saying; 'Well, it's what the butcher *sent*, Madam.' Lower down is one of Fürer-Haimendorf's pictures of a Konyak Naga boy, and alongside it a very touched-up photo of me, with this caption: 'Gen. Ursula, Dainty as a Freshly-Laundered Handkerchief, Became the White Princess of Assam to Naga Head-Hunters like the Chief's son at Left'. Strewth!!! The most shattering paragraph is this:

'Before she had been there very long, a Naga chief decided she would be an excellent addition to his bevy of wives, so he sent one of them to Ursula with the finest present a warrior wooer can offer – the freshly severed head of an enemy.

The diplomacy with which she rejected his gift and declined his proposal endeared her to the entire tribe. Eventually she learned the Naga language, became reconciled to the customs and got so inured to the idea of head-hunting that she rarely cast a second glance at the long lines of bamboo poles topped by skulls, which are common in the Naga fields.'

I should like at this point to indicate that the author's ideas on Naga custom are as inaccurate as those on my nature, career, and attainments, and that Laisong is *at least* 150 miles from the nearest area where head-hunting still occurs.

Further on, they claim Miss Bower was 'despatched to Nagaland with the admonition that the fate of the British Empire might easily rest on her slender shoulders.' This is news to the Army, and to me. If you can think of any adequate comment on that, it's more than I can – or, at least, one that won't scorch the paper.

The respite after all the danger, frantic activity, jungle school and VE celebrations, gave Ursula time to reflect, and one of her letters to Doris shed an interesting retrospective light on the untimely end of her Roedean schooling and the denial of a university education:

You say I was a mug not to go to Oxford! It was the very thing I DID want to do, and had meant to do the whole time I was at Roedean, until in my last year there, poor old Humps broke it to me that she simply couldn't raise the cash, what with the financial crisis and other commitments, as it would cost at least £300 a year for three or four years. She couldn't even let me have another year at Roedean to try for a scholarship. I remember some talk about getting the Bower side to help, but Grandad was so dead against Oxford as being a 'hotbed of socialism', and it all seemed pretty hopeless so I didn't kick much, especially as Humpus so obviously would have given it to me if she possibly could, and my fussing would only make her feel worse. So I just folded up like a wet umbrella and felt quite too, too bloody. I can't remember whether she told me not to tell the reason, or whether in quite such a wealthy school, I didn't feel like it, but I can remember being pressed to give the reason and refusing to say why I wasn't going; and getting very unjustly jawed in consequence on my unwisdom! I always thought that was a bit hard, considering it was the very thing I wanted to do above all things, and I was being jawed for not doing it! I laughed like a drain when I heard that the Tanner read out the *News Chronicle* account to the assembled school, because she gave me the prize jaw on what my ghastly future was to be because I wasn't going to the University. I could cheerfully have killed her in that hour; but she didn't know the facts, so what the

> hell! It really was a bit of a jar, getting pipped right on the post like that, when I was all set and had got my Exemptions (from the entrance exams) in school cert. I felt most extremely bloody about it all. What a curious animal one is at seventeen – or I was, anyway. I felt I couldn't have discussed it with a soul, it was much too much of an internal hurt and I felt like all hell when anybody mentioned it. Ah well.

One rainy morning in late May the dak brought a solitary letter. It was from a Colonel Betts, also of 'V' Force, and he wanted to come up to Laisong to catch butterflies. The area, he said, was home to some particularly unusual specimens – would she be able to help him with arrangements to stay? She sent back a note to say that she could and returned to her perusal of the daily papers.

She thought little more of the arrangement, as the monsoon had set in and the conditions for butterfly chasing were less than ideal. However, a fortnight later on 13 June, Namkia came in to report that a Sahib was about to arrive, in a tone, as Ursula wrote to Doris 'as though he were announcing the Loch Ness Monster'. With no forewarning of any other visitors, Ursula assumed correctly that this must be the eccentric butterfly man. What a nuisance. She went to the back door of the bungalow and peered out into the rain. Two bedraggled figures were silhouetted against the sky-line – one a tall, thin and distinctly damp colonel, the other a Gurkha orderly, smaller but similarly soaking. Ursula and Namkia ushered them in – the orderly went to the kitchen for some refreshment and Ursula served tea to the colonel in the bungalow.

Colonel Betts explained that he would like to stay for a few days. He had heard that Laisong was a magnificent butterfly ground and understood that only a few weeks earlier, SDO Perry, who was a keen lepidopterist, had seen four rare Calinaga butterflies on the spur and even managed to capture two. Ursula saw no reason to object as there was plenty of room in the camp – he could certainly use the place as his base, and if he gave her a little notice, she could arrange pack lunches.

The next day's weather was fine, but he seemed oddly reluctant to get out among the Calinagas and Stichopthalmia Howqa he professed to want to find. It was eleven o'clock before he set out. As days ticked by, he appeared less and less keen to go out at all, and Ursula was finding herself getting quite cross. On the fourth day she went so far as to chase him out of the camp, pack lunch and butterfly net in hand. She was in the throes of mixing a cake in the kitchen when Namkia turned up to say, most disapprovingly, that the colonel wanted to see her. She was covered in flour and quite irritable as she put down the bowl, dusted her herself off and went out to find out what he wanted. Back ridiculously early from his butterfly hunt and rigged out in his best uniform, she found him pacing up and down. With only half an ear on what he was saying, her thoughts mainly on the cake she had abandoned, they walked through the garden and had just reached her very pleasing display of cannas when, as she wrote to her mother, 'I realised to my amazement that I was on the business end of a proposal of marriage'.

The next few minutes were a blur and 'a bit chaotic':

> At the next lucid interval, we were in the bungalow. We seemed somehow to have become engaged. I was not at all certain it was what I intended – I had, really, been thinking about the cake. But this was hardly the moment to explain. He was so terribly

> pleased about it all. It wasn't, either, as though he weren't a suitable colonel. He was a charming man. I couldn't think offhand of one that I liked better. Still, it did all seem rather sudden.

After years of the faithful and dogged Pat courting her, a man she had met just four days before had proposed and she had accepted. The term 'whirlwind romance' is hardly adequate to describe the turn events had taken:

> Then he kissed me. He was tall and strong. A chair got in the way. The scene resembled a struggle more than an embrace. I was in panic lest Namkia come in. My staff held strong views on that sort of thing, and should he draw the wrong conclusion – he certainly would – the Colonel was in for a mass assault. But the embrace concluded, the crisis passed and nobody came in.

This anticipated disapproval was a bit rich given the normal Naga proclivities – but then there was one rule for Nagas and one for Sahibs.

With the formalities over, Frederick Nicholson – known as Tim – Betts, had a chance to tell her about himself. As Ursula saw it, 'His story was the final touch, but I was past the stage of being surprised, the heels of the world were uppermost, we were all mad and a little more insanity couldn't matter.'

Suddenly, on just four days' acquaintance, Ursula found herself engaged to a man she scarcely knew. With a marriage some time in the future agreed in principle, the tension relaxed and there remained a few days of Tim's leave in which he and Ursula could get to know each other.

Tim started with recent events and worked backwards. Ursula was fascinated to know what had driven him to visit her and with no pretensions to having turned up disingenuously with lepidoptera in mind, Tim came clean at once. His interest in her had started eighteen months before when he had joined 'V' Force and heard of the 'Naga Queen' – the lady guerrilla who lived with the Nagas and had so gained their trust that they were willing to fight with her against the Japanese. He had resolved to meet the legend in person, but events had overtaken him.

His camp had been overrun by the Japanese and, having managed to escape, he set out for Kohima on a three-week trek through Japanese-held territory. Two hundred miles later, he arrived exhausted and starving – just in time to be shipped out to a hospital before the siege began. After a long convalescence, he retuned to 'V' Force and saw that Bill Tibbetts, a subaltern in his detachment, was being sent up to support Miss Bower. He'd been very tempted to cross off the initial TIB from Tibbetts' name on the orders and go himself – but he thought of the ruse just a little too late and Tibbetts was already preparing to leave.

When Tibbetts returned, his reports of Miss Bower and her Nagas had only served to fuel Tim's curiosity and his determination to meet 'the Naga Queen'. However, events conspired against him, and when Ursula went on leave and visited HQ in Comilla, he missed her by two days, and again when she was staying in Calcutta. A full year later, Tim's unit was in Shillong for a refit, although there was talk of 'V' Force being disbanded altogether. If this was the case, this would be his last chance to meet Ursula, and as he had some leave due, there was no time to waste. Tim had never been the marrying kind before – or rather, he had never met the right woman – but over time the idea of marrying this exceptional female had become more entrenched. He had always been the outdoors type, and he suspected that the Naga Queen would have more in common with him than any other woman he'd met, so he made up his mind. Even if she proved to be unsuitable or unwilling, his time in Laisong wouldn't be wasted, as it was famous butterfly country.

He'd sent his letter, and had been delighted to receive her speedy reply. Tim applied for leave, and the CO, not keen to grant it, asked why he wanted to go. Feeling it was pointless to dissemble, he answered simply that he wanted to reconnoitre the Naga Queen with a view to possible matrimony. Stunned, the CO had no words with which to refuse, so Tim packed his butterfly-hunting kit and his smartest uniform and set out for Laisong.

The journey was difficult and hardly propitious. Due to a delay, the rains had broken and it was bucketing down as he arrived in North Cachar with his orderly. Going on foot towards Laisong via the Tolpui pass they paused for a breather, and dripping wet and tired, Tim took stock of his situation. He must be mad. Chances were that she would turn out to be a ghastly, hard-faced, horsey-toothed Amazon whom he wouldn't want to marry anyway. And she could just as likely send him away with a flea in his ear for being so presumptuous. Unable to make up his own mind as to what to do, he decided to draw lots with three straws. Long straw, she was a harpy anyway, middle length, she would be his dream woman – but wouldn't have him. If he drew the short straw she'd be a perfect peach – and she'd say yes. Tim drew the short straw. He pulled on his green beret, drew himself up straight and marched on to Laisong.

The short straw seemed to be holding good, as the Naga Queen who greeted him was hospitable, welcoming, efficient – and absolutely the 'peach' he had hoped for. Settled into quarters, bathed and in dry uniform, he joined Ursula in her basha and talked for a while by the fire. He confessed to Ursula later that he had not been with her more than an hour when he decided that he was utterly smitten, and began to plan a schedule for proposing – while still maintaining his butterfly-hunting camouflage. Ursula thought him 'an extremely nice fellow, very easy to get on with, and just as nice as Albright, CO Scott, Tibbetts and all the others I had come across in the unit.'

Tim's butterfly ploy was hard to sustain, as Ursula attested to Doris in a letter written in August, when eventually she felt confident enough to announce what had been going on:

> The next day, very reluctantly, he went off to the jungle, and was back again as soon as he decently could – much to my annoyance, as I was busy! I noticed, too, that when I was pointing out the tracks on the map, his hand kept straying rather near mine; but such vagaries are not uncommon among officers who have been too long in the front line, and he did not seem to be at all the sort to start serious trouble, so I just kept my hand away – and the second time I moved it, he took the hint.
>
> The next day he crawled reluctantly off to the jungle again (I thought I had never seen so dilatory a butterfly-hunter – I must have been extraordinarily obtuse, but I never realised what was up) and was back, once more, long before dusk, this time with a butterfly or two to show. The third day the same thing happened, but

> this time he came back when I was busy in the cookhouse, baking. He asked to see me and when I came out, rather hot and floury, he had already changed and was striding up and down the strip of grass by the one flower-bed with the air of a man with something very much on his mind. We started quarter-decking up and down alongside the garden. He started to explain why he had really come, and at about the fourth turn up and down, I found myself in receipt of his proposal, and he was asking me if there was 'any hope?' Well, I really thought he was a very nice fellow and that we had a lot in common, and that when we knew each other a bit better, we should very probably find grounds for matrimony – and I was just starting in to say this as tactfully as I could, only I don't think I can have put it very clearly, because it got through to Tim after the first sentence or two that I had more or less said 'yes', and any carefully-phrased conditionals I may have put in after that failed entirely to penetrate. He looked exactly like a man who has been hit on the head with a blunt instrument – so much so that I began to wonder whether he had only proposed because he had run out of other conversation!

Tim had got his answer – but confronted by this unexpected success, he took a moment to prepare for his next move. Ursula continued to explain to Doris:

> Well, I don't really know what happened in the next few minutes. Tim didn't know whether he was on his head or his heels. Anyhow, we got back into the bungalow, and the next thing I remember is being kissed like blazes, which to my intense surprise, because I had hitherto thought it a nauseating and overrated pastime, I was enjoying. Then he grabbed his signet ring and shoved it on my finger, and at that point, I got my first wave of panic and began to feel I was selling myself down the river and up the garden path, and it was about time I started to think it over. Tim was in Seventh Heaven all evening, talking about plans for the future. 'We'll this' and 'we'll that' – and my feet were getting metaphorically colder and colder. I spent the hell of a wakeful night. Whiles I thought, 'Hell, marry him. What are you fussing for?' and whiles I lay wondering how on earth I was going to call a halt to this rapid descent into the abyss! The same thing went on in varying degrees on the 17th and 18th, and on the 19th we went up to Hangrum together. During the night I got so fed up with that something ring, I took the darned thing off, but I felt it was such a damned mean trick to hand it back before I had really thought it over, and it was much better to let it pass and consider the whole thing dispassionately after he had gone – so I put it on again after breakfast.

Ursula wanted to put the brakes on and consider, and was determined not to be hurried into something she might regret later. An engagement – a good long one of at least six months – ought to buy her the time she needed, so having stipulated this, she saw Tim off:

> We marched up to Hangrum and about 5pm he set off back to Laisong, getting there late that night – it is the very devil of a road – and next day double-marched back to the railway and went off to Shillong. That same morning I hung the darned ring round my neck on a string, where it was out of sight under my shirt, and went

on with my normal avocations, feeling, nevertheless, not at all sure about the course upon which I had so blithely embarked.

Tim's leave was over and he returned to his unit. With the caveat of a long engagement, and furtively wearing Tim's ring around her neck, Ursula had the prospect of three weeks before their next planned meeting in Shillong, during which to consider his proposal.

38

Two Weddings

Ursula was still adamant about a long engagement and prepared, should she change her mind, to call the whole thing off. For this reason she made no mention of budding romance when writing to Doris. As there was no need for secrecy anymore, and her men were now 'running about with blooming great badges all over them', she could tell Doris that General Slim had endorsed her CO's recommendation that she be honoured for her war work, and she had been awarded an MBE – Namkia had been given the British Empire Medal.

She did mention that she was trying to get on with some writing:

> but for a remote hilltop, this place is a ruddy Piccadilly, first the C of E padre, then a 'V' Force colonel on leave and hunting lepidoptera, and now a senior official, who is actually quite a young man. They are all very nice, and I have had several 'treasures', some chocolate, which I have hardly seen for years, sherry, the loan of books, all of which mean a good deal in the wilderness, so I mustn't complain.

Tim wrote from her camp in Laisong, the night he had left her in Hangrum. If Ursula had misgivings, Tim had none:

> I love you! This would have been one hell of a letter, at least three stars on the Cold Comfort Farm scale, but the return journey took longer than I expected, and I only got in, somewhat footsore, about 10pm. I simply hated leaving you. This last week has been the most wonderful one I have ever spent. After these years waiting around, wondering if the sort of girl I wanted to marry would ever turn up, I was beginning pretty well to give up hope!
>
> You say you had a hunch about the Nagas – well, I had one about you when I first heard of you. But the prospects of ever meeting you seemed quite remote until I heard a chance remark that you were back in Laisong. That sounded a break in my direction on the part of fate, and I determined to play it for all it was worth. It seemed an entirely forlorn hope, as I am very far from being a professional ladies' man, and sadly lacking in graces, charm or appearance. But I had to try it, and after I had met you and spent one evening with you, I realised you were all and much more than I had ever hoped for. Here was I, at the end of a period of life with the prospect of having to pick up the strings alone – not so young and with very little idea of what I was going to do, and dreading the prospect of wandering about indefinitely and alone…

Unwittingly, avoiding bravado and bluster, he had adopted the approach most likely to endear him to Ursula. She kept the letter for the rest of her life.

Tim was frantic to convince Ursula that he was no impulsive fly-by-night – that he really meant every word he had said and wanted, without any shadow of a doubt, to marry her:

> I am afraid I rushed you terribly, but in the circumstances, what was there to do? Had I not done so, our ways would have parted and the chance would probably never have come again, and I should have been regretting my lost opportunity all my life. I have tried to show you myself in these four or five days as I really am. I know only too well I have little to offer a woman. Having lived so long on my own, I am selfish and self-centred, not particularly gutful and lacking in enterprise. But with a girl like you as a partner, I am sure I should be quite another man, as there would be something to live for, and if you are prepared to take me in hand and train me, I think there is every chance of my making a good husband. I cannot expect or hope for you to fall seriously in love with me, though I have myself got it in a way which astonishes me – I who thought I had long left the romanticism of youth behind. But a sincere friendship and companionship on your part would be all I would ask, and I think it will grow as we know each other better. So, I beg of you, vehemently, not to be moved unduly by the cold light of reason and caution which might prompt you to think now I have gone and you have time to consider that, 'here comes this totally strange man, who owing to his importunity, the isolation and the fact that I haven't seen a fellow countryman for some time, has rushed me off my legs into an evanescent "board-ship affair" which cannot last'. I know well it is a hell of a gamble on your part, but give me the chance and I will do my best to see you never regret it. I don't mind telling you I had a heart attack when you hadn't got my signet ring on at breakfast. I thought, 'She's repented of it in the night' – and it was an unimaginable relief to see it on again when we set out.

Tim had also promised confidentiality – except a mention to his commanding officer that marriage might be in the air and a confiding of his hopes in a letter to his mother – so when Ursula and Namkia went down to the railway at Badapur Junction to meet Tim almost three weeks later, she had assumed that no-one knew of the engagement. It must still be six months, she insisted, even though Tim came with the news that he had been posted to Burma, and felt they should marry at once. On the drive to Shillong, after waiting for a large military convoy to roll by, Tim pulled out to pass a stationary saloon car and in it were Philip and Pam Mills. Ursula jumped out and ran back and, in the briefest of conversations, laid out for Pam her quandary about the engagement.

For all Ursula's determination, the Millses shook her resolution. Tim had met them before (he and Mills were both old Wykhamists) – and he had recently visited them to tell them of his hopes – and they had been delighted. They were the best friends Ursula had in India, and they were absolutely convinced it was 'right'. As Pam pointed out, she had married Philip Mills the eighth time she had seen him, and though she had had cold feet right up to the wedding, she had found it entirely satisfactory. She had discovered she was very fond of him as soon as they were married, and had continued to be so ever since. As marriage was much of a gamble anyway, she advised Ursula to go ahead and marry her 'long and earnest swain'.

Ursula cabled her mother on 6 June to say that she had got married the previous day, then in a letter two days later explained the whirlwind courtship and marriage:

> I thought it over for two days, and agreed on third to get married forthwith. We've got a special licence, as the chaplain knew Tim's people and Mills vouched for me. Mrs Mills made all the arrangements and was acting bride's mother – you couldn't have had a better deputy – and we had quite a smart wedding in Shillong on the 5th. HE the Governor and Lady Clow were there, all Tim's brother officers (mine too) and various old friends who happened to be in Shillong. Mrs Mills did marvels and was most wonderfully kind and helpful – dress, flowers, reception, trousseau – all were produced out of nowhere. We had an arch of kukris, Namkia and the dakwalla on guard, and a Jap sword to cut the cake (which was made at 48 hours' notice). We left on 6th for Calcutta, where we now are, to try and wangle leave for Tim before he joins his new post. If we get it we hope to do a trek in Sikkim by way of honeymoon. We are very well suited in tastes and inclinations, both loving trekking, the wilds and adventure generally. He is shy and rather a man's man, but very amusing, and a darling.

It was late August before she could tell Doris about the wedding itself:

> I had moved to a room in the officers' hostel and spent the morning of the 5th in packing, had an early lunch and a bath, and started to change. Mrs Mills came along to help me finish dressing. She said my hands were shaking. I hadn't noticed it, but I was not surprised. I felt slightly sick, and *how* I wanted my mother! Well, with the inevitability of Fate, along came Mills in the bridal car, and we rolled slowly down to the church, for we were a bit early. Mills was very fatherly and soothing. I needed it. Then we drew up at the door and we got out, and when we got into the door and I saw the serried ranks of the congregation and knew the moment had come, I had the most dreadful wave of panic – an awful feeling that the whole thing was a most ghastly mistake, which it was now impossible to rectify. I saw Tim, looking like a distant pine-tree, turning round to see if I'd arrived, and being fiercely eyes-fronted by his best man, who is rather shorter than I am, and looked about up to Tim's waist. Then Mills was marching me up the aisle to *Here Comes the Bride*. I don't know whether I was going red and white by turns, but I certainly felt like it. Poor Tim, apparently, had the most dreadful wind-up, when I reached the chancel steps or whatever it is one reaches, and Mills parked me. Tim moved up alongside and as close as he dare get, presumably to grab me if I bolted; and my sense of reality was suddenly restored by a whiff of a certain scent. He had been in such a state of nerves that the best man had had to give him a stiff brandy in the Club bar! My sense of normality was restored with a run – this was clearly a true Bower wedding, running well to form. It ran even truer in a minute, for having handed over my bouquet to Mrs Mills, I suddenly found an acute drip on my nose in the middle of a prayer. The bridegroom looked round to find me with my head bowed on my clasped hands, apparently overcome by the solemnity

> of the occasion. Not a bit of it – I was neatly but unobtrusively wiping the drip on my knuckles.
>
> It all went off without a hitch, except that the ring was rather a job to get on, what with my hand being sweaty and Tim's shaking, but it went, and there we all were in the vestry and signing papers, and then they queued Tim and me up and ordered us out down the aisle. From that moment I think I was reconciled to matrimony. Out we came down the aisle to *Lohengrin*, past Namkia and the dakwallah one on either side of the church door, like Gog and Magog, under an arch of kukris and into the car, and away to the reception. As we came up the front steps into the hall of the hotel, a bearer met us with two glasses of the hock cup we had managed to raise. A charming old custom – and oh, how I needed it! Tim's went back like nobody's business, so I gather he needed his too.

After the reception it was back to the hostel, amid showers of rice and the clattering of an old boot and a tin can with which Tim's friends had customised the car:

> I found it extraordinarily embarrassing having a strange man in the room. After all, I hardly knew him, and we had never been properly introduced… I needn't have worried, because I discovered, just as Mrs Mills had prophesied, that I really was very fond of him and that he was an absolute lamb – and that it is all quite different from anything that ever happened before, and I can't even understand it myself. It just happened that way, and here we are – I love him most frightfully.

There followed a few days in Calcutta during which Tim and Ursula shopped for a wedding ring and replenished their diminished wardrobes. As Ursula admitted to Doris,

> In Calcutta, the climate (and time) being what they are, I had only a nominal need for night wear, but it is as well to have something to put on when the bearer brings the morning tea.

She continued, 'I still have many of my old things, but I have changed my shape and got a good deal slimmer; no doubt they will come in handy for maternity wear, however!' Having lived with a total disregard for the niceties and luxuries of life, marriage had given her a sharp reminder that she was feminine – not just a decent chap among her fellow officers and Naga colleagues. Doris had quickly asked her what she would like as a wedding present, to which she responded;

> The thing I should like more than *anything* would be a fitted dressing case, or a nice dressing-table set – all my things are so old and worn and shabby; it would be *lovely* to have nice things!

On 16 July they set off into Tibet. It was steaming hot in the valleys and the ridges, humps and bumps of the foothills offered climbs twice as challenging as the Assam Hills – and the leeches were at least four times as bad – but none of this damped the Bettses' ardour.

Having been unable to ask the bride's mother's blessing prior to the marriage, Tim wrote to Doris to explain his impulsive behaviour. He owned up immediately that it was far from an unpremeditated performance on his part – he gave his version of their first meeting and her consent to an engagement – and how the Millses had tipped the balance in his favour:

> It must seem to you that she had taken a terrible risk, but we are neither of us children, and have seen a good deal of life, especially in the last few years, and know what we are about, and you may understand that there is nothing I will not do, within my power, to make her happy.

Given the whirlwind nature of Doris's own first engagement, she could hardly demur.

The honeymoon gave Ursula and Tim an opportunity to get to know each other – and they returned to Calcutta on the first week in August a very happy item. Tim reported to his office – but no-one seemed to be expecting him, so they booked into the Grand Hotel and contacted old friends. Ursula discovered that Tim's cousin's wife, a Mrs Morshead, had been Ursula's particular friend on the boat coming out to India in 1937. However, on the 8th, Tim's office ordered him out to Lashio, and the newlyweds had to part. 'Tim went off early on the 11th and found his office had laid nothing on at all, came back searing and went off again by taxi, chewing his pipe and looking straight in front of him – he hates goodbyes.'

Back in Laisong, Ursula reflected on the events of the last six weeks. She sent Doris wedding photos – her first glimpse of Tim:

> I am sending you two photos of Tim and myself – you may notice a change in your Winkle. The standing one makes me look rather like Princess Juliana, but it's very good of Tim – except that his face really goes in and out in crags instead of being so long and smooth. As for the sitting one, I seem to have bobbed into the picture by accident, with a cry of 'Yoo-hoooo!!' I have also had the proofs of the wedding photos, which I will send you for interest's sake, but I don't think they are quite mantelpiece standard, having been taken by the local Indian Cecil Beaton – though the one of Tim and me leaning coyly on each other isn't so bad. There is one of us, the cake and the two Nagas. It is quite a good likeness of the cake.

As she concluded,

> Oh cor lumme, what a flap and excitement it has all been. Still, I think I'd rather have it that way than a long planned engagement – and it was a thrill all right. Romance with a capital R – and I love him so.

Ursula wrote to reassure the rest of her family that, mad though she had always appeared to them, her marriage was based on something better than impulse. To Granny Bower she explained the uncertainty about Tim's future employment and where they would end up:

> We don't know what his job will be like, or when, or whether I shall be able to join him, but he will let me know as soon as he can, which cannot be for a month or so. Meantime, we have had a glorious and most wonderfully happy time together. I am very, *very* fond of him, and we have a tremendous amount in common.

To Aunt Mary Bower she described the wedding – and oozed happiness:

> I soon found the indefinite something about Tim – my long, lean, brown, freckled, pipe-smoking Tim – the indefinite something, I say, which had led me to take the plunge in defiance of all prudence and reason, was *far* more than a liking. I was most desperately fond of him. So here we are – Tim away to Burma, beret over one ear, pipe jutting sternly, and gazing firmly to his front as the taxi bore him away… My dear Aunt, I feel that the last six weeks have really been rather a wild kind of dream. I don't feel in the least married, though I presumably am, as I am definitely wearing a wedding ring that wasn't there before. I am also learning to answer to cries of 'Mrs Betts', and quite often get my new signature right first go. I think you will like your new nephew a lot. His photographs don't flatter him. Tall and lean, build not at all unlike Graham's, he's rather rugged in the face, very sunburnt, with deep-set blue eyes and light brown hair – now getting a bit grey – a great sense of humour, very quiet, very kind, very much a man's man. He is a keen ornithologist, and hobnobs with finches and choughs, as well as hunting butterflies (including Ursula Cacharensis). He loves dogs, horses, the country, Africa, the jungle, trekking, the sea, and adventure generally. In the middle of the Darjeeling Club he discovered a whole bookcase of periodicals and journals, so the happy honeymoon couple spent evening after evening sunk in complete silence, he reading the Bombay Natural History Society's Journal, I the Royal Geographical Society's.

The war in the Far East was still unresolved. American troops had been 'island hopping' across the Pacific, reclaiming key locations such as Iwo Jima and Okinawa. Plans were afoot in the United States for a full-scale invasion of Japan and while Ursula and Tim were on their honeymoon trek into Tibet, US aircraft had been bombing cities across Japan to take out strategic targets in a softening-up process.

It was in early August that President Truman gave an order that in his eyes would end the war without risking the thousands of casualties, not only from America but Britain and the Commonwealth that would inevitably be incurred during a troop invasion of Japan. On 6 August the first atomic bomb was dropped on Hiroshima and, as this didn't elicit an immediate surrender from the Japanese emperor, a further bomb was unleashed three days later on Nagasaki. The horrendous impact and staggering loss of Japanese civilian life that followed shocked the world and forced the emperor to surrender. All of a sudden the war was over.

At the end of July, Tim had headed off from Calcutta to Burma, leaving Ursula to return to Laisong with Namkia and Haichangnang. Their two weeks together were enough to convince her that she'd found a kindred spirit. She had only to recall the occasion when, high in the Tibetan mountains, the whole party had had to take a half-hour roadside halt while Tim chased a Camberwell Beauty butterfly around a chorten to see that they had much in common. 'We both seemed to be mad along the same lines, so it appeared a very suitable match.' Namkia had been speechless with amazement when Ursula first announced her intention to marry their butterfly-chasing visitor, and he and Haichangnang had been equally bewildered to find themselves accompanying their newly-wed employer and her husband on a trek into Tibet.

The day following her return to Laisong, she glanced out of the window of her basha and watched as a procession of her staff formed up in the lines of their own accommodation and moved with an air of disconcerting formality through the camp towards her. From experience, such a gathering was generally the prelude to some sort of petition. It occurred to her that they might be about to ask for a pay-rise in view of her new status as a married woman. The staff arrived in her living room and formed up in a line, each face turned solemnly towards her. Namkia didn't keep her waiting. He stepped forward and looked her in the eye. 'The Sahib is all right,' he pronounced. And with that, the staff turned and trooped out, Namkia having spoken for all of them. Ursula knew that a major hurdle had been overcome.

Life among the Nagas took on a different aspect – not just because she was married, but more because of the new relationship that had been consolidated by the war. The Army had helped the Naga people in ways that the British administration had been unable to achieve in the pre-war days of mistrust and recrimination. They had relieved the famine, brought in effective medicine and by Ursula's single-handed efforts, a new atmosphere of co-operation and trust had been established. By her own admission, she felt that she had been making some headway with the Nagas before the war, but afterwards, the rapprochement was even better.

Ursula returned to her anthropological observations, and made arrangements to tour the area. It was during this time that, knowing her to be on her own, Mills contacted Ursula, inviting her to spend a few days touring with him. At that time Philippa, Mills' fifteen-year-old daughter, often used to accompany him on local tours, helping with dispensary work, while her two younger sisters remained with their mother. Ursula joined Mills, Philippa and their tour party for the first three days. She had got to know the whole family, especially enjoying the company of the intelligent and like-minded teenager, and during these days their friendship was firmly cemented. It was with regret that Ursula parted from the Millses and struck out alone on her scheduled tour. The ensuing incident became part of both the Mills and Betts family histories.

A day after leaving Mills, both parties having set out in opposite directions, Ursula awoke in the night, disturbed by a very vivid dream. Humpus had appeared to her and said that she must turn back because Philippa had become gravely ill. There were by now two days' march between her and the Mills party, but Ursula upped sticks and marched back to find Mills. When she arrived she found Philippa delirious with a high fever, diagnosed as cerebral malaria or meningitis. Ursula accompanied Mills on the forced marches back towards the Brahmaputra where there was a semblance of civilisation and proper medical aid – but this took three days. By the time they reached the doctor, Philippa was beyond help. Mills had the grim task of returning to his family in Shillong with the body of his daughter. For Geraldine Mills, just three at the time, her first vivid memory was of her mother walking down the garden path with her older sister as she told her of Philippa's death. It was a loss from which Mills never truly recovered, but as Ursula had been so closely involved, it was one which strengthened the bond between her and the Mills family. Sixty years later, Geraldine remains in touch with the Betts family and remembers with affection the extraordinary friendship between Ursula and her parents.

Tim came back from Burma 'for keeps' in spring of 1946, just as Haflong was holding its VJ Day celebrations. He found Ursula organising the arrival of the dancers and village people of Magulong.

Magulong were Zemi Nagas, but their village was in Manipur state, outside British India, so after Ursula's first encounter with them in 1940, she had little contact with them – until, that is, she and Bill Tibbetts were recruiting for 'V' Force. One man in particular, Khutuing, had reported to her at Tamenglong, and he remained the 'V' Force contact. Now he led the troupe which was to join their celebrations and Ursula had her first chance to experience Magulong's dancers in 'full fig'.

It was acknowledged that the best Naga dancers were the Zemi – and Magulong, very proudly, knew that they were the best of the best. Their arrival had a lasting impact on Ursula:

> We saw them as they really were. They came down out of the hills like a gale from the past. They were Naga incarnate, tremendous, rip-roaring savages, men who had taken heads but danced like Nijinsky. For drive, for discipline, for skill, for sheer zest, they made our North Cachar Zemi look like a flock of sheep. Oh, they were heady wine, were Magulong – a rich and earthy vintage, splendidly barbarbous!

In an article for *London Calling* – the overseas organ of the BBC – Ursula wrote:

> We heard a noise like an army on the move on the path below the camp. The villagers all turned out, my staff of eight Nagas came running out of their huts and the dogs all began to bark, and then up from the head of the path came the Magulong dancers. And what a sight they were! They were brown-skinned and beautifully made, the men sturdy and muscular and the girls shy, shapely little things; they were all in full dress and singing, a brilliant, beaded, feathered crowd, dressed in vivid native cloths, scarlet, black, salmon-pink, yellow, and earthy brown. Some of the men carried head-hunters' shields tufted with black human hair which swung like tassels as they walked, and all had polished spears which they spun in their hands, so that there was a flickering haze of light down the whole length of the column.

Once officially received in Haflong the next day, Ursula handed the dancers over to the hospitality of government interpreters:

> The Magulong people had danced since the time they could toddle, and they were so steeped in music that even in normal life they were as likely to sing things at you as say them, which was a little disconcerting till you got used to it, and rather like living in a musical comedy. For the same reason, it was one thing to start them dancing and another to stop them. When the audience went home at eleven o'clock, the Magulong were only just getting into their stride. I hung on until about one o'clock and then went off to bed. At dawn the next day they were still at it. Then, when the

> sun was well up, they took their spears and shields and filed away down the hill, a long and magnificently barbaric line of them.

In early May, Ursula and Tim set out on an extensive tour, starting east towards Magulong. As they paused near the village, the sound of singing reached them from across the valley. With the song of their own Naga escort going out to meet the welcoming party, their arrival in the village was a joyful event. As soon as they entered the main street they realised that some celebration was in the air. The village council were all sitting in a row – at least forty bottles of zu were laid out and a small mithan was tied to a post. One of the elders explained that the people of Magulong knew that Ursula and Tim had been married under Sahibs' law, but they felt that she, as a Zemi, should be married by tribal rites too, and they, the Zemi of Magulong, were proposing to do so.

As Magulong got ready for a massive wedding, news came that Tim had a new post in the North-East Frontier Service. The Indian Government would be unable to employ Tim permanently because of his age, but they were keen to offer him a finite contract. He had been allocated the Subansiri Area, essentially an unexplored tract towards Tibet – a posting they had hardly dared to hope for. In a letter Ursula had received from Philip Mills the previous November, he had mentioned his trip to the tribes in the area, 'I've seen the remarkable Apa Tanis, and I must say, their country is rather like Conan Doyle's *Lost World*.'

They would need to leave in just a few days – but in the meantime, there was the wedding. Khutuing officially adopted Ursula, giving her the Naga name 'Katazile' – 'Giver of All'. Tim presented Khutuing, as Ursula's adoptive father, with a spear as a symbolic gift of respect and the sum of 100 rupees as her marriage price – and Khutuing gave Tim a special crimson betrothal cloth, particular to Magulong. On the day of the ceremony a cock was killed by the village priest and the omens taken from the position of its crossed feet. The bird was then cooked and laid out in a dish which, along with a symbolic rice basket representing wifely duties, was borne before them from Khutuing's house to the camp. The rice basket should have been just part of a collection of axe, hoe and spindle, but there had been no time to assemble them. The meat was laid out in the hut – the first formal meal of their Zemi married life – and the wedding was complete.

The celebrations started at four in the afternoon with dancing in the huge, dark smoky morung. It was a ritual untouched by time or external influences, and it continued until the sun went down, until the moon set and the sun rose again. Only at ten o'clock, at the request of the bride and groom, was the party disbanded:

> Grouped about the doorway, they sang goodbye. They ended at last with the ho-hoing – the *heroa-kai* – that wild, ringing barbaric chorus which I think would rouse me out of my coffin. They fairly threw the notes out, chord on chord, magnificent, savage, with the clang of bells. Up went a quivering arm. The whole band checked, on one sustained note. A second's pause; then 'HOI!' It was finished.

Next day Khutuing accompanied Ursula and Tim back to Laisong. He wanted to accompany them to the railway and see them on to the train – to shake their hands as they left:

> There was a special significance in that gesture. We were not just two white people who called him 'Father' for fun, but were linked to him in a relationship of much greater emotional depth. The handshake was the public expression of this.

At the station, as the train rumbled in, they hurried to load their luggage and claim their seats – then stepped down to say their farewells. He spoke simply: 'Go well, son-in-law. Go well, my daughter. Bring my grandchild to show me if you can.' And as Ursula watched him turn with his porters and head through the bazaar, she realised, seeing his head bent down, that he was crying.

39

Tibet

In leaving Laisong and uprooting to the Subansiri Area in Tibet, Ursula and Tim were inheriting a potentially hot political potato.

China had long laid claims to Tibet, and in 1910 had invaded, deposed the Dalai Lama and taken over the capital of Lhasa. This sounded alarm bells with the British – not least because China had previously laid claims to the buffer states of Nepal and Bhutan. It was now of prime importance to explore and survey the North Assam Hills and lay down navigable roads. The area which lay deepest within the hills, the Subansiri region, however, remained uncharted, with no roads through it. In 1914 a convention between India, China and Tibet was negotiated, defining the frontiers between India and Tibet along the Great Himalayan Range. Tibet was pleased to have its border recognised, but China refused to sign. With other matters to deal with – not least the First World War and then the arrival of war in the Far East in 1941 – China and the border wrangles were put on a back burner. However, in 1943 China made another grab for Tibet and issued maps showing Tibet as a Chinese province – indeed, their maps drew the border of Tibet 100 miles south of that laid down by the convention, so also claiming part of the Indian plains. The situation was delicate, since China was an ally against the Japanese – but India would not be robbed of territory, so Britain renewed its efforts to explore and develop the Subansiri Area of the Assam Hills.

Philip Mills was put in charge of this tricky frontier area – if anyone could deal with the people and enlist their help, he could. The country had no proper tracks, and with the high rainfall and loose nature of the soil, it was almost impossible to build roads. This meant animal transport was well-nigh impossible, so it was down to human porters. He overcame the problems sufficiently to establish outposts on the three known routes through the hills – the Lohit and Siang valleys and the Dirang Dzong track, and along the border laid down by the 1914 Convention. He then asserted India's right to the territory between it and the plains and had the line marked at accessible points as the official frontier. Even with this done, the Subansiri region remained unexplored – so he contacted his old friend from the Pangsha expedition of 1936, Baron Christoph von Fürer-Haimendorf, and asked him and his wife to undertake an official expedition into the region.

They set off in 1944 to contact the Apa Tanis – very much an unknown tribe – and returned having cemented good relations. Soon after, at the Apa Tanis' request, they went back with an administrative officer and some military police to deal with the aggressive incursions by Dafla tribesmen from the north-west of their valley, and to release some Apa Tanis whom they had taken prisoner.

The Haimendorfs reported back to the government that of the two main tribal groups, the Apa Tanis and the Dafla-Miris, the latter were aggressive, unstable, riddled with blood feuds and quarrels – which led to kidnaps, enslavements and ransoms. Their communities shifted and reformed with alarming frequency in the areas around the valley in which the Apa Tanis lived. These people were a complete contrast – peaceful, settled, and living in just seven large, strongly built village communities, from which they cultivated their flat-bottomed valley. It was among these peaceful people that the government wanted to establish communications.

Their best plan was to conquer the area by gradual infiltration, starting with a permanent post as far as possible into tribal territory. This would remain manned, even through the rainy season, so there was no opportunity for the area to slip back into anarchy. To do this, permanent supply and communications lines had to be set up. Tim, as Political Officer, was to move straight into the hill district with a small staff of interpreters and a platoon of military police. He would select a site for the post then receive a year's stores by air-drop, and thus provided for, would travel among the tribes, setting up friendly relations, repainting the tribe's perceptions of the government, and learning the terrain before making any attempt to administer the area. The Assam Rifles detachment would enforce the 'Pax Britannica' and defend the outpost and its lifeline back to the plains.

Just as Ursula had understood that it would be disastrous not to deliver on any promise she made to the Nagas, it was impressed on Tim that he should make no commitment which he could not fulfil. However, due to the volatile nature of the Daflas, any such failure would not just be disastrous – it could be fatal.

Here was a chance for real adventure – and, given the warlike nature of the Daflas, Ursula also anticipated an enticing level of risk. The land itself was a mass of knotted mountains – a terrain sufficiently hostile to have deterred exploration hitherto – but now it had been newly gazetted. Tim was to be the first Political Officer and Ursula, with her pedigree of successful dealings with local tribespeople, was to go with him. She described the area as 'the very stuff of dreams – an anomalous survival into the twentieth century' – and she couldn't wait to set out.

Kitted out with such cold-weather clothing as could be raised from the bazaars of Shillong, Ursula and Tim set out by lorry through the grasslands, into light pine woods. From here they moved into the jungle of the Assam valley, and north across the river, eventually taking a sidewheel steamer up the Brahmaputra and arriving, three days' journey out, at the North Lakhimpur Circuit House by truck in semi-darkness. Looming beyond them were the huge dark mountains of the outer ranges surrounding the area.

The light of morning revealed a dirty house, airless and infested with bugs. Thirty paces away were stinking servants' latrines, and the ditch in front of the building buzzed with flies drawn by the carcass of a cow. In these inauspicious surroundings Tim prepared to receive his staff – the Assistant Political Officer, Rajuni Gogoi (an expert on the Daflas); the Assistant Surgeon, Dr Bhattacharjee, a Bengali who had toured with the Haimendorfs; the Transport Supervisor, Siraj-ud-Din, an energetic and fiercely loyal Mohammedan; and a group of interpreters. The latter were all Daflas, the notables being the Head Interpreter Kop Temi and his lieutenant, Bat Heli. The former was in his mid-fifties, dignified in European dress; the latter was much younger, a dyed-in-the-wool Dafla in full tribal dress of tunic, helmet, necklaces, body armour, wrist guards and sword.

A major problem soon emerged. Tim was to identify a place in the hills for the RAF's Dakotas to drop supplies in the second week in November, so needed porters. As Rajuni knew, chances were the hill men wouldn't come forward. During the preceding two years a number of exploratory expeditions had called for porters – it had been tough work and they weren't keen to turn out again.

Kit was a problem too, in the post-war disorder and shortages. Recruits and equipment, once acquired, would vanish inexplicably – sometimes together. They would have to repair their existing cameras, as no new photographic kit was available – but even these would be useless without film. The whole enterprise seemed doomed until, at last, in late October it all came together and they were away.

The main party loaded up, Ursula rounded up their dogs and the three Nagas who would accompany them, and they set off from Lakhimpur. Unlike the inviting warmth of the Naga Hills, these mountains seemed to resent the intrusion – it was a foretaste of the territory and the problems it would cause. The skeleton of a trader who had died en route left a lasting impression. The flesh had long gone from the bones and in the cool damp, forest ferns sprouted around the shoulders and tendrils grew through the ribs. It was a lesson to learn quickly – this land was harsh, hostile and unforgiving, and if a man weakened, he would quickly be drawn in and broken down to nothing.

As the straggling party pitched camp and Tim fished for their supper, he heard a distinct drone. It was the first reconnaissance flight, looking for signs of a dropping zone – not expected for at least another five days. If no recognised sign of them was visible, with signals on display when the second recce came over the next day, the airdrop would be cancelled and the whole year's work would be scrapped.

They had planned to be a good twenty miles further into the area, so Tim decided that if they had no porters by the afternoon, he and the Assam Rifles would go ahead and try to find a rendezvous by forced march. Tim was expecting to have to opt for the march – when eight Daflas hove into view and in no time they, Tim and two Gurkhas set off into the fading light.

At dusk Siraj came back with fifteen recruits – and the promise of twenty more next morning – and to Ursula's amazement, all arrived for an early start. Ominously, they heard the hum of approaching aircraft and all was quiet as they waited … and at last the hum grew louder again and the aircraft headed back. Ursula knew that they'd spotted Tim's party.

As Ursula's group marched on, three Apa Tanis came towards them and one almost jostled Ursula off the narrow path. Bat Heli shouted to him to give way and he grudgingly moved aside – then paused. He realised what the party was and asked for the Sahib. Bat Heli said the Sahib had gone ahead. 'Where's the Memsahib, then? They said there was one coming.' As Ursula recorded in *The Hidden Land*,

> There was a general guffaw. The man looked amazed and two or three people pointed me out within a yard of him. He looked me up and down – heavy sandals, ankle puttees, drill trousers and an old army shirt – much as I might study a circus elephant, and then said: 'Huh! She looks just like a man. She's much bigger than the

> one who was here last year.' The outraged porters chivvied him off down the path and cut short this interesting comparison with Betty Haimendorf. Siraj, much upset, said, 'These Apa Tanis have no manners. They are an impudent people.'

The supply drop went ahead over the next few days, but despite the large number of villages around the Panior Basin, there was no approach from the local tribes – then several days into the drop, Tim came charging back to the camp. A huge official party of headmen was approaching. Now was the time to set out the political presents and prepare a welcome. Ursula and Tim were still struggling with the sticking lid of the chest when the first man arrived.

Kago Bida, the head of the Kago clan in Haja, stood almost six feet tall and cut a weird and fantastic figure:

> His lids were heavy and drooped over full eyes, giving him a reptilian look. There was a blue tattoo mark under his lower lip; his skin was fair and the mark showed up clearly. His hair was black and long and plaited in a horn on his forehead – not the heavy Dafla knob, but in the lighter, more complicated Apa Tani knot, and a foot-long brass skewer was thrust through it. He wore a scarlet Government cloth draped in a short tunic, below which was a perineal band and a perspective of bare, pinkish leg which reminded one of a cock ostrich. He was formidably armed; a dagger hung round his neck on a string, he carried a Tibetan sword on a baldric ornamented with a tiger's jawbone, and he wore a hairy black palm-fibre rain cape; a saucy little white feather fluttered from his cane hat, contradicting the implied ferocity below.

His demeanour was sullen and non-committal, but with him was a small, elderly man with a clown's face. He was Chigin Nime: priest, warrior, and councillor of Duta village – and one of the most influential men in the Apa Tani Valley. His welcome was effusive. He rushed towards them, arms outstretched and hugged the new Political Officer and the Memsahib. He grasped their heads between his hands as he patted them with cries of joy – and he turned to accord Siraj the same greeting – but he, shocked by such lack of decorum, had made himself scarce.

A cordial and liquor-lubricated conference began, with much polite chit-chat – then one man, Toko Bat from Talo, cut to the matter in hand. 'Let the foreigner say something sensible. Will the Government hear our cases, or will it not? And if not, what is the use of his coming here?' They wanted adjudication on their feuds, but Tim had no time to get involved. Certainly his ultimate object was to make his new outpost a neutral sanctuary where feuding factions could meet and settle their differences peacefully – but first the outpost had to be set up. If Tim didn't agree to their request now, he might lose the much-needed local labour.

All eyes turned to Tim, who sat back, smiling enigmatically. Ursula wondered what on earth he could pull out of the hat to fix this impasse – and then she heard what he had evidently noticed before. It was the drone of aircraft, and as the crew pushed out the bales of supplies over the nearby dropping area, long parachutes opened up to drift the packs gently to the ground. Pass after pass came over, with all eyes turned to the sky in rapt amazement, watching as case after case of sugar, butter, tea, kerosene, condensed milk and more came down. As the last plane turned away, the whole party started away to be the first to tell the story at their home village. Without even the formality of a goodbye, they were gone. Only Kago Bida and Nime remained – the latter ecstatic and elated, and the former more reserved – but still unable to stifle a shy smile. As he left, Bida pushed a fat, grimy, naked fellow tribesman towards Ursula with a few barked orders – and Ursula realised she had been given one of Bida's serfs as a souvenir.

Ursula and Tim set out to see the Apa Tani Valley, nestling in the centre of the Dafla-occupied hills. To reach it they hiked through mountain forests with lush alpine-style flora and orchids growing wild. Their first view of this haven of civilisation came as a revelation. A vista suddenly opened up below them – an expanse of orderly, cultivated fields and scattered villages through which the Kale River and its tributaries flowed. It was like a hidden Shangri-La. This was territory explored only by the Heimendorfs, and the Apa Tanis were understandably suspicious as they entered the first village – Haja:

> The street before us was twenty feet wide and looked, as it wound away, like a drained canal. It was solidly walled on either side by bamboo houses on piles; each house had an entrance balcony reached by a notched log ladder, the steep-pitched roofs were thatched, and the eaves came nearly to the ground. In no time the locals were gathering on their balconies to see the strangers. There were Apa Tani men in their normal near-nakedness; some wore cloaks, a fine bordered cope for the rich and quilted rags for the poor, and every grown male had the tribal belt, the girdle of scarlet cane strands with the long lobster-tail behind. Small boys had miniature cloaks and a single strand of red cane, and the little girls wore a cloak and a bell. Then there were the women. Filthily grimy, like all Apa Tanis, their greasy black hair was screwed on top of their heads in a pointed knob; they wore bunchy hand-woven skirts and quilted jackets, both sooted dark grey. Their necks were hung and their ample bosoms loaded with string upon string of blue beads, their faces were tattooed, and their noses were turned into hippopotamus-snouts by large black resin discs thrust into the pierced wings.

Tim was prompted to speculate what happened if they got a cold.

When, the next day, they peered out from their tent in the Haimendorfs' old campsite at nearby Duta Pape (rhymed with 'harp'), they found the Apa Tanis flooding across the fields towards them.

> They crowded round our fires and elbowed us out; the place seethed with tousled and verminous heads, sooty faces and grubby grey cloaks; men were shouldering, crushing and peering. The camp was swamped. There were rude comments and they laughed in our faces. We were Wild Men of Borneo, apes in a cage to be teased, jeered at and prodded. Most primitive people are formal in their manners – after all, an insult is more than likely to get one killed – but the lower-class Apa Tani, secure in his hidden valley and God-given conviction that his tribe is the hub of the universe and the only true human race, is the worst-mannered creature in Asia. Almost as bad as their manners were their thefts and their filth.

After the Apa Tani had rifled through the camp, spitting and pilfering as they went, Ursula wrote feelingly,

> by nightfall I loathed the Apa Tanis, loathed them singly and collectively, from unpolished brass hair-skewer to calloused and grimy bare heel, and I didn't care if I never saw another.

However, in Bobo they were received with respect and hospitality – and they left the Apa Tani Valley in a more optimistic mood. These people were the peaceful counterparts of the feuding Daflas – as far as the 'hearts and minds' work at the core of Tim's posting was concerned, the Apa Tanis would be the easier of the two to win over.

Tim soon located a suitable site for the outpost, just above the Dafla village of Talo, overlooking a meeting of routes, and giving a good vantage point of Talo itself, which was suspected of being at the root of a number of local raids.

The Betts' household, with attendant staff and their Assam Rifles escort, moved to the new site, named Kore, and set up camp. They pitched tents, cooked over the fire and went to bed 'with a pleasantly pioneering feeling'.

Gradually the outpost took shape, but the hoped-for log cabin evolved into a much less windproof building. The only solid timber was too far away to be brought in – so it had to be giant bamboo, lashed together with coils of green cane. The final building comprised a bedroom with two camp beds, tin storage cases, cane carrying boxes and some nails in the walls for hanging clothes; a bathroom – small and dark with a canvas tub for a bath which was emptied by tipping up over a hole in the floor; an office with bamboo shelves, a box for Tim's botanical specimens, and a desk made from a large box-lid rested across two tea chests, and 'the Great Hall'. This latter was big and draughty, its windows unglazed, and was destined only to be used for major gatherings, hearings and meetings.

The Bettses celebrated Christmas 1946 by raising the Union Jack over Kore:

> It stood out bright and strong against a clear blue sky and we all stood round below and drank its health. It was a symbol and more than a symbol. For three months we had fought and struggled to bring it there, and to bring with it that for which it stood. In its shadow the tribal warfare, murders and kidnappings of the Dafla country would not be tolerated, and law-abiding men of whatever race or tribe would be free to travel the King's highway in safety. Tribesmen could come in to where it flew and settle their disputes peaceably without fear of assassination. It stood for law and order amid anarchy and peace amid bloodshed, and all of us – Tim, myself, Rajuni, Temi, Siraj, Heli, Europeans, plainsmen and tribesmen alike – cared very much indeed for all that it represented.

Overall, there was a sense of mistrust of the government and its agents. Past British expeditions to the area had left making no attempt to establish any permanent authority. It was for this reason that interpreters were so hard to find. They had worked on previous expeditions and been involved in adjudicating over disputes – then, when the expeditions had left, the interpreters had suffered recriminations. None of these men was keen to get involved again, and others saw what had happened in the past and felt similarly unenthusiastic. If Tim was going to succeed, he would need to convince the local tribes that the government would make a permanent investment in the area.

Kore was one signal of this intention, as was the setting up of a household and employing locals. Ursula got to know the Apa Tani women who carried out the tribe's trading, and made every effort to operate within their barter system, despite much profiteering and sharp dealing on the part of the women. They would arrive, heavily tattooed, black plugs in their noses and, as Ursula had to admit, 'lamentably plain', bearing a sad collection of wilting greens, some smoke-dried rats, pumpkins, and other undesirable wares. These they would trade for tobacco leaves, kitchen salt or, occasionally, a few annas in cash.

On 2 January 1947 Tim and Ursula set out north, towards uncharted territory, through hostile country. Tim insisted that they travel without armed support, despite warnings from locals about the violence of the Hidjat men – but nothing happened. The villagers, far from being aggressive, were curious and nervous. All the same, the trip was beset with local difficulties, each daring Tim and Ursula to put a foot wrong – but on every occasion, the sound diplomacy and local knowledge of their staff interpreters saved them from errors of protocol.

In areas outside the influence of the government, slavery was common. In the Palin Valley they saw the saddening plight of people kept in abject poverty, robbed of their dignity and wearing only flimsy rags – but they knew that they could not act for the slaves unbidden, and to interfere would damage the fragile trust that they were working so hard to build. There was a two-tier class system where a notional nobility of well-off, free families lorded it over the servile poor – but for now Tim had to stay on the sidelines.

At Beuri they met a stumbling block – the clan operated a very profitable trade-block between Tibet to the north and the tribes to the south, and had gone so far in trying to protect this control as to try to conceal the very track approaching their village. When Tim visited the village with Chigin Nime, the trip was effectively stymied. The best agreement they could wrest from the headman was that he would grant Chigin Nime safe passage north if the rest of the party turned back. Nime was keen to go on and reconnoitre on his own, risky though it would be – so Ursula and Tim resigned themselves to returning to Kore.

The pitfalls of bringing order and justice to the Daflas and Apa Tanis soon became apparent. The less sophisticated tribesmen saw the government as a big, stupid beast which they could trick into taking their part, right or wrong. Tim was never free of importunate litigants, perverting the course of justice with evasions of the truth, wilful misunderstandings and obstacles to discussion and settlement. Ursula appreciated Tim's phlegmatic approach: 'They would have driven a less even-tempered man than Tim to frenzy, but they were lucky, as Chigin Nime pointed out, in having a Sahib who tore his own hair instead of theirs.'

By May Kore was becoming well established, with Ursula's plot laid out to grass with a flourishing kitchen garden and orchard. In six months they had achieved a lot:

> The porter track was through, staging-camps had been built along it and another half-year's rations had been dropped from the air and were safely in the Yatchuli store.

> Raiding had been stopped along the track and within patrol-range of the post, and there was a mel daily in the Dafla interpreters' quarters. The line of communication was still precarious and porters were still short, but at least a part of our dream had taken shape. Kore, our own creation, was a living, coherent entity, a valid community, a growing and expanding cell, which acted and interacted with the body of the Subansiri Area.

Six months on, there was a marked change in the Apa Tanis' attitude,

> We had travelled with them, joked with them, been in danger together, been wet and hungry and cold, had sat on dank logs with them in Dafla fields and waited for the porters, had ploughed through knee-deep mud and crossed perilous bridges and ferries. Since the New Year alone, we had marched nearly a thousand miles with them, for we were walking a steady average of two hundred miles a month. On these cheek-by-jowl treks there was no room for sham. You came to know people as they were and you liked them or you did not.

The Betts' household consisted of Hage Tara, an eighteen-year-old who became their chief interpreter, three Nagas, three of their original Dafla staff and four Apa Tanis. As time went by, the interpreters, as befitted their office, remained the soul of propriety and rectitude, while the rest proved as full of foibles as had Ursula's Naga staff before.

At the beginning of May, Tim and Ursula visited the Apa Tani Valley again. It was like June in England, the trees in full leaf and the landscape bursting with colour and energy. 'The wind rustled in the pines, the air was warm and sweet, the young rice in the acres of rice-fields was brilliant with colour, and fat white clouds were sitting about on the mountains beyond.' Their aim was to find a site for a new government camp.

> We passed down brush-fenced lanes which might have been in Cornwall, we rested in bamboo-shaded alleys at whose mouths the flooded fields glared in the sun like white-hot metal. The Apa Tani guides cut us pine branches for us to sit on; the needles were young and silky and the cut ends smelled sweetly resinous. Between the half-grown trees of the wood we could see green pastures and grazing cattle. Overhead was the shimmer of pines, round us as we lay, the men sprawled in perspectives of cane hats, red belts and tails, and bare, copper-brown buttocks, and away at the head of the Valley, framed between distant wooded hills, the snow-peaks showed cool and unattainable. It was the last really happy day we were to know for a long time.

The fly in the ointment was India's imminent independence. The committee convened to determine the fate of the hill tribes was touring Assam in May, and Tim went to meet them in Shillong, leaving Ursula with Dr Bhattacharjee, Siraj and the Assam Rifles. It was important to maintain a presence in Kore, especially during the rains, when previous government parties had decamped. In Tim's absence, word reached Ursula of a gambu in the Apa Tani Valley. This was a mass duel, held to settle feuds between villages. The idea was to provide a swift solution to a grievance so that the Apa Tanis could resume their cultivation. If one party did not accept the decision of a mel, the situation would escalate to a gambu – which would be either unopposed or, more seriously, opposed.

An unopposed gambu took the form of an armed demonstration against the recalcitrant litigant – attacks on his property usually ended in his humiliation and the sequestering of his property. An opposed gambu was likely to result in casualty or even death – and it was such an event that an interpreter announced to Ursula that she must go to Pape at once, where the gambu would take place the following morning to settle a feud between a man from Bela and one from Duta. The latter village was hell-bent on crushing Bela, and having rallied other villages to support them, they wanted their gambu.

Ursula arrived in time to see the heavily armed war party from Duta arriving. A group of Bela elders approached the assembled hordes, bringing a mithan and offering to pay a fine to restore the peace, but the Duta warriors had put on armour and come a long way in hot sun, and they wanted their gambu. The Bela men, it seemed, were at home, scared out of their wits. Ursula and Dr Bhattarcharjee were astounded:

> It had not occurred to us that anyone, even the Apa Tanis themselves, could consider this comic-opera affair a deadly serious military demonstration, for compared to war as we unfortunately knew it – or even as the Daflas or the Nagas knew it, when it was quite bad enough – this was nursery charades.

The growing battle line now stretched to a quarter of a mile. A contingent from Hong hove into view, and a group from Hari made an elaborate charge, pikes lowered, flashing daos and making an aggressive 'rrrrrrrrr' sound, then marched back to rejoin the ranks. These village charges went on for an hour, while Hong discussed their allegiance. The village was divided over their support of the gambu – and the matter had come to blows in which the Bela-friendly faction was driven back home. The Hong men were now howling for reprisals against their own people who had tried to hold them back – and against Bela as a whole.

The main body of warriors had enjoyed their sabre-rattling outing but were now all for settling for a mithan and a fine, but the Hong contingent urged them on to wreck Bela's fields and groves. Even Duta, at the centre of the original dispute, had had enough and were heading home – but Hong formed up to charge. It was only a feint, but as they turned back, the last few men kicked up a shower of dry earth behind them in a crude gesture of insult.

The remaining groups gathered round the Bela elders, accepted and killed the mithan and set up symbolic tripods to denote a peace treaty. Bela had been subjugated – but Hong wouldn't recognise the treaty and it was only through the mediation of one of Ursula's interpreters that they were persuaded to hold their protest outside Pape instead of in Kore. Ursula later reflected, 'As it turned out, the Apa Tanis were going to be very sorry for that gambu before we were through.'

40

Indian Independence

Indian Independence, scheduled for June 1948, was suddenly brought forward. No-one knew what was to happen to the North-East Frontier area – or what the policy of the new Indian Government would be:

> Plans were disrupted and everything was at a standstill. The RAF was to go and there would be no airdrop in the autumn, for no civil firm had been found to undertake it. Tim's contract had been cancelled, and as India was a second home to us, he had applied to stay on there instead of transferring to a British colony; there was, however, no guarantee that he would be employed, and we should probably be workless and homeless in a month.

Their endeavour to bring trust and peace to the Subansiri Area had been in vain:

> What was unbearable was to know that we had failed. In our battle with our gigantic task we had worked twelve hours a day and seven days a week for three-quarters of a year, fighting our way from crisis to crisis while new obstacles and frustrations rose at every turn. We had gone hungry and cold and dirty, we had slept on the ground and under the sky. Now the flag flew over Kore and the long hours through which Tim had kept his temper were bearing fruit – not for nothing had the Apa Tanis dubbed him the 'Ui Sahib' – the Sahib who, like their own benevolent god of the heavens, was never angry.

Ursula received Tim's news from Shillong with despair:

> We had won over our people only to be the means of their betrayal. All that we had promised them and that they had believed, had been turned to lies by people far away, people who would never see them – but it was we in Kore who would take the blame. We had come to care very much indeed – no! That is a miserable understatement. We had come to care passionately, vehemently, fanatically for the Subansiri Area and its people, to care as the unemotional inarticulate Briton is supposed to be incapable of caring. They meant more to us than anything else in the world – than home, prosperity, security, children or comfort.

Ursula tried to maintain normal routines – and one morning, in Duta Pape, a headman from Haja arrived and offered her a slave boy to buy. He had been orphaned so went to live with an elder brother – who was a cattle rustler. The seven-year-old had been captured as a bargaining tool against his brother, and put in the stocks, but had managed to escape. He was retaken, but when his brother was killed, there was no-one who would want to ransom him, so he was sold on for his potential as a slave, and had ended up with the Haja headman.

Back from Shillong, Tim learned that his contract had been extended by six months – however, he would have to administer the neighbouring Balipara Tract as well as the Subansiri, so they set out to explore the territory. On the return march to Kore, Ursula found one of their camp stops particularly unforgettable:

> Even at the time the experience seemed curiously intense, the senses unnaturally sharpened, and yet nothing happened to mark it; it was simply another camp. Tall, isolated trees like Scots firs rose out of the dry grass; their trunks were straight and branchless, almost to the top, but high overhead their limbs and stiff foliage made delicate, unreal pattern against a pale evening sky sown with faint stars. As the darkness deepened and the firelight began to tell, our tawdry tents and shelters took on a new quality; the fires glowing in the dusk were sources of magic and wonder, transfiguring rather than revealing the figures – sepoys, porters, tribesmen – which moved round them, so that they became inhabitants of another and more marvellous world – creatures of high romance. When night shut firmly down and the stars, grown big and bright, glinted through the remote roof of leaves, a wind came rushing down the valley. It whipped the fires into sudden life; the fir-branches which built them roared into flame, whirling tourbillions shot skywards, the red-barked branches overhead leaped out of the dark, the half-seen foliage tossed and, far above the fiery caves and the flames, swarms of sparks, like fireflies hurtled into the windy blackness.

The sight of the Apa Tani Valley as she turned a corner at the edge of the forest never lost its magic:

> It had never ceased to amaze me and leave me staring and silent, unable to comprehend but wanting to wrap up the incredible moment of experience and take it home to wonder over and treasure. For the Valley was beautiful beyond belief. It was lovely with the wild, unearthly beauty which belonged to the Subansiri Area alone and to nowhere else, a frightening beauty, a beauty so grand and terrible that we had no right to see it. We had strayed into the world of the Gods and were tasting forbidden pleasures.

It was an enduring vision Ursula would always carry with her as a reminder of their Subansiri days.

Late in 1947, Tim negotiated a peace treaty between the Licha Daflas and the Apa Tanis. He and Ursula saw this finalised in Kirom, and then went to help in the rebuilding of the Pape camp. They were unaware at the time, but this was one of those pivotal moments on which lives would hang. Instead, they were happy at the prospect of the exploration ahead.

At Pape they started constructing a hut which would afford some proper shelter. The result of their labours was not what they had planned – but they loved 'Crazy Gables' for all its faults. Ursula described it in a letter to Pam Mills:

> The Naik who put up the framework couldn't tell a fifteen-degree slope from dead level, and the floors and the roof-beams are too 'Olde Worlde' for words. The front veranda is ten feet off the ground to start with, and swoops upward like a rocket-launching ramp. The south-east corner of the bedroom is a foot higher than any other and the front gable zooms upwards like the roof of a Zemi dekachang.

Tim felt that he could be spared to go back to see the relief of the Assam Rifles garrison near to Kore. It would take only a small detour to inspect the annual repairs to the Panior Bridge, and he left Kore in November, expecting to be gone a week, and Ursula went to Duta Pape.

Just four days after Tim left, Ursula was awoken before dawn by a frantic Koda. Someone had been badly burned in Haja – she must go at once. She gathered a pack of ointments and bandages into the first-aid kit and set out. She found the patient in a terrible state – much of his body was a sheet of burns:

> Face, chest, arms, thighs and feet were skinned and sloughing, eyelids and ears were blistered, eyebrows and lashes were gone, and on the outside of his arms, which he must have thrown up to protect his head, the burns had destroyed the skin and bitten deeply into the flesh and muscle below.

Reports of the British leaving India had reached the Daflas, and they saw this and Tim's recent departure with the soldiers as heralding the end of government control. Tragically the spies who reported this didn't stick around long enough to see the incoming relief. They saw, instead, an opportunity to settle old scores, and a Bagi man had recruited some Kirom Daflas to help him take revenge for a twenty-five-year-old grievance against two households in his own village. The Apa Tani man whose burns Ursula was treating had been staying overnight with friends when, just before dawn, the house was set on fire. The raiders had fired the exits, and were cutting down anyone who tried to break out. Women and children ran screaming through the inferno and four children were roasted to death. Eventually the death toll was around twenty – mostly women and children. Horrified at the ramifications, Ursula hurried back to Pape to write a report to Tim.

It emerged that all the men of Kirom were implicated. Most of the people who were missing from Bagi had resurfaced from the woods, but one man had been captured by the Kiroms. With Tim back and the Assam Rifles relief in situ, the Apa Tani villages began to hum with excitement and the prospect of some serious retribution.

Ursula and Tim knew that news of his return with the troops would have reached the Kiroms. As she surmised,

> It must have come on them like a thunderclap; they had miscalculated horribly; they must have felt that the gods had cheated them. They knew what happened to villages which defied the Government, for the mild punitive measures against them in 1945 had frightened them beyond all reason. Ambushes they understood, raids and counter-raids they knew, but disciplined, organised, steady, rifle-armed troops were as terrifying and incomprehensible to them as a Martian horde.

In a panic, they threatened to burn Kore, murder Tim and sell Ursula as a slave if the government took action against them. Tim declined to respond at all, so the Kiroms' threats got louder and more vicious.

The new Assam Rifles men were mere rookies – and twenty-five of them had replaced the fifty old hands, so Tim was not entirely confident in his military back-up. However, he felt that a major raid was unlikely. Ursula stayed in Pape, going to Haja to dress the burns every day, while Tim went back to the heavily guarded Kore to organise a patrol.

Tim had just left when Rika rushed in to Ursula to say that Kirom meant to attack her camp that night. It was too late to send for Tim to come back – but there was always the chance that the rumour was a lie. Ursula had to weigh up the possibilities. As she confided to Rika, 'I've got a shotgun and cartridges. Let's hope they don't come.'

Ursula assessed her defences, and was less than confident:

> The house was damnably inflammable and, to make things worse, the space between the piles below was stuffed with dry grass for thatching. I walked round all the rooms and looked out of the windows, studying the routes to the ground. It was a long jump, but with a foothold outside I could make it at a pinch. I took out the shotgun and cartridges and put them on the floor by the bed, and then crawled into my sleeping-bag and lay there, thinking. I wasn't particularly scared, but I didn't like the situation much either. The only comfort was, funnily enough, that there was nothing to do about it, for the way out was to take shelter in Haja, and that would have let the Daflas get us on the run. 'Either they'd raid or they wouldn't,' I said to myself among the blankets, and if they didn't there was nothing to worry about. If they did, I could worry about it when the time came.

Ursula woke to a cold, grey morning, and another episode in the war of nerves was over.

Ursula learned that Kirom men were going to gather at the house of the man who had instigated the raid, and share out the loot – so if Tim timed it right, he could take them in one fell swoop. They decided that the patrol should start from Pape – but with a suitable ruse as a cover-up for the movement of troops. Tim would arrive ahead of them and let it be known that a contingent of Assam Rifles were on their way to give one of their popular entertainments. Meanwhile Ursula sent out Apa Tani staff, in on the secret, to find someone to guide the patrol to the right house.

As the Assam Rifles arrived, Tim prepared to leave, his carbine slung on his back and his kukri in his webbing belt. Ursula watched as he and his patrol disappeared into the darkness. She returned to Crazy Gables, which felt uncannily empty. 'I realised I was frightened for him. I wished I had borrowed a rifle and gone with him.' She dismissed the staff and prepared to sit it out alone.

Thirty hours later Tim was back – exhausted but triumphant. The Gurkhas had dashed in one door of the house, driving the Kirom men and their Bagi host out the other way, leaving behind a small baby of about fifteen months, whom they later identified as a survivor of the Bagi raid. There were signs that the Kirom men and their sympathisers were rallying, so Tim's men withdrew, taking the baby with them. For the cost of one minor casualty, they'd put the wind up the enemy, burned down the house of the instigator, destroyed his livestock and garden, fired a granary full of looted grain and rescued a captured child. The government had regained the initiative.

All was well when the grandmother turned up to claim the baby. However, the Kirom arsonists were still mainly at large, and Tim was pleased when news came in that three of them would shortly be visiting Talo. His men surrounded the house and captured one man as a bargaining tool – and once again, Kirom reacted aggressively, threatening to torch the Great Hall. Ursula and Tim slept with their guns by their sides and with buckets of water to hand, and only undertook the journey between Pape and Kore with an armed escort.

Suddenly Tim gained a trump card. Siraj had spotted a lad in Talo – the son of a Kirom ring-leader, Licha Tasser. Siraj gave no sign of recognition and hurried back to Kore. Although Tim was due back later that afternoon, there was no time for delay, so Siraj gathered up three unarmed sepoys and an interpreter and returned to the house in Talo on the pretext of a social call. They settled by the fire with a drink and, when the lad joined them, they quickly pounced on him and took him back to Kore. When Tim arrived the hostage was in safe custody.

Word travelled quickly, and the door of the Kore lock-up had scarcely closed on the lad when the Kiroms freed the porter they had taken captive. Tim released the first prisoner, but was adamant that if Licha Tasser wanted his son, he must surrender his red cloth and come to Kore under safe conduct to see Tim about the Bagi raid. Tasser was not accustomed to straight dealing, so suspected a trick – and for some days he wavered. Tim was quite prepared to sit it out, so he and Ursula set out on tour, leaving Kop Temi in charge. It was now too late in the year to follow the Haimendorfs' route to the Upper Khru region, but the Miri posa had to be paid, and the route, far out to the north and east, would make a good short tour – a final trek 'to say farewell to the cool, bright winter days, the long, leg-aching marches and the star-roofed, firelit nights'.

41

Leaving Tibet

There was a special poignancy to the tour as Ursula and Tim set out in early December. All along, they had hoped that the new Indian Government would offer Tim a permanent post so they could stay in the area – but now they accepted that they'd have to leave – and sooner rather than later.

All the same, there was much to celebrate. After months of struggling against the innate mistrust, deviousness and hostility of the local tribes, the barriers had dissolved and in their place were a sense of trust and genuine comradeship.

It was a tour Ursula would always remember – one out of so many. This was the steepest country they had ever tackled – the southern flank of the valley was 7,000 feet high and from it there jutted ridges with knife-like edges, divided by deep ravines. In this extreme terrain, they covered just seven miles in eight hours on the first day.

The Miris were charmingly laid-back, and two days of litigation passed in leisurely fashion, after which Ursula and Tim crossed the swirling current of the Kamla. The days disappeared in the sweat of steep climbs, long walks, camp chores – until, south of the Kamla and setting up camp at the more northerly village of Rakhe, Siraj, who had come out to meet them on the return leg of their tour, delivered a mail-bag of letters, parcels, newspapers and magazines. Suddenly they realised it was Christmas Eve.

Every step back towards home camp was a wrench:

> At Bua, reality closed in. It was the last Miri village, and the fact brought it home to us suddenly that we should never in all our lives see another, never sweat up and down these interminable ridges with our tail of porters following us, never again know the freedom, the friendship, the share in adventure. Our days in Eden were numbered and the desolation beyond loomed frighteningly close, a grey desert of days at which we could hardly bear to look.

The camp was pitched – Ursula and Tim slept on the ground in an open tarpaulin shelter rather than in a standard tent – and night fell. The last night in Miri country was unbearable, and as the fire burned low and they crawled into their sleeping bags, Ursula was beyond consolation. 'The pain of our loss was so great that I could not even cry, and I lay and watched the stars walk along the far hill until, in spite of myself, I went to sleep.'

Three days later they were back in the frost-covered Apa Tani Valley – it was white from end to end, with every pond frozen and icy splinters sparkling on the path. It was a Christmas card scene, and the interpreters who came out from Pape to meet them looked absurdly like robins as their red cloths bobbed through the frosty landscape.

Tim coughed and coughed throughout the next day, and by evening he had a high fever and retired to bed. Ursula recognised the quick, shallow breathing of pneumonia, so she dosed him with sulpha drugs, then settled down to watch him overnight. She knew how weak Tim had been after his long, hard war, and having come straight to his posting in the area, had little time to gain weight and strength. Their last sixteen months had been physically and mentally gruelling and she was scared sick that he might not have the reserves to beat a serious bout of pneumonia. She laid up wood for the fire, spread out her bedding and prepared to watch through the night.

Tim's breathing was normal in the morning, and despite a graveyard cough, nothing could deter him from getting back to Kore. Ursula followed him a day later with the heavy baggage and arrived in time to put him to bed again, this time racked with bronchitis.

Licha Tasser's son was still in the Kore lock-up, as he had not yet complied with Tim's stipulations. However, with Kore about to be disbanded, Tim let it be known that he was going to send the lad, still in custody, to the military base at Lokra, and this prompted Tasser to send in his red cloth, along with a rather inferior mithan. Tim let the lad go with a sigh of relief.

They had to close Kore down – and the first sign was the demise of the garden which Ursula had tended so lovingly. It was heart-breaking to see the orchids they had brought back from Rakhe putting out new roots, knowing they would never see them flower. The weeds were already creeping over the vegetable patch – which would never be planted again. Soon the marked graves where they had buried their dogs would be grown over, 'Nagi, my own little soft Nagi, black and gentle and kind, with a coat like silk, and Tim's beloved Tessa, the golden, foolish puppy. Heartbreak and happiness and tragedy were buried here'. Kore was dead, and they would spend the rest of the winter at Pape.

At least Ursula and Tim had a house there, so they enjoyed a residential status when the Morrum festival came around. The year before they had been alien spectators, but now they were part of the feast and the fun – and were honoured guests, even with their cameras, at many private celebrations. Then came spring, with pussy-willow, wild violets, peach trees in bloom and all the lush promise of colour and fruitfulness in summer. From the balcony of Crazy Gables, Ursula could look out on the froth of white blossom on the old crab-pear trees, standing stark against the dark pines behind. The rhododendrons, primulas, flowering cherries – the blooms were a splash of brilliance against the powder-blue hills – it was all unbearably beautiful – and soon to be lost to them forever.

Trouble was brewing in the rest of the valley. It was a political matter between Bela, Haja, Hari and Hong who had co-existed harmoniously for centuries, and three more groups of newer settlers who founded their own villages of Duta, Mudang Tage and Michi Bamin – collectively known as Dübo – and asked to join the alliance. Not all were agreeable to this, but a compromise had been reached and all was well until Duta's gambu against Bela. Bela had capitulated and accepted the tribal verdict, but felt that the very act of the gambu had been in breach of the spirit of their original agreement. They told Duta that they would be rejoining Hong and Haja to celebrate the big Mloko festival. Duta became increasingly aggressive and announced that if Bela made the threatened Mloko visits to Hong and Haja, they would attack the processions.

All was quiet at Crazy Gables. Tim, now on paid leave, had gone to Haja, Ursula was knitting by the fire. At half past nine, Koda called Ursula outside – the Duta men were assembling, just fifty yards away, all armed up for another gambu. From the Duta groves came the sound of bamboo being cut for weapons. 'Here, before our eyes, an entire village was wasting the treasure of generations, sacrificing the patient, slow-growing accumulation of uncounted seasons to egotism expressed in a collective adult tantrum.'

Tension escalated as the other villages were drawn in. Bela, which had split its loyalties in the original treaty, was now in a state of civil war. Tim returned to Pape and learned that Hong women had apparently been molested in the fields by Mudang Tage, so Hong men retaliated in kind against the first Duta women they could find. By lunchtime there were reports that a Bela raiding party had attacked a Duta field-gang, and by mid-afternoon, the whole valley was a tinder-box.

Temi called a meeting the next day, for which delegates slunk in furtively to avoid Duta aggression. They agreed unanimously that no-one wanted a war, and all were prepared to invest time and reason in reaching a solution – but as Duta was not represented, they could not even agree a temporary truce. The next day Ursula and Tim went out under the pretext of shooting pigeons to keep an eye on Kop Temi as he went, otherwise unescorted, to a road block set up by Mudang Tage. As they had suspected, it was manned by young toughs, all up for a fight, who would have shown little mercy to a lone, unarmed interpreter. En route home another Mudang Tage gang sprang out on them, but checked when they saw their guns. Ursula was unimpressed: 'I have always disliked cowardly bullies, and I was beginning to dislike Mudang Tage and Duta very much indeed'.

Back in Pape, a large Bela delegation had come in, desperate for a solution. After the meeting, which made no real progress, Temi reported that he had urged Hong and Bela to make concessions so that Duta would have no excuse to attack – but again there was no agreement. There was just one day before the festival, and if no compromise were reached, Duta would attack – and there would be war.

Unable to influence events, Ursula and Tim went out the next day with a picnic. As they returned in the late afternoon, Temi came to meet them – with good news. Desperate to avoid conflict, the elders had reached a simple compromise. The ceremonial processions would be left out of the festival this time, so if there was still a problem, the Apa Tanis would have a year in which to sort it out.

The next day, as Ursula and Tim left for the north end of the valley they saw with horror the havoc that Bela men had wrought – they had broken down bridges, felled their trees and hacked down their bamboo. Retribution was inevitable.

On the way back, sounds reached them of shouting from Duta and their own camp. They broke into a run and looked across the valley to see the lines of irrigation broken by a huge column of smoke. 'For all we knew, the whole of Haja village was going up, and our camp as well. In the fields we met two fleeing women racing towards Bela, and they called out that trouble had begun.' A man rushing towards Bela explained that Duta, Mudang Tage and Michi Bamin had turned out in force to attack Haja. A large Duta contingent had clashed with Haja, leaving one dead and two wounded. The scene below them was one of disorder and destruction all around. At Duta's ritual tree an armed party was protecting a chanting priest in full battle-dress. Ursula wondered if they would turn on her two men, Buda and Rika, but was grateful to see two armed Gurkhas approaching to escort them in. 'We passed the Duta group with bare steel between us and them. The priest never turned his head but the warriors stood and glared.'

The smoke over Pape created a grey, premature evening and in the dull light the Haja servants stood huddled on the balcony of Crazy Gables, the Gurkhas on guard below. Tim and Temi joined a huddle of elders, deep in anxious discussion, and as Ursula looked out, she saw at least 200 Duta warriors, moving out along the narrow path towards Pape. 'We all stood and watched till the last warrior had gone and dusk had fallen in earnest and then we went indoors to piece together the tragedy. Tim lit the lamps and the sudden white glare showed our small company sitting grim and sober round the hearth.'

Early attempts by Hong to give peace offerings had been rebuffed, panic escalated among the villages and despite Kop Temi's best efforts, Duta launched a charge, sweeping past Pape camp, on towards the island village. In no time the Duta army and a small Haja contingent were facing each other in a pitched battle in the wet-rice fields.

The knee-deep, churned-up mud greatly limited their agility and hampered their reactions. Everyone watching hoped that they would exhaust themselves without anyone being seriously hurt, but then a Haja man, so bogged down that he couldn't take evasive action, took a pike in the stomach and fell. The headmen rushed in and prevented further fighting, but the Haja man was dying and two had been wounded. Blood would have to pay for blood and the tribal feud would disrupt the whole life of the valley.

Chigin Nime, as a Duta elder, had done nothing to calm the situation, so Haja was after him. Duta's allies gave heavy hints that if Haja cared to kill off Chigin Nime, they would consider the feud squared. To Ursula and Tim this was unthinkable – he had been their friend and guide for the last eighteen months, but there was little they could do to save him.

Nime refused all offers of help, but with Temi's mediation, he agreed to pay material compensation if Haja would agree – although he doubted that they would settle so easily now. Despite everyone's best efforts, by the afternoon, Duta was in a state of siege. The air was filled with shouting, incantations and the braying of war horns.

It struck Ursula as especially absurd that the two main protagonists were situated just a couple of hundred yards from each other. 'It was like Berkeley Square at war with Piccadilly, and they were playing their drama out in their backyards and gardens, within earshot of one another, in a miniature and domestic campaign. Perhaps that only made it more tragic.'

Duta, palisaded against attack, went on the offensive, staking the approaches with bamboo, laying ambushes on the paths into Pape and destroying Haja's bamboo groves.

Haja, who were celebrating Mloko without leaving the village, had to interrupt the festivities to set up defences. The atmosphere of aggression mounted:

> After dark they made life hideous by bugling and yelling till dawn, partly to keep awake and partly to impress Haja with their efficiency and general frightfulness. This cacophony was the last straw, Duta's crowning contribution to the ruin of the Apa Tani Valley, to the destruction of peace and loveliness and an innocent, primitive Arcadian beauty which the world could ill afford to lose.

Their last days were ticking away – but right to the last minute the Apa Tanis were unaware that Tim and Ursula were leaving, but when they realised, there was bewilderment and real distress. So great was the villages' reliance on them that Haja even offered them a free labour force to keep the camp going. Even another month would help steer them through the trouble – but they could not undermine the new Political Officer, wherever he was. As Ursula wrote to Haimendorf,

> Nobody in authority has the faintest idea of conditions in the Subansiri. Nobody now cares either – not a hoot – what happens to the hill men. How is one to explain to the Apa Tanis, when under Philip the whole be-all and end-all of work in the Subansiri has been the hill men's welfare?
>
> I have been ten years now with tribal people, and the future seems an utter blank. An ability to deal with savages has no commercial value. How is one to explain, too, that that kind of work in human relations and human values can be the only work worth doing – a thing outside one's whole self, a thing one could not give up if one tried. Something besides which no other kind of existence is life at all? For a full year I did all I knew to win their confidence and bring them round, and at the end of it, believe that I had failed – that one could not have with the Apa Tanis the same relations, the same friendship and loyalty, the same comradeship, that I had had with the Zemi. As late as Christmas, I told Tim, in a moment of despair, that if I were to be struck by lightning, the next minute all the Apa Tanis would worry about was who was now going to issue their pay and rations! But I did them a gross injustice, as the last three months have shown. For all their apparent faults – and many of these faults only by our standards – I love them, and they have forgiven me much. Since the New Year there has been an immense change in our personal relations with them, and a great increase in mutual understanding and trust.

Now, the Apa Tanis were terrified of the vacuum the Betts' departure would create, as no resident officer had been appointed and it seemed that this might never happen. Temi was staying, and so were the Assam Rifles, but since the start of the crisis, they had relied on Tim as their guardian and mediator. As Ursula reflected, it was one of the Subansiri gods' ironic jokes that they should have succeeded in what they had set out to do only in the very hour that they had to leave.

As they went to say goodbye to Hari, the valley seemed normal enough – apart from the racket made by the Duta warriors. It was a desperate and heartbreaking moment as they climbed to the rim of the valley for the last time, and Ursula could not bear to look back. 'The forest closed in behind us, shutting the valley in, shutting us out, and we walked forward through the centuries, in a thin, unkind rain, towards the alien and bitter present, and the strangers who were our own kind.'

The Apa Tani servants accompanied them down to North Lakhimpur on the Brahmaputra, where they were to board the steamer. The truck dropped the staff back on the track towards Kore, and only Dr Bhattarcharjee came to the jetty to see them off. Ursula was desolate:

> Buda had been the last to part and had stood on the truck steps to say his goodbye long after the others had turned and gone; it was a curiously touching gesture, for we had never suspected the fat, reluctant Buda of much attachment to us. And now all that was over, and we should never see any of them any more, and there was nothing left except the dwindling figure of the doctor, still waving his white handkerchief in infinitely pathetic farewell.
>
> I looked at Tim. There was nothing to be read there. We were both wrapped in our separate miseries, cocooned and bundled in wretchedness. I knew that a part of me was dead – had died of grief on that long road of parting between the Valley and the plains. The woman who had been me was gone and a remnant, a ghost, remained.

42

Back in England

In post-war England in 1948 there was a shortage of housing following the Blitz, taxes were extortionate, food was still rationed and unemployment was rife. To Ursula and Tim, back among 'their own kind' after years in the wilds, this was an extreme culture shock – they'd scarcely seen a white face in years, or heard English spoken. What used to be familiar was cold and almost hostile.

Tim, weakened by pneumonia and bronchitis, was very sick indeed and was immediately hospitalised, leaving Ursula alone to consider their future. Much had changed since she had left in 1939 – not least the deaths of her father and Humpus – and she found her surroundings unbearably claustrophobic:

> Everything round me seemed to be unreal; life was nightmarish. The English hills were too close. I wanted to push them back, to have space, to have forty and fifty miles of clear air between me and untrodden mountains. We had been torn up by the roots. The wound ached unceasingly. People talked kindly, could not understand – were bewildered. We had come home; what could be the matter? How could one explain that home was no longer home – that it was utterly foreign, that home was in the Assam hills and that there would never be any other, and that for the rest of our lives we should be exiles?

To Ursula, the wild and naked tribesmen were 'bone of our bone, flesh of our flesh' and had provided her with an insight so precious into the condition of all human life, and taught her something which could never be unlearned. 'Truly we were cast out of Eden. Willing or no, we had eaten of the Tree of Knowledge and we knew that, across the barriers of caste and custom and colour, human beings are one, all struggling along the same dark road.' Ursula's only small glimmer of consolation was the conviction that her time among the hill tribes had made a real difference.

The misery, emptiness and frustration drove Ursula to seek solace in something philosophical:

> Of all that we had seen and known, nothing remained but the intangible. Each fact of being makes its own impress on the shape of Time. It is and passes, and sinks into oblivion, and falls down to the bottom of Time like a dead mollusc to the seabed, but because it *was*, because it *existed*, the shape of things is eternally and irrevocably altered to an infinitesimal degree. Nothing can ever take away that fact of being. We had gone, we had striven, we had tried, we had loved the tribesmen in spite of ourselves and they

> had loved us, and though everything else might perish – our bodies, our memories – nothing could ever wipe out and destroy that.

Ursula contemplated the future. There was no network by which she could learn the outcome of the Duta–Haja feud – or even know what was going on in her old camp of Laisong. Once, in August 1947, Ursula had received a letter from Namkia – now 'Political Jemadar' in Impoi – giving her all the news of her former household. Now these old familiar friends were beyond contact and, from being at the heart of the lives of these people, she and Tim were shut out.

She left London to visit relatives out of town: 'The train slid on, gliding in and out of patches of morning mist. For a horrible moment I knew that I had died and that this was my own particular private hell.'

Now, with no work on which to focus his determination, Tim fell victim to an alarming variety of tropical viruses and parasites and remained at the School of Tropical Medicine, so Ursula took up temporary residence in London with her mother, whose second husband, Eric, had died after a long battle with cancer.

The daughter who had returned to England was very different from the one Doris had seen off to India in 1937. Living in London and being married was what proper daughters did, and was something Doris could relate to. After years of strain, relations between Ursula and Doris blossomed. Doris was a very youthful fifty-four and was not one to languish too long in widow's weeds, and the London social scene was a salutary antidote to loss and loneliness. Fairly or unfairly – but certainly without rose-tinted glasses – Ursula summed up her mother's new interest in her. She rather suspected that, given her recent rise to public renown, with her MBE and the award of the Lawrence of Arabia Memorial Medal, her mother relished the kudos of wheeling her out at cocktail parties.

Ursula worked through the notes, artefacts, photos and films she had accumulated over the previous ten years, and after careful cataloguing, labelling and captioning, she donated them variously to the Pitt Rivers Museum in Oxford, the Cambridge University Museum and the Horniman Museum in London.

From being an aspiring novice in the anthropological field, Ursula had become one of the foremost experts on the Nagas and Apa Tanis, and with her passion for the subject and first-hand experience, she became a welcome speaker in anthropological circles. Giving talks would not provide an income, but Humpus had bequeathed her a modest sum – which was just as well. Tim, as he had written so apologetically to Doris, had no money and no immediate prospect of earning any.

At last Tim was well enough to travel, and they arranged to go to Kenya. Humpus' legacy helped with the initial purchase of a coffee farm and they travelled out in 1949, anticipating a return to a pioneering outdoor life. Although the Naga people were Ursula's first and greatest love, she was enthusiastic about tackling a new continent and new peoples, and the Bettses arrived in Kenya in a spirit of optimism.

Before long, Tim realised that he was not really needed to run the plantation. He had inherited a very able and experienced manager, so rather than dismiss him, Tim decided to get alternative work, and found a job in the veterinary service. Ursula had all the time in the world to start her new studies, but in the political climate of Kenya she found one obstacle after another prevented her from getting close to the indigenous tribes. Another factor – the prevailing social structure – imposed a restrictive stay-at-home baby-producing existence on womenfolk.

This was not Ursula's style, and to flout convention would only have caused friction, so eventually, thwarted by red tape and bereft of any occupation she could relate to, Ursula and Tim reached an agreement. Although money was tight, Ursula would return to London and take a degree in anthropology – with her enormous experience and the amount of fieldwork she had under her belt, she could move directly to a post-graduate diploma, which would only take a year. In this time she would also be able to write her book about the Nagas. It was not a question of the marriage 'going off' – the Bettses loved each other very much – so much so that Tim was prepared to suffer separation so that Ursula could pursue the one interest that illuminated her life. Besides, despite the new lease of life Ursula had bought him, Tim was quite accustomed to being alone.

By the time Ursula got back to London in late 1949, Doris was about to remarry. The gentleman in question was an impecunious peer who had spent his life very humbly under the name of Robert Vernon. When he proposed to Doris it was in full recognition of his impoverished state, that he offered her a title in place of hard cash. Shortly after Ursula took up residence with Doris again, her mother and Robert Vernon tied the knot and she became Lady Liveden. It was a truly happy match and Robert – 'Bobby' – was great fun and much loved by Ursula and Graham.

At the age of thirty-five, Ursula embarked on the further education she had missed as a girl. As a full-time student at the School of Oriental and Asian Studies, London University, she was delighted to find that her chief tutor was to be Philip Mills. With her old friend as tutor, she enjoyed one of the happiest years of her life outside the hills.

With her studies, her book to write and other articles and poems about the Naga Hills to occupy her, Ursula kept very busy. At the end of the course Ursula presented her thesis on 'The Village Organisation among the Central Zemi Nagas' and was awarded an academic post-graduate diploma in anthropology in 1950. She finished the manuscript for *Naga Path* and submitted it for publication – so there was nothing to keep her in England any longer.

Back in Kenya there was a happy reunion with Tim – but essentially she could never feel at home in Africa. She had a deep-seated gut reaction against it – 'It's a very old country, and it smells of blood', she claimed – but she persevered for Tim's sake. Tim enjoyed the outdoor life and riding out into the big, open country, but Ursula, although an adequate horsewoman, did not. Ursula again applied for permission to make a study of the Masai people, but was turned down. There was the same pressure to conform to the expected standard of female domesticity – and eventually she succumbed. Catriona Graham Arminell Betts was born in 1951, and remembering Khutuing's parting shot when they left Magulong, Ursula quickly sent word to him of the new arrival.

It was a crowning joy when Ursula received a parcel marked from the post office in Haflong. In it was a tiny Zemi Naga girl's dress and top, beautifully packed and sewn into a linen bag. Ursula was deeply touched when she realised that Khutuing must have walked for several days in order to reach the nearest post office, and arrange for its carriage out to Narok in Kenya – and then there was the journey back again. Just as Ursula had been given a Naga name, Catriona's Zemi name was to be Haihangile – 'a hundred times welcome'.

What Ursula would have loved most in the world would be to take Catriona to see her Naga family in Magulong – but already the area was becoming inaccessible in the wake of Indian independence. Instead, in May 1952, the Bettses took some leave and returned to the UK to introduce her to their English families. It was while they were in England that the simmering troubles in Kenya with the Mau Mau tribes came to the boil and widespread violence broke out. News reached them that the young son of the family on the neighbouring farm had been killed, and this changed Ursula's views on going back. Previously willing to face up to any enemy, gun at the ready, Ursula decided that although Tim was keen to go back, the Bettses as a family had had enough of trouble spots. It was time to up roots again, and from the safety of London make a measured decision as to what to do next.

For two outdoor hardies such as the Bettses, a suburban home and office job for Tim were not an option, so they decided to go back to Ursula's highland roots and began searching for a property in Scotland. They set out on a combined holiday and house-hunting trip. It was autumn, and most of the summer tourists had left, but there was one other guest in their B&B – one Hilda Murrell. They hit it off at once, and enjoyed days hill-walking together before crossing to Mull and finding their new home – Ardura – a rugged sheep farm with a dilapidated farmhouse.

Ursula described their new home:

> It was old; it was shabby; it needed far more spending on it than we had the money for. But – some places have magic. Ardura had. The house itself stood on a shelf jutting out from the steep southern face of Glen More, the great rift which almost cuts Mull in two. I say jutting; but in fact it was tucked into a shallow fold in the hillside to find such shelter as it could from the wild Atlantic gales which tore and funnelled down the glen. The core of it was probably an 18th century tacksman's house, in itself a rarity. This contained an Adam-style fireplace, which we thought an Edwardian decoration until a visiting expert told us otherwise. The walls of this central house were two-and-a-half feet thick, of a rubble core faced with boulders, a technique which I, as an archaeologist, know goes back to the Iron Age; and perfectly sound it is, until one has to put central-heating pipes through it. The old byres and steadings had been converted into kitchens and larders to enlarge the old house – and a fine kitchen it was; it was said and rightly, that you could dance an eightsome reel in it.

After many complications, the Bettses went north:

> We sailed from Oban at last on a wild, windy April day and chugged across the Firth of Lorne in the face of a flaying wind. We were emigrating – leaving the known mainland for the lovely, lonely Hebrides; the mountains of Argyll retreated into the grey haze and the peaks of Mull came out to meet us. The gulls swirled and cried about the boat. I felt cold and tired and scared.
>
> When we reached the house after a night in the local hotel, I burst into tears. In the eighteen months since we had seen it last, emptiness and wet had made havoc.

> Stray cattle had trampled the once-beautiful garden into a pitted mess; they had broken down the garden door, the strawberry bed was gone and the potting shed was a heap of ruins. Inside the building there was a reek of mildew and decay. The kitchen floor had rotted into holes, the wallpaper hung in strips and there were five leaks in the roof.

Ursula and Tim surveyed the ruin that was their new home – and there began a programme of renovation and repair. Hill farming on a remote island is no easy life, but Ardura, at Craignure, offered a greater than usual challenge. The restoration was hard work, but Catriona, looking back, remembered her parents having a lot of fun. One of the reasons for choosing this remote spot was to give Ursula an opportunity to write. To her surprise and gratification, *Naga Path* had been published in 1952, and she was already part way through a second book about the Apa Tani Valley.

In the Subansiri, Ursula and Tim had fulfilled complimentary roles and were a support to each other, but now Ursula found it hard to deal with the conventional business of being a wife. She threw herself into domesticity, making jams and chutneys and the odd cake – and also found time to organise the Mull Archaeological Survey. Eventually Ursula had some archaeological papers published and gave some lectures at Glasgow University, but shortly after they first moved, Ursula found she was pregnant. This wild, highland paradise was a perfect place for children to grow up – a landscape rich in history and legend – and Ursula felt at home and not at all unnerved by the spirit of the ancient island.

Catriona recalled a story of an unusual encounter during Ursula's pregnancy – perhaps her condition made her especially sensitive. It was part of the paeon of local legend that the 'seal-woman' of Ardura had special powers. It was well known that she had 'flippers' instead of hands – in essence, a birth defect – but despite this, she qualified as a doctor, using specially adapted comb-like extensions as hands. High above Ardura, where the seal-woman had lived at the start of the century, was an ancient, stone-walled well – and a stone seat had been set up there, in the seal-woman's favourite spot, dedicated to her memory. She was well loved, doing a lot of good work for the community – and local people liked to talk of her special affinity with animals. Stories about her abounded, such as the occasion when she boarded the ferryboat for the mainland on a stormy day, when the sea was surging furiously and threatening the safety of the crossing – and the sea fell calm as she appeared on the deck.

Ursula was resting on the stone seat by the well when she turned to her side saw a woman sitting next to her, dressed in a herringbone tweed skirt and wool jersey. They sat in companionable silence for a while, during which Ursula had plenty of opportunity to observe the woman's features. Ursula got up to leave and nodded her goodbye to the quiet woman then, a little way down the hill she was drawn to look back. The woman was still sitting there, and she half smiled at Ursula, who walked back to Ardura. On a hunch, Ursula phoned the niece of the seal-woman who lived on a nearby farm, and asked her to describe her aunt. The description she gave matched exactly the woman Ursula had shared the seat with – apparently she often appeared there to those sensitive enough to see her, and after that, as Catriona commented, 'it was always happening'.

43

From Nagaland to Scotland

Alison Betts was born in 1955, and having engaged a nanny, the Bettses applied themselves to the job of farming. Although it could never offer the challenges or excitement of the Naga Hills or the Apa Tani Valley, it was an outdoor life, away from 'civilisation'.

This 'easy' life was a real test of Ursula and Tim's relationship in which the balance wavered and changed subtly as circumstances affected them. Catriona found her father less complicated to sum up than Ursula:

> Tim was a lovely father. They were a complete foil to each other – he was very, very gentle, very laid back, funny. He was really quite a shy man – despite his proposal. He was shy at one level, but with a fairly mad streak which runs through the whole family. He was very much of his time – beautiful manners, very courteous. He was passionate about the outdoors, and determined always that he would never work in an office. He had done so for a short while and hated it. He was a very good ornithologist and as an amateur he published a huge amount. An academic would be proud to publish as many papers as he did.
>
> My mother was the dominant person in the relationship, without any doubt! You couldn't have two characters together who were as forceful as that, and they were a very good partnership. My father was worried that by getting married my mother would lose the opportunity of an academic career, and regret it – and he was concerned that she found the role of wife difficult.

However, Ursula did get down to some satisfying archaeological work – and to writing – but having directed her own anthropological career with such confidence, she was unwilling now to sacrifice her creative integrity to write for a mass market. Her second book, *The Hidden Land*, was published in 1953. Like *Naga Path*, it was written from the heart, with a scrupulous attention to local detail and it left in no question the passion with which they had worked or the desolation they felt at leaving. Her scholarly papers and lectures were lapped up eagerly in academic circles, but her fiction and anecdotal writings failed to hit the spot with the popular press. She wanted to write her own way, and on her own chosen subjects, so the agents' rejections were disheartening – and her failure to get published meant that she was not contributing to the family's income, so money was always short.

However, Catriona remembered a very happy childhood, with both her parents throwing themselves wholeheartedly into the life of the community, taking part in amateur dramatics and local arts groups. Tim dealt with the farm and Ursula wrote or cooked – and Mull was a wonderful, stimulating place to live. Catriona suspected that, had Ursula been successful in her writing, she would have been very happy – but for the memories of their life in the hills.

For Catriona and Alison, Mull was idyllic, with all the joys of their own ponies and the freedom of an outdoor life. When they weren't at the local school, both girls spent their days with Tim, out and about on the farm, or in the house with the nanny. In a way it was a very Edwardian childhood – but it was what working families did if they possibly could. While loving the girls very much, Ursula was not the sort to get into the nitty-gritty of child-rearing, so the girls would leave the nursery and Nanny at five o'clock in the evening to spend an hour with Ursula and Tim before bed.

Catriona as a toddler was a terror, so in the early days there was a succession of nannies – but it was not only Catriona which drove them to leave. Young girls didn't like being stranded on an island – it limited their social life – so Catriona and Alison enjoyed the ministrations of a procession of volatile and emotional foreign girls:

> There was Berit, the au pair who had black hair and green eyes, and was just recovering from a broken love affair. She couldn't stand me, but she used to walk around with Alison when she was a baby. She used to cover her with Chanel No 5, and wander about looking tragic. Then there was Maria, the Italian cook. My mother was hysterical about her – for her life was one long opera, and if we ran out of butter there was a major aria about it.

At last a nanny was found who was happy on the island, and could handle the girls. This gem remained with the Bettses until Catriona was about ten (she had gone to a boarding school, Butterstone, in Perthshire at the age of eight, but Alison was still at home). At this point Nanny had a heart attack and had to give up work – leaving the girls, now ten and seven, unsupervised in their island idyll. 'It was bliss – perfect bliss!'

Ursula came into her own on outings, holidays, or the trips back to school:

> We went to various places in Scotland – it was fabulous, because she would sing – we sang all the time when we were on Mull – Scottish folk songs. We had a whole repertoire and Mummy had quite a good singing voice (although my father's voice was lousy, and so was mine). Then there were poems – she'd learned them with Humpus, and could repeat all the Hilaire Belloc cautionary tales, which she knew by heart – and Lear's limericks … and a lot of rude ones too, although not so much when we were young children. It was a rich childhood in that way.
>
> There were stories too, because she had a terrifically retentive memory and a fund of knowledge about Scottish history. We'd be driving around Scotland and she'd tell us stories about the Jacobites and the Stewarts – our car journeys were just a feast. When you got her away from home and out of her study, she was fabulous company – we'd have such a great time.
>
> …I did sometimes wonder why I couldn't have a mother who did the washing – but she was an inspiration and so interesting – such fun. She was not like other people's mothers, but she more than made up for it in other ways.

Ursula's life would always be inextricably bound together with the Nagas. The farm was full of reminders of their time in the hills, and Catriona and Alison were brought up on a heady diet of Naga culture – however, Scotland was a long way away, so it was with absolute astonishment that Catriona, aged eleven, was summoned to the head-mistress's study at Butterstone. Her parents and some special visitors were there to see her. Ursula and Tim arrived accompanied by four Naga tribesmen, sombrely suited against the Scottish weather. Catriona was amazed:

> My parents turned up with four Nagas in tow. What a day – for an eleven-year-old schoolgirl who had been brought up on all the stories of things before she was born – and here in the flesh, in Scotland, on an autumn afternoon, were four Nagas!

These four had left their homeland and travelled across the world to contact Katazile – and to ask for her help.

Ursula and Tim had no way of knowing what would happen to the Nagas once the British left in 1948. Ursula, writing some years later, summed up the problem facing India when Britain withdrew from their country – and Nagaland:

> Arrangements had to be made for the future of the Nagas. The result was the 1947 agreement between the Naga National Council and the Governor of Assam, acting for the Indian Government. The District – the most developed and best-educated section of the Naga territory as a whole was included; the more backward groups of the Tuensang Area were, I believe, excluded at the request of the Naga National Council itself. The agreement, while certainly not conceding all the Nagas hoped for, was rather better than the responsible British officers expected; it certainly represented as much as could be exacted at that time from the Indian Government, and it made over to the Nagas most valuable tracts of forest which were a source of considerable potential revenue. It did concede to the Nagas a measure of semi-autonomy. Had both sides implemented the agreement in a liberal and constructive spirit, things might be very different today – but they did not, and speculation is vain. The agreement broke down because, to put it bluntly, both sides were greedy. Each hoped by abandoning it, to get more than it gave.

The Naga people had supported the British, fighting for them in two world wars, and accepting their protective administration – but they had always maintained their autonomy. They were most definitely not of an Indian caste, but more Mongolian in appearance – and prior to Britain's period of influence, they had never been governed by India. When the British left they didn't expect to 'revert back' to Indian government, as in their estimation there was no reverting to do.

Unfortunately, the new Indian government assumed that Britain was handing over the Naga territories to them – and the Nagas were outraged. India became very nervous and fearful of the Nagas' claims to independence – theirs was a particularly sensitive tract, politically speaking, forming as it did a buffer between India and her north-eastern neighbours – most significantly China.

In 1947, East and West Pakistan became established through partition from India, essentially on religious grounds. West Pakistan (now Pakistan) and East Pakistan (now Bangladesh) were Moslem, while India remained predominantly Hindu. India thereby lost control of two crucial buffer zones, so when Nehru came to power in India, he was anxious not to lose any more border territory, and would not contemplate Naga independence. As far back as 1947, there had been increasing concern among those who knew and cared for the Nagas that British removal would be disastrous for them. Ursula wrote:

> Since 1954 there had been intense concern about what was happening to the Nagas among those most connected with them – Dr J.H. Hutton, Mr J.P. Mills, Sir Charles Pawsey and myself. In 1947 a Naga delegation went to meet Nehru in New Delhi, and were not encouraged by his statement, 'I will use all the forces at my command to crush the Nagas'. But eventually an agreement had been concluded between the Nagas and India which seemed to offer real promise for the future. Mr Mills wrote to my husband and myself – then in the Subansiri Area of the North East Frontier Agency – that the agreement was as good as could in the circumstances be hoped for, and that it gave the Nagas a reasonable measure of autonomy and the return of valuable forests in the foothills. (The fear, of course, had been that the new India would swallow up the hill-people, to the complete destruction of their liberty and cultures; they had no place in Hindu society except as Untouchables.)

The concern Ursula felt was made worse after a rising against Indian intervention in 1956 – about which no firm details could be established. Eventually information got through which confirmed Ursula's worst fears. There were long lists of victims and incidents which, as Ursula said, 'if a tenth were true, were frankly appalling'.

Years then went by without information coming out of Nagaland, and Ursula was desperate to know what was happening behind the closed frontiers. It was in June 1960, when Ursula was on the Scottish mainland at a hotel in Perth, having just dropped Catriona off at school, that she was called to the phone. The caller was the Reverend Michael Scott – known to her by reputation only as a champion of the underprivileged in Africa. Ursula's immediate assumption was that Aunt Maud, who lived in South Africa and was openly a supporter of the United Party had got herself arrested and needed bailing out. However, the news from Scott was that the Naga leader, Phizo, had arrived in London, and wished her to travel to London to identify him for the authorities.

It was widely known that Phizo had gone over to the Japanese during the war. With the Japanese defeat at Kohima, Ursula had been warned that he might be heading in her direction – and if she or her men saw him, they were to shoot on sight. There were suspicions, too, about his involvement in the murder of political opponents. Now, claiming to represent the majority of Naga people, as leader of the Naga National Council, he was in England. Mills had died earlier in the year, and Ursula felt his loss deeply – and with this new turn of events, she would have to make up her own mind about Phizo.

Almost giddy with shock, Ursula told Scott that she would come to London, but needed to talk to Tim first:

> I drove back to Mull next day and talked the thing over with Tim. We would have given anything for Philip Mills' advice. But Mills was gone, and we barely knew Hutton and Pawsey. What were we to do for the best? Phizo, as such, was immaterial. What did matter was the safety and well-being of the Nagas.

Ursula travelled south and performed the necessary identification for Phizo to stay in the country. With formalities out of the way, at a meeting held out of town, Ursula had a chance to talk with Phizo alone:

> A path ran out to the riverbank and he and I walked there for hours, by shadowy alleys among the bushes and along a deserted path on a raised embankment. My chief memory is of utter incongruity. It was fantastically illogical that the Nagas – the people who, after husband and children, probably were closest and meant most to me – should come back into my life like this, in the person of Phizo and in the unlikely setting of a luxurious English country house.

The truth was worse than anything Ursula could have imagined. Since the Indian Army had arrived in 1954, the soldiers had molested Naga women, pulled down houses, and burned villages. Through all this the Nagas did nothing. However, if this continued, the Nagas would effectively be wiped out, so the Naga Home Guard was formed, which fought under cover against the persecution, torture and killing.

In London, Phizo contacted David Astor, then editor of *The Observer*, and persuaded him to smuggle a reporter into Nagaland, so the Home Guard could show him at first hand what was happening. The man chosen for this mission – a potentially deadly one if he were to be discovered by the Indians – was journalist Gavin Young, and he visited Ursula for briefing. Ursula was delighted to help, and she settled down to tell him about the Nagas with excitement at the recollections – and sadness at what her adopted people were suffering.

In early May 1961, under close protection, Young travelled with the well-organised and disciplined men of the Home Guard and learned of the suffering, the cover-ups and the Indian duplicity.

Gavin Young's articles in *The Observer* exposed the situation in Nagaland for the world to see, and at last the appalling abuse of human rights was made public, crying out for action – but still the British authorities did nothing.

In spring of 1962 George Patterson, *Observer* correspondent, went out to India to cover the crisis from outside the borders – and sent back disturbing reports, which Nehru wrote to Astor to refute. The Indian Government's stance was that Phizo and the Naga Home Guard represented a small and violent minority in Nagaland, and, embracing the peaceful majority as Indian citizens, 'the Indian Army will remain in Nagaland to protect our own people against the violent element', according to Indian Foreign Secretary Desai. He further insisted that Nagas were Indian, and that the whole matter was an Indian problem, of no concern to any outside country or group. *If* any Nagas had been hurt, it was because they were 'hostiles' or 'hostile sympathisers who only form 5–10 percent of the population'. He dismissed the list of atrocities drawn up by Naga General Kaito as being a routine military document, of no particular significance.

Some years before, Phizo and Yongkong, an Ao tribesman and minister of the underground Naga movement, had left war-torn Nagaland via Pakistan, where the pressures of international politics intervened and they were detained under house arrest for four years. Yongkong explained the reasons for this:

> We came to Pakistan expecting that we should be free once we reached that country, but now we faced politics. The reason why the government of Pakistan detained us was that they had their own problem of Kashmir. The Pakistani government knew that if the Nagas were given their freedom, they would solve their trouble before they could solve their problem of Kashmir, and they were worried about their standing in the eyes of their own countrymen. That was the reason why we were detained for such a long time, when our whole country was burning. Mr Phizo was very disheartened, and some nights he came and knocked at my door. He would say, 'Yongkong, the situation at home is such – suppose something should happen to me? Will you promise me that you will not give up?' So I said, 'No, uncle, I will not give up.' Thousands of lives could have been saved by Pakistan if we could have been able to let the world know that India was killing the Nagas. Then India would have hesitated to kill more people.

Eventually the Pakistan government released them, and Phizo gained a false passport:

> The Pakistan government really thought that with that passport he could not reach Europe. When those officers met Mr Phizo in London, they said that they were sure he would come back to Pakistan – and that they were waiting for him. But he escaped. Such miracles happened to us.

Thus Phizo managed to reach England, and he worked for the Naga cause from his office on Vauxhall Bridge Road, South London, trying to negotiate for peace talks and an end to immediate hostilities.

In the meantime, back in the Naga Hills, Yongkong and three other influential Nagas from various tribes were preparing to follow Phizo to England. They were General Mowu Gwizautsu (General Mo), a Western Angami, General Kaito, Yongkong, and Khodao Yansan (the last two being members of the Naga National Council) – all with a price on their heads and wanted by the Indian Government. Surviving heavy fighting, they managed to enter East Pakistan and from there board a flight for England.

44

The Nagas in Trouble

Ursula learned of the delegation's imminent arrival and through official channels it was ascertained that, providing the delegation arrived before 1 July and had affidavits sworn by someone of standing who knew each of them well (they seemed prepared for this to be Phizo), there was a good chance that they would be let in. These were duly submitted, but then the Home Office raised their terms. They wanted sworn statements by the mother or father of each Naga, and not only that, but someone to identify each relative. The government's stance suggested that they didn't want to handle this political hot potato – and the fact that Nehru was in London attending the Commonwealth Prime Minister's Conference might also have influenced British policy.

Eventually the Nagas landed at 'London Airport' at Heathrow. *The Daily Express* covered their arrival:

> **Nagas held at airport**
> **'We are British' fight**
> For seven hours yesterday, four bewildered Naga tribesmen at London Airport tried to prove that they were British subjects. But Home Office officials remained unconvinced. And last night, the talking marathon over, the tribesmen were taken to an airport detention room.
>
> The four, who defied the Home Office to come to Britain to plead their case against India, 'are being held while their documents are being examined', said an official. Hour after hour, they argued that they were British. Legal advisers, officials of the National Council for the Study of Group Rights and the Naga leader in London, Mr Angami Phizo, also argued on their behalf. The main difficulty is in proving they were born in the British section of Nagaland – no birth certificates being issued in that country. The four men had to hark back to childhood memories in an effort to establish the district in which they were born, said one legal adviser, Mrs Blanch Lucas.

The piece concluded with a comment from Patterson, 'It is obviously a matter of high politics and not of legality. We knew that India had told Britain that it would be an embarrassment for the Government in New Delhi if the Nagas told this country about Indian atrocities.'

The four Nagas were uncertain of their fate as they waited at the airport. Surely it was unthinkable that they would be sent back to Nagaland – which would be tantamount to a death sentence. It was not surprising that the Nagas were confused at their reception.

Yongkong recalled that a BBC radio reporter had interviewed them at the airport and asked if they had expected to be detained on arrival in Britain:

> We said 'No'. When the British left India the officer had said, 'Any day, any time you come to our country, you will be most welcome'. We told the BBC our story. They asked us why the Naga people wanted to be independent, so we said that the Nagas were not asking for independence from India. 'We ARE independent. But we are not free, because the Indian Army is interfering with our way of life. Before the Indians came we had plenty of food to eat – plenty of everything. We were more than self-sufficient. But today the Indians have burned down our villages and everything has been destroyed. That is the reason why we came here to complain.'

Catriona filled in the behind-the-scenes details:

> It was realised that Ursula was the one person who could verify the fact that they had been born under the British Raj, and therefore they had a right to enter the country. High-level QCs were brought in – Louis Blom Cooper got involved – and my mother rushed to London, together with a very formidable lady lawyer. There's a wonderful photograph of them. My mother was not a small woman, but this lady was even bigger – and there were the two of them going off to do battle. She got to see them at the airport and asked them the appropriate questions, and was able to tell the authorities that they had been born under the Raj, and proved that they were – so they were allowed to enter the country. But it was touch and go. It was enormously stressful, but it was also very exciting for her, and she loved being involved with the Nagas again.

The Naga delegation finally headed for the unfamiliar but welcoming shores of Mull. The *Oban Times* carried a picture of the men with Ursula:

> Pictured boarding the *Lochearn* at Oban on 22 September are the four Naga leaders who have been in Britain to gather support for their country's fight for independence from India. The Nagas were on their way to spend a few days in Mull with Mrs Ursula Betts, Ardura – seen with them – who during the last war was awarded the MBE after leading the Naga head-hunters against the Japs in Burma. The Nagas hope later to go on to New York to seek UN support for their plan for independence.

After the stress and uncertainty, the warmth and hospitality in Mull was wonderful and the Nagas enjoyed hunting and fishing with Tim, and evenings round the fire, giving Ursula the background to events since she had last been in Laisong. It was both a joy to have contact with Naga people again – and a heart-wrenching agony to learn what had been happening.

Yonkong recalled the visit:

> That was the beginning of our association with Mrs Betts – a mother to all of us. We were fresh and new to the West, and it was she who integrated us. She left her husband and house – and her husband was looking after their large farm on the Isle

> of Mull – and from that day onward, she became a part of us – part of the delegation. She organised everything for us – and she was our life.

They unfolded a history of unimaginable events. Despite all the Nagas' efforts to negotiate reasonably, Nehru regarded them as ignorant savages and ordered stringent measures against the Naga National Council. It was unthinkable for Ursula and Tim, remembering their co-operation and mutual support for the Assam Rifles that they had been turned out against the Nagas. They had fought on the same side – when there was no compulsion but loyalty to do so – and the Nagas had died in numbers for the British cause. Now the Assam Rifles had been set against them.

In late 1953, forced labour had been introduced in Nagaland, and the village elders, placed in an impossible position by being required to carry out the Army's punitive measures, resigned in their droves. The fabric of village society was crumbling – but with the increase of atrocities committed against women, homes burned and villages looted, the Nagas began to build resistance. Eighty members of the Naga National Council were on the Indian Army's wanted list for apparently provoking the insulting mass walk-out at Kohima – so the NNC went to ground.

More Indian troops were sent in during 1955 – but by this time the Nagas were arming up and resistance was escalating. By 1957 the war – for it was nothing less – had spread throughout the Naga territories and India had resorted to extreme measures to quash resistance. Two Naga dobashis overheard confidential discussions of a meeting of Indian officers at Nokklak Camp to disseminate government policy, at which orders were issued to

> Kill the fifteen Kilonsers of the 'Free Nagaland' government, with their families and children; kill the national leaders and the leading members of communities; kill off 10,000 to 15,000 Nagas to scare them into joining the Indian Union, and unlimited number if they refuse; pressure on population through destruction of granaries and food-stores; kill or dispose of Christian leaders and Christian Nagas where found. Eradicate Christianity from Unadministered Territory; kill anyone refusing to co-operate with Indian forces.

This policy would quickly eradicate Nagaland or bring its people to their knees. Forces arrayed against Nagaland at that time numbered five and a half divisions of the Indian Army (although they would only admit to three), tanks, artillery, Indian Air Force helicopters and rocket-firing jets, fighter-bombers, 30,000 armed police and ten battalions of the Assam Rifles. All this was ranged against 40,000 men – not all armed, and not all in the field at the same time. They had rifles, automatic weapons, light machine-guns, trench mortars and grenades, along with some home-made weapons and sporting guns. Ursula was wracked by the violence against her people.

To make sure she had all the facts told her by her Naga guests – and rather than have to scribble notes – Ursula taped their reports of events in their homeland. All four men told of horrific experiences and considered themselves fortunate to have got out alive.

The men stayed on Mull for a month, pouring out their hearts in endless talking, and their visit cemented enduring friendships which thrived despite the difficulties of distance and the problems of communicating from within Nagaland. Memories of the days in Mull were handed down to the families of Mowu and Kaito who returned to Nagaland, perpetuating Ursula's legendary status for another generation, who would in future write to Ursula and Catriona with a genuine sense of kinship and love. Mowu himself wrote to Catriona, reminding her of the status conferred on her by her mother's relationship with the Nagas. She recalled:

> In December 1962 I received a letter, which was an extraordinary one for an eleven-year-old girl to receive. I always treasured it and I have it to this day. 'Are you coming to Nagaland as a Naga princess? Your mummy was known as the Naga Queen during the last World War. I wish you to come and see me like your own brother, and help our people.'

Yongkong and Khadao settled in London and remained in constant correspondence with the Bettses and, interviewed in 2005, Yongkong recalled visits to Mull and the kindness and sense of kinship with which Ursula always treated him.

One Christmas at Ardura, Ursula remembered an emotional charge in the atmosphere:

> After Christmas dinner, we listened to the Queen's speech. We drank the Queen's health after the National Anthem, Alison taking the part of the youngest subaltern (at seven and a half!). Then Yonkong suddenly said, as we rose to leave, 'Let us sing *God Save the Queen* again'. We, being self-conscious, casual Britons, would never have thought of doing so on our own, but we halted where we stood, Tim, both the children and I – and sang it with him in all sincerity and fervour.

Ursula felt strongly that Britain had let the Nagas down. She and Tim embarked on a campaign of letter-writing, lobbying and 'educating'.

Events on the Indo-Chinese frontier had taken a serious turn at the end of October when the dispute which had been simmering over the border, high in the Himalayas, escalated into heavy fighting. India had declared a state of emergency – bringing the two nations just a step away from all-out war. The Chinese threat brought a more urgent problem. Fighting had reached the doorstep of Nagaland, and Ursula was painfully aware that, with the Naga leaders out of the country, the men on the spot were likely to be tempted by the short-term advantages of accepting aid from China in exchange for unhindered access through Nagaland to India. There was also the possibility that, even if the stand-in Naga leaders on the spot resisted Chinese offers of aid, they might have that aid thrust upon them whether they liked it or not.

Phizo too saw the need for positive moves towards a solution, and he sent a confidential telegram to Nehru. 'At this critical time for both Indians and Nagas we propose a ceasefire and amnesty for all Nagas. We are prepared to postpone settlement of our future political status until Communist invaders have been repelled.' He received no response to this, however, or his next communication.

The big problem for the Naga delegation was how to get the two generals back into Nagaland to monitor the response to the Chinese problem. A major diplomatic drive was soon under way – with Burmese goodwill, the men could be back in around fourteen days, otherwise the estimated journey would be around three months, by which time the situation in Nagaland might have become out of hand. Having met Slim and hit it off so well during the war, Ursula quickly arranged to meet the now Lord Slim, and had great hopes, given his appreciation of the Nagas' loyalty to Britain, of his influential support.

In the meantime, following Gavin Young's undercover trip to Nagaland in 1961, Ursula had prepared a summary document *The Commonwealth's Unknown War*. Her first concern had been to set the public straight about the Naga people:

> The Nagas are no longer a remote and picturesque mountain people, incapable of political organisation. In the last sixteen years they have met the challenge of changing times by a stupendous leap forward, springing in less than a generation from what was virtually an Early Iron Age culture into the mid-twentieth century.

She explained at length the progress of the Nagas and concluded,

> Backwardness there still is, but the effective Naga of 1961 is a literate, politically-conscious Christian, with as passionate a national feeling and desire for independence as a Pole or Irishman; and it is as such that one must deal with him. Anything else is fantasy.

She had speculated India's ability to sustain the military pressure on Nagaland indefinitely – unless some external threat such as China were to make them divert their troops to a more urgent struggle. At that time, around 2,000 Naga guerrillas were engaging some 30,000 Indian troops, and India would be very reluctant to confront China while Nagaland was still actively hostile. 'A contented and peaceful Nagaland would be a valuable buffer-state on this vulnerable border, and it is for all parties concerned – and that includes the Commonwealth – to review the realities of the situation and find a way to lasting peace.'

Despite all their letters, reports and statistics, the Betts–Astor team's appeals fell on deaf ears – because international powers were unanimously unwilling to interfere in what they were content to regard as an all-Indian matter.

Tragically for the Nagas, it suited the great powers not to dig too deeply into their tribal history. An avowed understanding of the tribal origins of the Nagas and the fact that they had never been part of India before the British administration, would have made it much more difficult to leave the matter to India to resolve.

Given Phizo's war history, Ursula nursed ambiguous feelings towards him. From anti-British turncoat, siding with the Japanese when the war was going in their favour, he'd made a *volte face* to return to the Naga fold and take office as president and leader of the Naga National Council when the British left. This duplicity had been the cause of her dilemma when he'd first arrived in Britain – but he *was* their only representative who could champion their cause now.

Phizo's diplomatic approaches, however, were high-handed in tone, and dogmatic in insisting on full independence, even if total autonomy was not necessarily what the majority of Naga citizens wanted. By his inflexibility he made it impossible for India to give ground without losing face – so it was deadlock.

It grieved Ursula that Hutton and Pawsey were standing back from supporting the Naga cause because of their doubts regarding Phizo's leadership. So distressed was she at the Naga's plight that she gritted her teeth and wrote to Hutton, who had made clear his misgivings, to justify her stance:

> I venture to write to you as I cannot help feeling that you and Sir Charles Pawsey and, indeed, official opinion in general, consider that those of us who are endeavouring to back the Naga National Movement are a lot of sentimental cranks who had very much better in the ultimate interest of the Naga people, leave well alone.

She wrote eloquently, citing instances where the collapse of the colonial empires had thrown up a whole string of highly undesirable characters – 'Nkhrumah, Hastings Banda, Jomo Kenyatta, Cheddi Jagan, to mention only a few, who have had to be made the best of, and who now strut the world in the odour of respectability.'

As she saw it, Naga supporters could stand back and hope that, under the attrition of India's oppression, the majority of Nagas would eventually capitulate – but this might take years and suffering would continue. Alternatively, they could publicise the Naga cause and shame India worldwide. Sadly, if the Nagas were involved with Communist China, the USA would be only too pleased to send aid – but the international community was reluctant to offend India.

Ursula rounded off her missive:

> Unless India can be persuaded to come to terms with the rebels under some neutral guarantee, the latter dare not for their lives' sake give in, and would rather die fighting than surrender and be shot. I entirely agree with your remarks about Phizo's proper role. Naturally he won't see it in that light, but one can only hope that if by any stroke of fortune there did seem some chance of India relenting provided Phizo was out of the way, it would be possible to find some other leader who was more acceptable.

During the course of 1963, the Betts' working relationship with Phizo became more strained. They'd known him to be an extremist – a volatile hard-liner whose obduracy could well be costing his people at home dearly – and eventually she and Tim felt it best to work independently for the Naga cause – however, on Sunday 1 December 1963, Nagaland was inaugurated as the sixteenth State of India under a puppet government headed by Mr P. Shilu Ao.

Despite Nagaland's new status as an Indian state, the war with the Indian Army continued. Notionally there were to be 'democratic' elections in Nagaland early in 1964, however, Yongkong wrote to Ursula in mid-January to let her know that the Home Guard had blown up a bridge between Kohima and Imphal, cutting off the latter from the rest of India. 'At election time it is really difficult to fight the Indian troops for fear of heavy retaliation against the civil population.'

All seemed very gloomy – but Yongkong's high spot in January was a visit in London from the thirteen-year-old Catriona, who had already become part of the Naga family. 'It was so nice to see my beloved niece … the time was short, but it was precious.' For Yongkong and Khodao, Nagas alone in England except for

Phizo, Ursula and her family were their only anchor. With alarming snippets of news reaching them about events at home, beyond their influence, contact with Ursula was a lifeline.

Since the Bettses ceased to work with Phizo, Yongkong and Khodao remained their only source of Naga news – and in return, Ursula gave moral support and friendship – the best she could do for the people she loved so much, embodied in her two Naga protégés.

No longer commuting between Mull and London, Ursula had time to write. In the wake of the war with India, Ursula put all her historical and anthropological knowledge and her unique personal experience of the Nagas into a third book – *The Naga Problem* – but this was never published, although it seems unlikely, given the deeply entrenched preconceptions, that any single written work could educate the outside world and influence the fate of the Nagas.

Having failed to get her short, anecdotal pieces published, Ursula turned to fiction – short stories inspired by her travels around the highlands. From years before, as far back as Ursula's eerie experience with Doris at the vitrified fort, she had been aware of the ancient spirit – or even spirits – of the wild Scottish landscape. As Catriona pointed out, Ursula, while having to acknowledge her own psychic sensitivity, was adamant that no mumbo-jumbo should interfere with the solid facts of proper archaeology. 'Later in life she would go ballistic if anybody started talking about ley lines or anything a bit fey within the scope of archaeology – and yet there were things that happened that she couldn't deny.'

Ursula kept having psychic and supernatural experiences, and in September 1963, presumably at Doris's request, Ursula tore herself away from the Naga campaign and accompanied her on a trip to Italy. After a week in Venice, they moved to a fifteenth-century hotel, four miles up the River Arno from Florence, which was ideally placed for their cultural exploration of the city. Ursula recorded the events at the Villa La Massa for Catriona many years later. She recalled how Doris had, on several occasions, seen a very solid-looking girl with an American family staying at the villa:

> Granny remarked that the American newcomers had two daughters. She'd been going down the stairs when they overtook her, the younger one hopping and skipping and bouncing down, the way kids do, and the older one, who was about twelve, running down a trifle more sedately. They were quite obviously sisters, both with long, light-brown hair tied with a ribbon, Alice-in-Wonderland fashion. Both were dressed alike, in dark-blue velvet frocks, Daniel-Neal style – close-fitting bodices, full skirts, Peter Pan muslin collars and short sleeves with muslin cuffs. Granny noticed them particularly, as they were just the same age as you and Alison were then. Then they disappeared out of sight round the turn of the stair. They were within a foot or so of her; the light on the stairs was good, and she saw nothing to make her think that there was anything odd. We went in for a drink, and there was the younger child (whom we later found was called Lisa), but no elder one. Same thing at dinner. Going to bed, Granny opined (I think she'd taken rather a fancy to them) that the older one must have been taken ill.
>
> It wasn't till about the third day that it dawned on us that there *wasn't* a second kid. It was just before dinner, and I remember our sitting on our respective beds

> and trying to make head or tail of it, and Granny saying over and over again, 'But I saw her! I saw her!' And undoubtedly she had, for several seconds, on a well-lit staircase, at a range of about a foot.' She concluded, 'Anyhow, the only sense that we could make of it was that the Barclays had quite recently lost a child – Lisa's elder sister – and that Granny, in some inexplicable way, had seen her, large as life and twice as natural.'

Ursula combined her knowledge of ancient sites, folklore, and her familiarity with the frisson that supernatural experiences provoke, to write short stories set in the Scottish highlands. There was the enigmatic *Dun of No Name* and the chilling *The Other Bed*, and undoubtedly Ursula had a real talent for creating atmosphere and suspense, building up tension and spinning a good yarn, so it's surprising that her stories were not published. In the case of some of her tales this may have been because of her stubborn refusal to kowtow to populist tastes. A literary agent's rejection letter summed it up:

> I personally enjoyed your story, *The Well of the Truthful Heart*, very much indeed, but I am afraid I must return it to you as it is not quite the type of story that editors are looking for. The main difficulty is that your writing is rather on the long side for the plot that you have written up. By this I mean that you have included a great deal of descriptive narrative, and I am afraid that the reader's interest is not held. The majority of the magazine fiction that is published is very slick and sophisticated.

All the same, Ursula continued to write, for her own entertainment. She had a vivid and fertile imagination, and her stories for adults and children would probably have found their proper publishing niche today – but in the 1960s there was less scope for variety.

Eventually, in 1968, Ursula completed a full-length historical novel, set in the first century AD when, 100 years after Julius Caesar's first exploratory visit, the Romans returned to conquer Britain. *The Black Charioteer* was painstakingly researched, and she adhered meticulously to the details of the tribes, their lifestyle, the names of the ancient kingdoms within Britain and even details of arms and warfare. Over the months it took her to prepare and write, Ursula would frequently get disheartened. Catriona recalled, 'My father and I would cheat. She'd get despondent and throw the whole thing in the wastepaper basket, and he and I would wait until the coast was clear and then we'd tiptoe up and get it out again. Then we'd wait until she'd calmed down, and give it back.'

Ursula felt, with all its historical weight, it was a book for adults, however, through the combined deliberations of agent, publisher, illustrator and Ursula herself, it was finally re-categorised as a historical novel aimed at teenagers. Furthermore, it was decided that *The Black Charioteer* should be published under a pseudonym. Ursula opted for the old family name, Paterson – and at last, at the age of fifty-five, Ursula was in print again.

For Tim, running the sheep farm was very physically demanding for a man in his early sixties – three or four times a week, he would walk ten miles a day, and he spent at least one day a week up in the hills. Then in 1967 an accident changed Tim's life and made him and Ursula reconsider their future. They had recently bought a highland pony, 'Dundee', for Catriona, and his former owners had trained him to drag deer on hunting trips. Tim had found a dead cow up the hill, and Tim took Dundee out to bring it down. He had hooked up the cow on a rope attached to Dundee's harness, when the pony suddenly took fright and bolted. One of the hooks holding the cow flew loose and ripped through Tim's calf, tearing it open and leaving him on an exposed hillside with a gruesome wound.

Tim managed to get back and was whisked away to a mainland hospital, where over six weeks he underwent skin grafts and extensive rebuilding of the tissue of his leg. The prolonged separation underlined just how strong their partnership was – but also how vulnerable and dependent Ursula had become. She may have worn the trousers in the household, but alone and facing the prospect of Tim coming back permanently disabled – or perhaps not at all – Ursula was devastated. Although Catriona preserved most of Ursula's writings and letters, she found the letters she had written during Tim's time in hospital and deemed them too heartrending to keep. It was a time of unbearable sadness for Ursula and she missed Tim to a degree that she, and later Catriona, found quite frightening.

Tim returned to a rapturous welcome after more than six weeks away – but he was weak and struggled to keep up with the farm work. In addition, Doris contacted Ursula to say that Bobby was ill, so after much discussion, the Bettses sold up and settled near Doris in the New Forest.

45

The Last Years

Ursula and Tim packed up their wild and weather-beaten farm and decamped to Stocks Cottage, Burley in the New Forest. Sadly, the rapport which had grown between Ursula and Doris now fizzled out, and while she helped and supported Doris during Bobby's illness and death, she was just going through the motions. Perhaps the permanence of their new living arrangements, near to Doris and back in 'civilisation', reminded Ursula of her childhood and teenage unhappiness, and it fell to Catriona and Alison, by this time in their teens, to visit Granny Doris.

Tim escaped by going out riding – but Ursula found village life very limiting. Catriona recalled,

> My mother was never one for small talk – she was bored by it, and bored by all the bridge and coffee mornings and pony clubs, and she wasn't prepared to play that game either, socially. It was all impossible for her unless she was lucky enough to fall in with a kindred spirit – or anybody with an enthusiasm. She loved people who had an enthusiasm about their subject, even if it wasn't necessarily her subject.

Ursula and Tim didn't really fit in, although Tim adapted rather better than she did. Her solace was in staying in touch by letter with her Naga friends, or their descendents – for Haichangnang and Paodekumba had died in the mid-fifties – and keeping up with the Naga struggle through Yongkong and Khodao. The fight against Indian oppression continued throughout the seventies, and Ursula still received heartrending news of violence and torture – but in spite of this, there was some progress and development, and she sent money for educational and cultural projects.

Ursula had made her mark in the academic world with her anthropological work, and now there were occasional opportunities to visit institutes and societies where she could mingle with some stimulating characters. Although quite reticent and shy in social situations – a trait which had never changed from as far back as her debutante days – Ursula came into her own in academic or working environments, and this sustained her through the first years in the New Forest.

When Tim died of a stroke while out riding in 1973, Ursula lost her mainstay. For him it was mercifully swift, but for Ursula it was terribly sudden and a harbinger of unbearable loneliness. He was the one kindred spirit who had shared so much with her – a love of wild landscapes; a passionate devotion to the tribal people whose trust they had earned, and whose loss they had weathered together; a dedication to his ornithological and entomological studies – in fact, every aspect of their lives together.

Tim's spell in hospital in 1967 had been a grim foretaste for Ursula of life without him, and when it became permanent, she was beyond consolation.

Occasionally Ursula escaped the parochial confines of Burley, and spent holidays in Shropshire with Catriona. On one such occasion she arranged to meet Hilda Murrell – the friend they had met while house-hunting in the highlands. Although, to Ursula's great regret, Hilda never visited them on the island, they always kept in touch by letter. On moving to Hampshire, Ursula and Tim had inherited a neglected garden and they consulted Hilda's expertise about their roses.

When Catriona moved to Shrewsbury, she and Hilda met often and the two became very attached. It was thus a very cordial reunion when Ursula travelled to Shrewsbury to stay with Catriona and deliver a lecture in October 1981, and renewed her friendship with Hilda.

A year later, staying in Shrewsbury, Ursula went with Hilda to look at churches and visited one – Church Preen – where Ursula had another of her psychic experiences. They had looked around the ancient building and were approaching the chancel when Ursula was stuck by a sense of terror – a manifestation of pure evil. She described it to Catriona later as being as if a fairy-tale genie was released from a bottle and billowed out in a cloud. Here there had been no cloud, but instead Ursula was conscious of a 'bubble of evil', which pursued them down the chancel steps and as far as the church door. Ursula, not especially fit, ran and ran, with Hilda following after her. It was never clear whether Hilda had shared Ursula's sense of this pursuing evil, but that evening while celebrating Catriona's birthday at a restaurant, Ursula was still so shaken that even Catriona could feel it. It was the following year that Hilda was murdered under the most shocking circumstances. Following a break-in at her house, she was abducted in her own car – then, three days later, her mutilated body was found in a copse.

Her death hit both Catriona and Ursula hard and, given the strange evil presence at Church Preen, both must have wondered if this had been a portent of her death. When asked to write about her personal memories of Hilda, Ursula summed it up, 'I cannot well express what I feel about the loss of Hilda. Something has gone out of life which can ill be spared, and gone in such a way that grief will always remain with it. I shall not forget Hilda.'

Having suffered from increasingly ill health, Ursula died of a heart attack on 12 November 1988. Tributes poured in from friends from as far back as Ursula's Roedean days, from academic admirers, and Bower relatives. All spoke of her generosity of spirit, her enormous enthusiasm for her work, her humour and courage, and the energy she gave to any gathering. The Dorset branch of Burma Star wrote, 'We shall always remember her as one who faced up to that campaign with outstanding courage and very special qualities of leadership and enterprise – forged entirely on her own initiative.'

Caroline, from the Du Croz side of the family recalled the traditional Bower joie de vivre:

> The Du Croz / White genes definitely affected the brain patterns most remarkably. It has always given me great pleasure and comfort, just to see any of them together – the mannerisms, habits of speech, so distinctive, familiar and full of enormous fun.

> When Ursula stayed with us a little while ago, she and Daddy sat either side of the table quoting, at length, 'The HunHunters' and other such nonsense. Some of them none too clean, of course. It was a hilarious evening, but the greatest joy was to see their glittering eyes and supercharge of vitality. The very closeness of that generation permeated all they said and did.

Janet Laurence, married to Ursula's cousin, Keith, captured the spirit of the day of the funeral:

> I admired her long before I knew she was to be a cousin by marriage. I read *Naga Path* when I was about seventeen. It was a wonderful surprise to find that the 'Naga Queen' was to become a cousin! What a great person she was. I loved meeting her and your father, and it was terrible when your father died. His funeral was one of the last meetings between us, and I felt afterwards that much of the zest of life had gone for your mother. I think they were perfectly matched. It was a lovely funeral – everything about it was right – and that lovely Naga farewell…

For indeed, three Nagas were there to say farewell to their greatest champion… Yongkong, Khodao and Niu-Lungalung. It was a chill November day, so the three wore their brightly-coloured native shawls over dark city suits as they and three British ex-servicemen carried the coffin in the New Forest churchyard of St John the Baptist, Burley. As Yongkong said, 'It was a great honour to be asked to be one of the pall-bearers, and it was very nice that there were us three Nagas there.'

46

Pilgrimage to Nagaland

At the time of Ursula's death, the fighting in Nagaland had de-escalated, after years of deadlock, and both sides had made attempts to organise 'peace-talks', in the interests of which the Naga Home Guard had laid down its weapons in a gesture of good faith. India had set up its own Naga government, controlling entry and exit from the country and effectively closing the region to westerners. For this reason, Catriona remained unable to visit her Naga 'family' and see her mother's villages.

In 1982 a Parliamentary Human Rights group compiled a report on atrocities against Naga people, which made horrifying reading – and still no direct action was taken by the British government.

One man who felt very strongly about the Nagas was Raymond Hutchinson, who remembered them from his time in Kohima during the war. One afternoon a week, he and Yongkong would stand, lobbying peacefully outside India House for the release of Naga prisoners, and an end to the oppression and killing. In this sense, he had started a Naga movement in the UK.

Throughout the late eighties the persecution of Naga dissenters within Nagaland continued, and came to the notice of David Ward, at the time an inmate of H.M. Prison Wellingborough. Ward had been born not far from Nagaland, and had grown up with Naga people around him. In1989 Ward started Naga Vigil as a volunteer group founded, perforce, in British prisons. The aim was to promote awareness of the Nagas' plight and spread information about past atrocities and injustice and the latest developments to human rights groups. From this small beginning, Ward soon had not just prisoners, but, in his own words, 'students, teachers, Ministers, academics, World War II veterans and many members inside Nagaland' involved in his cause.

Naga Vigil made it a priority to establish credibility with human rights organisations, and with the support of supporters 'outside', Ward set up projects, and fundraising operations to finance them, to give material help to the Naga people.

Those already interested in the Nagas – in their past loyalties to Britain and in their future – rallied in support of the group, including David Astor, Ebenezer Butler, Yongkong and Catriona, and all took on different aspects of co-ordinating operations. Ebenezer Butler took charge of the book collection for the Kohima college and despite many setbacks and much red tape, succeeded in getting a huge consignment through, beyond the closed borders. The books had been donated largely by prison inmates and a doctor at the college wrote to Ebenezer to say how impressed and delighted he was that prisoners in England cared so much about the Nagas.

In 1999 border restrictions were sufficiently relaxed for Catriona to visit Ursula's villages and meet the children and grandchildren of her oldest friends:

> I think there were three main reasons for going. The first two are rather romantic – one was sheer, unadulterated curiosity, having been brought up on a diet of Nagas since the time I was in my cot, and an odd sense of destiny, remembering Mowu's letter and his invitation to visit my Naga brothers and sisters. The third reason was a wish to do something positive to help.

Catriona was married in January 1999, and the service in the UK was attended by two Nagas – who startled her husband by suggesting that, as he was now married to a Naga princess (Ursula having been, of course, the 'Naga Queen'), he was now a 'Naga Duke of Edinburgh'. In honour of this, they presented the groom with a Naga shawl, traditionally worn only by those who have taken a head…

Later in the year Catriona and her husband travelled to Nagaland and had their marriage blessed in the same church (now a cathedral) in which Ursula and Tim had been married – and in whose register they found the entry from 10 July 1945. It was an immensely moving occasion. Representatives from all the Naga tribes attended, some of whom, in their seventies, had walked for two days in order to reach a road, then catch a bus and endure a thirty-six-hour journey on unmade roads, obstructed with monsoon landslips in order to be there. Catriona read a passage from the Book of Ruth – 'Thy people are my people'; one of the senior Nagas present read the verses on love from Paul's Epistle to the Corinthians, and David read Psalm 121 – 'I will lift up mine eyes unto the hills', which appears on the grave shared by Ursula and Tim in the New Forest churchyard. After traditional hymns – 'How Great Thou Art' and 'The Battle Hymn of the Republic' – the Nagas sang 'Jesus Bids Me Shine', to the English tune but in the Naga tongue.

The ensuing party was a three-day epic in the old Naga style, during which Catriona received deputations, bringing handmade gifts from different Naga villages. Most moving were those from Laisong, Pape, and Magulong where Ursula had lived and, in the case of the latter, celebrated her own Naga wedding.

Eventually, in February and March 2000, Catriona got to visit Ursula's villages in person. At that time it struck her that little had changed in these more remote areas since her mother's time there – so much of what Ursula had described was exactly the same:

> I talked to people who, if they didn't know her, their parents or grandparents had known her – and i'm in touch with Namkia's children and grandchildren. I went to Laisong and Magulong – Magulong particularly hadn't changed – I took some video footage and compared it with the cine film she'd taken, and apart from the colour quality and some differences in dress, the technology was just the same. Magulong was, and still is, a singing village. They sing all the time, as they speak to you. It's like being in an opera – they'll fall into song in the middle of a conversation, and they're brilliant dancers – and their textiles are fantastic. You could see the continuity in their genes too. Khutuing, the headman and my mother's adoptive father, was a very strong character – you had to be to become a headman, it was not

> a hereditary thing – and I could see those genetic traits in his children and grandchildren. They are natural leaders.
>
> The character of the villages was still the same too. Magulong is organised and disciplined, whereas Laisong, where my mother lived, was always a bit chaotic – and still is. After she and my father married, it was in Magulong that they had their Naga wedding, not Laisong – because I now understand that they would never have got it together!
>
> In Laisong they showed me cooking pots which my mother had given to one family when she left and distributed her possessions all round the village – they still had them after all that time. It was all completely mind-boggling.
>
> They gave me a fantastic welcome there – it was one hell of a party – and they did dances and held all sorts of celebrations – but in Magulong I was carried up the roadway in a sort of sedan chair by strong young Naga warriors, and was presented with a young mithan with a bougainvillea garland – an amazing reception.

She later admitted that the mithan was very small and rather startled, and her immediate reaction was that she would have liked to take it home … although she suspected that it may have been the main ingredient of that evening's feast.

In keeping with village tradition, Magulong had created a special dance of welcome, which, after performing it, they insisted on teaching her. In return, Catriona taught them the old Scottish standards 'Strip the Willow' and sword dancing, and she speculated on how future anthropologists would explain how the former headhunters of Nagaland came to know Scottish country dancing:

> They told me that when she [Ursula] left, she asked Magulong what they would like her to give them, and because in those days it was a hell of a long walk down to the plains to buy salt, they said they'd like salt. So she provided an enormous block of rock salt – it's a sort of greyish colour and looks like a dull, glassy coal. This was divided up between the families and they used it for medicinal purposes rather than for everyday cooking. One family showed me a fist-sized chunk of this salt, which they had handed down the generations. Now they say, with a wry laugh, that they can't believe that they didn't ask for a village hall or a school – but opted for salt instead.

They wondered in retrospect why they hadn't been more ambitious – although Catriona was not sure that Ursula would have been in a position to give them anything much more extravagant. Certainly, if Ursula had been able, there would have been no limit to her generosity – the Naga memory of her exceeded anything Catriona could have imagined:

> The reverence and love were even more than I had expected. It knocked my socks off. I couldn't believe it was happening, either. It was bizarre and fantastic – and I found my mind veering off to totally trivial and unworthy thoughts such as, 'I wish the girls in the office could see me now' as I was being carried up this path. And then I'd come back to feeling so very moved and touched by it all – moved to tears by the effort and love, and the degree of honour. The relationship she had with the

> Nagas WAS extraordinary. They're a very honourable, passionate, loving people and they remember her with such HUGE affection. It was fascinating finding out from their perspective what they thought about her, and what children and grandchildren have been told by their parents. The good thing was that she was such an event in an area where not much has happened since, that stories have been passed down because they are worth the telling. My turning up was like being the daughter of a local myth.

Catriona came to understand how it was that Ursula could so seamlessly slip into a role of leadership among these people. Where work was concerned Ursula was always assertive, and she was even more so – to the point, Catriona suspected, of bossiness – with the Nagas. Catriona found this echoed in herself – it was a need to get one's point over and be upfront about it. She also observed, on arriving back in England, that no-one could relate to the intensity of her experience – 'no-one had any hooks to hang it on', as she expressed it. It helped her understand Ursula's sense of isolation, and her dependence on Tim as the one who shared that vital part of her life with her.

Catriona stayed among the Naga people throughout March and in April addressed the Zeliangrong Students' Union Congress. Her aims were to give something positive into the growing community, and make a real difference. She began by recalling her mother's love for the Naga people – and how her years living among them were, without doubt, the best of her life. Nothing later could match that happiness for Ketazile, and in the months before she died she used to tell Catriona that she dreamed often of a range of beautiful, green, jungle-covered hills which she called 'the delectable mountains' – which surely were her beloved Naga Hills.

When she returned to England Catriona took up the Naga cause, putting into action several practical projects for helping the Nagas in a non-political way, including the construction of good roads and wide-reaching education to promote their already sustainable economy. Her visit had enabled her to understand so much more about her mother and her relationship with the Nagas, and finally, given her an opportunity to do something positive for the people her mother had loved.

In 2006 Catriona visited the villages again – this time without quite as much pomp and ceremony. Laisong had grown to 2,000 inhabitants instead of around 800 as in the 1940s – but the character of the people was the same. They were reserved at first, but then extraordinarily warm and welcoming.

More anecdotes emerged – some the memories of over sixty years. One man recalled how, when she left the village for the last time, Ursula had donated her khaki drill shorts to him – then a small boy. The shorts were of a generous size, so he divided them in two – he wore one leg and a friend wore the other, and it being just after the war, they played soldiers…

Another elderly woman remembered that Ursula had given her a newspaper when she was a little girl, and she and her friend had made it into skirts in which they paraded proudly round the village. While in Laisong, Catriona stayed in the house of Dinekamba's descendents – the family were full of memories. Ursula had given Dinekamba an umbrella – the first in the village, and he was as pleased as punch with it. Rain or shine, he would walk round the village, umbrella raised high – thus causing much mirth among the village girls, who called him 'The Umbrella Man'. She had also given him soap, previously unknown in the village, and when this scented Romeo had visited the girls' dormitory to go courting at night, the girls held their noses, asking 'what's that awful smell?'

With their customary candour, the villagers looked Catriona up and down and said, 'You are thinner than your mother, and not as pretty'. To which she was tempted reply that she was some twenty-five years older than her mother was when she lived in Laisong … however, that seemed vain and small-minded. What mattered was the memory that lived on, of the Englishwoman who had become a Naga legend – and in a land where there were no monarchical titles, had more than lived up to her nick-name – the Naga Queen.

Index